# FAMILY
# SURVIVAL
# GUIDE

# FAMILY SURVIVAL GUIDE

## THE BEST WAYS FOR FAMILIES TO PREPARE, TRAIN, PACK, AND SURVIVE EVERYTHING

MYKEL HAWKE AND RUTH ENGLAND HAWKE

Skyhorse Publishing

Skyhorse Publishing books may be purchased in bulk at special discounts for sales promotion, corporate gifts, fund-raising, or educational purposes. Special editions can also be created to specifications. For details, contact the Special Sales Department, Skyhorse Publishing, 307 West 36th Street, 11th Floor, New York, NY 10018 or info@skyhorsepublishing.com.

Skyhorse® and Skyhorse Publishing® are registered trademarks of Skyhorse Publishing, Inc.®, a Delaware corporation.

Visit our website at www.skyhorsepublishing.com.

10 9 8 7 6 5 4 3 2 1

Library of Congress Cataloging-in-Publication Data is available on file.

Cover design by Brian Petersen
Cover photo credit: Ruth England Hawke

Print ISBN: 978-1-5107-3794-5
Ebook ISBN: 978-1-5107-3795-2

Printed in China.

DEDICATION

We'd like to dedicate this book to our parents, both in the UK and the US; we love them so very much. And to the folks who were like parents to Myke: the Hoosacks, the Stankas, Earl, Pete, Yedidia, and Ken.

We'd also like to make a special dedication to the handful of friends who helped us survive one of the toughest times of our lives: the Bolls, the Gabels, the Diazes, and the Erickson clan.

# TABLE OF CONTENTS

# FOREWORD

Jᴀᴍᴇꜱ Mᴏʀɢᴀɴ Aʏʀᴇꜱ

I wish the *Family Survival Guide* had been available when my now-grown sons were children. Although I am a generation older than Mykel, many of my experiences are similar to his. Like Mykel, I served with Special Forces (Green Berets). And also like Mykel, I have had an avid, lifelong interest in survival.

By the age of ten I was wandering the woods near my home town on my own, camping with little more than a blanket, a tin can for a pot, a knife from my mother's kitchen, and an oilcloth tablecloth for a tarp, while hunting rabbits and squirrels with a homemade bow. By thirteen I had roamed over much of my Midwestern state, camping in whatever wild country I could find.

Although I learned a great deal during my military service, like Mykel, I wanted more knowledge about primitive survival. Over the past half-century I have at times lived with so called "primitive" people on three continents, hunted, fished, and foraged with them and learned the lessons they had to teach. So you may ask, with my experience why would I have needed this book?

I raised a family and taught my sons what I thought they needed to know in order to survive in the wilderness and in the world. But I always had nagging doubts: did I make it fun, will they remember the stories I told to illustrate lessons, and most importantly, did I teach them enough, did I forget to cover something? I often thought I should have taken the time to write down an organized teaching plan for my boys. But due to the exigencies of operating an international business and dealing with the day to day affairs of a large family, I never did. That's why I wish this book had been available then.

In this book, Mykel and Ruth have brilliantly organized military experience and harsh real word experience to create a potentially lifesaving manual. They have done so in a non-militaristic, unpretentious, down-to-earth style that makes essential topics easy to access and absorb for anyone, especially including children. In the first few pages Mykel sets out the primary goal of this book: "The worst case scenario you can ever imagine . . . Your child is lost and must survive on their own at least long enough to be found." That's a nightmare scenario for any parent. And sadly, every year, children do get lost, whether from wandering off or getting separated from the group. And every year, some kids do not get found.

And as is pointed out early on, everything in this book comes down to fulfilling one mission: helping your child survive alone without you. Certainly that was my worst nightmare when my boys were children. I think it is for many parents. Chance cannot be ruled out, and anything can happen to anyone. But chance favors the prepared, and learning the lessons found in the *Family Survival Guide* will materially weigh the odds in your favor, and in favor of your children.

The book begins with critical components of real world survival, components not detailed in many other survival books. These include how to analyze your capacities, how to organize a hierarchy of decisions, and how to make plans based on the Special Forces methods that have enabled many to survive extreme conditions in far flung corners of the world.

Many survival books focus on making fire without matches, building shelters, and other basic skills, but leave out the most critical skills—the mental ones. Chapter by chapter the *Family Survival Guide* covers all basic, and some advanced, survival skills and needs and does so in a manner that is both easy to understand and easy to recall.

In addition to the excellent organization, Mykel and Ruth's prose style makes this book a stand out, and makes the lessons memorable. Here's an example:

> Only taking what you really need and know that what you took, you really use, because you are going to carry it in that *life-sucking tick we call the rucksack* and every ounce of weight with no pay off, is an ounce of weight that wears you down and when things get tough, that wear and tear comes into play and makes difference in a big way.

I hadn't heard that phrase, "life-sucking tick," since I was in the army, decades ago. I laughed out loud when I read it because it brought up memories of slogging through rough country with a monster of a rucksack draining energy from my exhausted body.

In one pungent, visual, and memorable phrase Mykel and Ruth sum up what I devoted an entire chapter to in one of my own books: travel light, carry only what you need, not what you *want*. That lesson is doubly important for children.

If their little rucksack is too heavy for them they will soon learn to hate it and will leave it behind at every opportunity. Mykel and Ruth explain how to ensure that your children have what they *need*, and a few things that are fun for them, so that if an extreme situation arises they will have the tools they need to survive.

This is an important books for all parents. Even if you don't go camping or spend much time out of doors there always comes at least one time when a kid wants to go snowboarding, skiing, river rafting, or hiking with friends.

That one time is often when it all goes wrong. I once witnessed a fifteen-year-old boy die of hypothermia. He had been snowboarding, got off, and got lost. The search and rescue team found him after he had spent two nights alone in the mountains. He was still alive then but so far gone into hypothermia that he could not be saved.

The rescue team was in tears. His parents were devastated. This boy was at no time more than a mile from the lodge. He was wearing jeans and a cotton hoodie—normal clothing for a teenaged snowboarder, but nonetheless clothing that helped to kill him by getting wet and not drying—as cotton does. He had no outdoor skills. He didn't know to stay in one place so he could be more easily found. He had no idea about lost proofing, route finding, or signaling skills. He didn't know how to build a fire, or even to carry the means to make fire. As a member of the rescue team, I watched the fear in his eyes as the light died from them. I don't ever want to repeat that experience. That's an experience that no parent wants to have. Unfortunately, kids die like this every year. But the *Family Survival Guide* contains critical knowledge and skills that can enable parents to avoid such horror and loss.

Even if you're an urban family with no interest in the out of doors, learning these lessons will teach self-reliance that carries over into everyday life. That's what we all want isn't it: self-reliant children who will grow into competent adults fully capable of dealing with life's vicissitudes? Accidents happen. Cars crash in remote areas. People become stranded. Kids get lost on vacation. Technology does not solve all of life's problems. Although the writing is humorous, make no mistake, this is serious life-saving stuff.

I intend to give each of my sons a copy of the *Family Survival Guide* to aid them in teaching their children, my grandchildren, life skills. Each of my sons is fully capable of surviving harsh circumstances. But like me, they can make good use of this book to organize their teaching and to pass on knowledge and skills that may one day save the lives of my grandchildren.

Whether you're new to survival concepts or an experienced hand, the *Family Survival Guide* is a valuable resource. You may have seen Mykel and Ruth on television in their show *Man Woman Wild*, or in one or more of the many other shows they have hosted. Unlike many other television "survival experts," Mykel and Ruth really are authorities. They are, as the saying goes, the real deal. Mykel's credentials are exceptional. His lessons are solid. His character is exemplary. Mykel won't let you down. Neither will Ruth.

Mykel and Ruth operate as a team. Together, they bring you a fine book, potentially a lifesaving book. It belongs on every parent's bookshelf, or better yet, in their hands.

# INTRODUCTION

When I was growing up, I was very poor and at one point around age fourteen, I spent a winter homeless and had to survive on the streets. That experience caused me to develop a keen sense of survival and a strong desire to learn more about how to survive. My extremely harsh upbringing further led me to join the U.S. Army Special Forces, also known as the Green Berets. While I was a soldier, I was required to attend the high risk survival school for special operations called SERE, which stands for Survival, Evasion, Resistance, and Escape. This school is considered by most special operations to be one of the hardest and certainly most emotionally stressful schools the military has to offer. I loved it and I learned a lot there, but I also believe that in some areas I didn't learn enough. The primary issue that I felt was lacking was the focus on survival.

The course is three weeks and a majority of it is classified, primarily because of the topics taught. The survival portion, however, isn't classified as no one owns those skills and anyone can learn and apply them. The course naturally has a heavy emphasis on this things that soldiers need—a Code of Conduct, information about the Geneva Convention and Rights of Prisoners of War, etc. So, that didn't leave a lot of time for survival topics. And most of what was taught still centered on gear that soldiers would naturally have on them such as canteens, canteen cups of metal for boiling and cooking, water purification tablets, a knife, a lighter and or magnesium bar, ponchos, poncho liners, good uniforms, boots, and other such gear.

Since I had learned some survival on my own as kid and then a lot more on my own as an adult, I was disappointed that SERE didn't teach a lot of what I call "primitive" survival; that is, surviving without any of that gear. Since those days, SERE instructors have added more of those skills in the course, at least enough to familiarize if not actually teach primitive skills, like friction fires for example.

As a result of not getting enough of what I wanted to know, I began a lifelong study of survival. I culled information from everywhere: from books, from pros, from subject-matter experts, country folk, indigenous peoples, and tribal elders. I also spent a lot of dirt time, with trial and error with a lot of mistakes, miserable tests and flat-out failures. But those were the things that I learned the most from: failing.

From all that, I set about teaching survival professionally in 1994 with an adventure business called "Specops, Inc.," a common term for special operations, and we only hired special operations veterans as our cadre. As I taught, I found couples and families were often interested in survival and that there were really no schools designed specifically to prepare a family for survival as a unit. It was from these observations that this book was born.

We hope that parents and kids can learn, practice, work, and play together as they make themselves better prepared for anything life has to throw at them. The reason survival became a lifelong passion for me is that the lessons learned can be useful to anyone, as everything a person does in life is about facing challenges, finding solutions, and overcoming obstacles. That's what this book is about: giving families the confidence to face problems and create a plan. At its core, this is a book of hope—that with it, there is always hope that you can make it, so long as you remember the cardinal rule of survival—NEVER QUIT.

# CHAPTER ONE

# WHAT PARENTS NEED TO KNOW

*When catastrophe strikes and the power goes out for a prolonged period, things can get nasty. Enrolling your child in a martial arts class can provide him or her with some valuable self-defense skills. Bridget here got a black belt in karate. She's now in high school and her dad Jeff tells me that should the need arise, she can beat up any person in her class, which I'm sure he finds reassuring! (Photo credit Gemma Sells)*

This chapter is going be a bit long, so settle in for a bit. It's important to pay attention as this part will pretty much dictate how you approach all the other components of this book and what things you focus on getting and doing to prepare your family.

First things first, the right mindset or mental approach is a fundamental necessity for everything else. We always say that you fight like you train and if you train sloppy, you'll fight sloppy. So be sure to keep it fun for the kids, since they learn best when they are at play. But make no mistake, the training you are giving them is absolutely a matter of life or death.

Next, my background is Special Forces. We Green Berets always jokingly call ourselves "Uncle Sam's Extremists." While there is humor in that quip, as most of our men are more mature than the average soldier, Green Berets are foremost family men, and learned men, with advanced degrees. Additionally, through our recruitment, training, and design, we are meant to go into harm's way with just a few men against unknown odds, and we're in it for the long haul, meant to stay until the job is done. No other special operations forces have that intense mandate. So, right up front, I am going to embrace that touch of extremism but also strive for balance in all I teach. Nevertheless everything shared here is with the absolute worst case scenario in mind. If you can face that, you can face anything.

Now, when Special Forces gets assigned a mission, the very first thing we do is look at the operation and ask ourselves, *what is the very worst case scenario*? Then, we prepare for it. The next we ask is, *what is the most likely scenario we'll face*? And that's what we plan on happening. Then we walk ourselves through the entire operation as best we can imagine it—from start to finish, including everything that might go wrong along the way. We make a plan for all that, then we continue planning until we reach the end of the scenario.

Additionally, we'll do an analysis of ourselves—a brutally honest one, because the only ones we're hurting are ourselves and our team mates if we're not honest in our self-assessments. We analyze our fitness, experience, skills, talents, limitations, weaknesses, and physical abilities, as well as what we think the mission will require and what we need to do to not just get ready for it, but to meet it, beat it, and overcome every single obstacle that gets thrown at us.

Then we look at our logistics, we ask the following: what supplies do we think we need and what do we really have? What do we need to acquire? What training do we need? Skills to learn? Skills to refresh? Info to read? Knowledge to review?

Then we start gathering reading materials, tools, training manuals, and supply packages. Then we begin to make ourselves ready for our mission by rehearsing anything and everything that can happen. We rehearse like our lives depend on it, because often enough, they do.

Now I say all that so you'll get an idea how Green Berets approach training and then you can modify and adapt it for your skills, abilities, your needs, and your family's abilities.

So now you're ready to do an analysis of your mission and operational capabilities so you can figure out what to get and what to do.

For the sake of simplicity, I am going to operate under an assumption that yours is a two-parent family. However, there are plenty of single parents out there trying to tackle the challenge of preparing their family for anything and everything, so nothing in here will be prohibitive for a single parent. However, often enough in extreme situations, you may find another adult being attached or accompanying you and so, it's not a bad idea even for the single parent, to factor the possibility for a second adult option into the equation.

That mainly means having a backup back pack so they can carry extra supplies for the team (family group) and carry their own needs like bag, tent, and the like so they're not a burden on the rest.

The next thing in your assessment is looking at your kids. How many do you have? How old are they? What are their personalities like?

You want to start with thinking like you're going on a one-week camping trip. What do you need for them? How much can they carry? Even the youngest child can usually carry something, even if it's just a small pack with water, food, and a poncho.

Next, you have to analyze your activities as a family. Do you mostly stay home? Do you take road trips, boat or plane trips? The reasoning behind this is that it will drive some of how you pack, what you carry, and what you plan for training.

Then you have to ask yourself, what are the risks you'll potentially face? Do you live in a part of the country where fires are a threat? Or where flooding is a major risk? Earthquakes, mudslides, volcanoes, tidal waves, flash floods, droughts, blizzards, hurricanes, tornadoes? Or is there political unrest or some kind of warfare? Ask the tough worst case scenario questions, and make a plan for them and how to handle them.

One of the most important decisions that any family can make is whether to stay or to go in the midst of a disaster. This choice will drive everything else that you do or don't do.

In general terms, it's almost always better to stay put. Be it at home, your hotel, or cabin, in a car, boat, or plane, with your relatives or friends, or where ever you happen to be staying. The reasoning behind this is that you are already there.

Generally speaking, if you are somewhere, you know something about what's around you and it's easier and safer to hold tight from right where you are.

The other reason staying is usually better is that movement takes work. It means you have to carry stuff, be it a backpack or car. That you'll inherently have to limit what you can carry and means leaving some things behind and that means having less. With mobility there is a direct correlation trade off to quantities of supplies; there is no way around that. When you stay put, you can stockpile.

Movement also means you risk exposure to some danger with every moment you are not stationary. This doesn't mean you're not at risk if you're static, but in that case you have an advantage; you can look and listen to what's around you and if trouble approaches, you can be take the appropriate action to defend or escape.

But here is where the real rubber meets the road for any parent—facing the worst case scenario you can ever imagine: your child is lost and must survive on their own at least long enough to be found.

That's a nightmare scenario for any parent. And sadly, every year, a few children do get lost, be it wandering off or getting separated from the group. And every year, some kids do not get found. But luckily, everything in this book comes down to one mission: to help your child survive alone, without you.

So, start your mental planning right now and ask yourself, how would you prepare your child to survive if they are alone and lost?

And do not let your child's age discourage you. Even a young child can be taught certain things within their ability to learn that can dramatically impact a favorable survival outcome if they get lost.

On this point the first things you should think about teaching them is what they can do. For example, you can teach even the youngest child to stay put if they get lost and to start making noise, calling for help.

The next thing to think about is, what you can give them and what they can carry and potentially use. For example, you can make sure they always have a survival necklace that has a whistle for daytime and a flashlight for night. You may also want to give them a small bag to always carry so they have some essential supplies. Also, make sure to brief them every time you go out, what the "break-in-contact" plan is, that is, what to do, and where to go if they get lost or separated.

Even in the Special Operations world, Special Forces are considered deep planners. The reason we do this is two-fold:

1.  We know that no matter what you plan, all plans can fall apart.
2.  Secondly, we expect to take casualties, we know things will go wrong, equipment will fail, or people will get hurt. Anything can happen, so we plan for it.

That said, we use a five-point plan for every mission and that way, even if only one man is left alive on the team, he knows what to do and he can complete the mission. And this is what you want to do with your kids.

For this, we use the following system: P.A.C.E.GTH.

Normally this means:

- **Primary:** This is what we use for the most likely scenario and ideal situation. Everyone knows what to do, where you're going, what their roles, duties, or jobs are, and how everyone hopes things will end up.
- **Alternate:** This is just a standard backup, or a simple alternative that can be put in place. A good example is Dad is in charge of the first aid, but gets sick, so Mom takes over. Or, the little kid on the team can't walk any more so Dad carries him.
- **Contingency:** This is when something seriously goes wrong. For example, the son breaks his leg. Mom splints his leg, the daughter makes a crutch for him, and Dad carries his backpack and the family moves on, but at a slower rate with more stops and maybe rests a day or two before continuing on.
- **Emergency:** This is something really bad happens, say, someone falls down in a ravine and can't get out. Then someone has to decide to make a run for help while the others stay and try to support the injured person.
- **Go to Heck or "WCS" (Worst Case Scenario):** This is for when everything goes badly and you have to take an extreme action. For example, a bear attacks your camp and everyone has to abandon camp. The plan might be for everyone to meet at the last river crossing five hundred yards away at the big boulder. Once there you can re-group and decide the next course of action.

By having a five-point plan for every phase of your operation, you will have the very best chances of success and survival. Especially when you make this a lifestyle habit to always keep your kids informed.

It also begins to instill a sense of confidence in you and teaches good leadership and thinking skills to your kids. In short, there are no down sides.

So try to make it a habit to make a five-point contingency plan for a break in contact every time you go out.

For example, you and your family are going to a large state park for a hike. If you get separated, tell your child the following:

P: Try to find us on the direction of travel for fifteen minutes maximum.
A: If you can't find us after that, stay put for one hour.
C: If we can't find you, try to get back to parking lot if not dangerous.
E: Make noise, call for help, blow whistle, and seek any adult or human to help.
WCS: Plan on staying put overnight, make a signal, make shelter, and be sure to hydrate.

The other part of this equation is that no matter how young your child is, by teaching them the most they can handle and with each year that goes by without event, you can teach them another skill that may help them to survive on their own.

To help you figure out the appropriate skills that you should teach your children, there are a wealth of films, books, games, and apps you as parents can use to train yourselves and stimulate thoughts for planning for the worst-case scenario.

Of course, a lot of what you choose to use will be based on your interests, the locales you frequent, what you think your threat/challenges are, what you think your personal weaknesses are, and those of your respective family members so as to make them training films to help make your team better prepared.

Here's a good list of resources to start out with. Although it isn't comprehensive, all of these items will certainly help you get on the right track:

## Films

| | |
|---|---|
| *The Road* (2009) | *The Jungle* (2017) |
| *All is Lost* (2013) | *Into the Wild* (2007) |
| *The Mountain Between Us* (2017) | *127 Hours* (2010) |
| *Castaway* (2000) | *The Grey* (2011) |
| *Robinson Crusoe* (1997) | *Alive* (1993) |
| *The Book of Eli* (2010) | *The Way Back* (2010) |
| *Kon Tiki* (2012) | |

There are many other films out there that address survival in one way or another, but many are very Hollywood—that means, not to be used for teaching realistic techniques, but still good for learning principles. Even some of my old favorites do not hold up to my now, wiser understanding of what is needed in real survival situations. Neither *The Man in the Wilderness* (1971) nor *The Revenant* (2015), provide much realism.

Consider using some of the above films to teach your kids the rights and wrongs of survival situations. These kinds of family viewings are great for bringing the family together, getting everyone in the right frame of mind for training, and helping in times of duress by providing a point of reference and ideas.

# BOOKS

Of course, I'd be doing myself, my family, and my publishers a disservice if I didn't give my own books a plug, but that doesn't exclusively drive my decision to share them here. What does motivate me to let you know about them is that they are genuinely good resources.

I have written a few survival books. The largest and most in-depth one is *Green Beret Survival Manual*. I consider it to be useful since it covers a lot of things not normally referenced by other survival books and it discusses a lot of myths. In addition, it also covers a lot of things no other books cover such as nuclear, biological, and chemical weapons, as well as all types of warfare. It also discusses great medical topics from amputations to cannibalism. It's an easy read and a good reference book once read. It's one downfall is that it's too big for the field.

Luckily, I have a handbook that is lightweight, water-resistant, and suitable for carrying in a backpack. This tiny book is helpful to put in a kid's pack so they have a reference should they find themselves isolated and alone.

I also have written a book on the edible plants of America. It combines the real world, hard-won lessons from a decade long veteran homeless man with my own well-studied expertise.

In addition to my own, there are some other books that I like to carry in my emergency bag as they are tiny and efficient. One is the *SAS Handbook*, which has great knowledge and tons of tiny pictures that help illustrate important survival techniques. Another is *Food for Free*, as it's filled with good photos and simple info. The book is European-centric so not all the plants that are referenced apply. Nevertheless, this book will get you prepared, and is good to refer back once a year and pick up what you may have missed.

While there are dozens of other books out there, I recommend steering away from most celebrity books in general, as many are not real survivalists, but were made so by television. However, one celebrity whose books I do like is Ray Mears, whose best-known work is *Bushcraft* (2002). The primitive skills that he references in this book and his others are very useful in the field.

## Games

Rather surprisingly, there are some very good board games based on survival. Most involve some form of zombies, the apocalypse, are set in the future or in the ancient past or in a completely fictional land. While these things do not hold my interest, it's good to know there are plenty of options that fit you and your family's needs, especially if it gets the kiddos interested in survival.

I'm a fan of simple and think that cards work great. When out in the field, you can play dozens of different games with cards. Plus they last, they're light, and they're versatile.

Now, when it comes to electronic survival games, there are literally dozens out there and there are more popping up daily. Again, most have some trending themes like zombies or aliens, but they are fun and have some education value. But they won't serve you much out in the wilderness or if the grid goes down.

## Apps

There are tons and tons of apps available and these will be a part of our lives for many years to come in one way or another. I'm a fan of apps that do things for me, like language translators, compasses, maps, etc.

However, I'm not keen on giving up access to my data so I steer clear of the free apps which are ad based and I tend to go for the higher-priced, best-rated apps that have a good track record for fixing bugs and a good history of keeping the app up to date.

The big thing I advise when it comes to app selection is to make sure the apps work even when you're not connected to the internet.

The chances are, when you need a survival app, you'll likely be lost and/or remote, far from Wi-Fi or access and very likely will be low on power or well on your way there. So, get the apps that work independent of Internet. It's beyond the scope of this book to recommend every useful app since they come and go so quickly and there are new ones added almost daily.

Here is a short general list of apps I consider good to have:

- Maps: Global, national, and especially local
- Language: For any you think you might need
- Weights and Measures: For converting distances, drug doses, etc.
- Weather: These will often download a thirty-day prediction
- Tides: Very important for if you are around salt water
- Moon phases: Critical for night movements
- Almanac: Both World and Farmer's are good to have
- First aid: Download the best one for your needs and skills
- Survival: Download the best ones for your needs and location
- Morse Code: Best to have those that can send and receive
- Flashlight
- Plants: Regional edible and medicinal plants are best

## Toys

When it comes to toys, there are many things that can be bought or made. I will cover toys more in the activities chapter as the list requires a little elaboration to see how the tool becomes a toy.

A lot of things I grew up with are not standard anymore, like slingshots, dart guns, and bows and arrows, but these are absolutely great fun for kids and they are equally essential tools for survival.

In some ways, parents have it easier nowadays as there are so many gadgets and programs out there to make it better for teaching and supplying our kids. However, in other ways, it's tougher as kids have more video games, greater internet access, and a lot of more pull for their attention. Because those things provide so much short term and immediate gratification, the kids are more reluctant to break away from them for long enough periods of time to learn these skills that could save their lives.

Most folks delude themselves by thinking, "It'll never happen to me." And while that is possible, it's ever more probable that something will happen to everyone at some point in their lives. And with more and more people on the planet, when there are disasters and more people are affected. And sometimes, that could mean more people will seek to exploit others in order to better their own desperate situations. When times get dire, people can become very mean. This is but one more thing you must gently break your kids into: the notion of facing such challenges.

Nowadays, we tend to have many logistical things sorted out for us. To help make our daily lives easier, we have firefighters, paramedics, police, grocery stores, restaurants, mechanics, and tradesmen of all sorts, as well as a lot of technology. But what if you didn't have them? Would you and your children know what to do?

Luckily, you can teach them. First, stage a camp out in "Fort Living Room." Turn off all the lights, water, heating, and the like, using nothing from the house that you normally would. With these conditions, how would you make food and get water? How would you use the bathroom and deal with trash? How would you wash clothes and dishes? Just do this for twenty-four hours the first time, then a month later try it for forty-eight hours.

The next step is to camp in "Fort Backyard." Make it fun, but don't violate the rules; use nothing from the house in terms of running water, stoves, fridge, bathroom, cooking, or the like. You fight like you train. Train to survive. Write down all the things you wanted or forgot or needed. Then add it to your plan and future packing list.

The next steps are car camping, taking what you need. And then figuring out what you really need, and don't. A simple overnight will suffice for starters. Just go out that morning, set up camp for overnight, spend the day, and go home. You'll learn a lot and most importantly, by starting slow, you'll be keeping it fun for the kids.

The next time, make it a bit longer, and make sure the kids are briefed well in advance. They have their own lives and the more you can give them time to get their heads around things, the more acceptance and the better performance you'll get out of them. Now, while I've taught survival to families for years, a lifetime of expertise is not the real secret of the advanced warning concept—military leadership planning is. You want to give your "troop" as much early warning as possible for any mission. In doing so, they can do more of their own preparation at their level, with the end result being a more successful operation for everyone.

The best way to ensure they "buy" into the idea is to get them involved. Ask them questions about what they think you should bring, what they think they can carry, what they want to do, and where they want to go. Of course expenses and budgets become a factor in the planning. So work within your finances but it doesn't cost too much to get out to the woods and camp.

The next step is the full camping out of your own backpack with your only mode of transport being your walking boots or shoes.

But don't fret. By now you and the kids will have warmed up to the notion and gotten comfortable with the concept of living out of your pack and in the wild. This is the point when it becomes important to pack well. Only take what you really need and will really use because you are going to carry it in that life-sucking tick we call the backpack and every ounce of weight is an ounce of weight that wears you down, and when things get tough, that wear and tear comes into play and makes a difference.

So, this is what it all comes down to: getting your kids to the point they can go out into the world prepared with supplies and then do what they need to do to take care of themselves and survive.

The next phase is to go camping, bringing everything but trying to use as little as possible and getting as much as you can off the land without dipping into your pack. Anytime you reach in is essentially a failure. But, it's better to fail and be safe. For example, if it rains and your lean-to shelter was not quite waterproof enough, so grab your poncho and throw it over top. That's okay. Learn and do better next time. Ultimately keep it fun for the kids but, as the parent, know that it was a fail and that next time, you have to do better.

*Jeff and Steph doing a brilliant job of managing a lively Den 7! I cannot express what a fantastic organization the Scouts are in terms of preparing children to cope in a survival situation and life in general. They have badges in backpacking, camping, kayaking, climbing, emergency preparedness, fire safety, fishing, hiking, lifesaving, wilderness survival, and orienteering, just to mention a few! (Photo credit Ruth England Hawke)*

There are lots of other skills that make your kids better at survival, but they don't all have to be tackled at once. Things like fitness through sports and other athletic actives like walks, swimming, and bike rides, all help get them ready. You can also get your kids into survival skills like fishing, hunting, foraging or gardening. Grow edible plants in your yard and let them start to learn to appreciate the earth and nature and the seasons and the cycles of life. Let them have pets, but also, expose them to traits of the animals, including animals habits. Let them learn archery, knife throwing, tomahawk throwing, or several other skills that are all good survival abilities and teach good hand-eye coordination. Some of these activities actually have clubs and competitions.

Use all your parental wiles to get them into activities that they enjoy and can help ensure their chances of survival should that "WCS" ever happen to them.

Also, skills like first aid, communications, and navigation can be their own standalone activities. They don't have to be on the camping trip and most likely are better off not being a part of it. They can be difficult and there is a lot to learn, so let them focus on one thing at a time.

Boy Scouts and Girl Scouts are very good programs to get kids into as they teach a lot of these things. Plus, it tends to be a lot more fun for the kids when they can share their learning experiences and fun with other kids their age and with similar interests.

# CHAPTER TWO

# WHAT KIDS NEED TO KNOW

*Being face down in the water underneath a boat is something no one wants for their child. But sadly it can and does happen so it's better to be prepared and to know what to do in those circumstances. The seventh grade student pictured here is being taught self-rescue by our friend Jeff Coit, an instructor at Red Wolf Wilderness Adventures in Brooklyn, Mississippi. Jeff says it's rewarding to see the students grow and accomplish so much in just a few days. There are outdoor centers throughout the country that teach valuable skills like these, and it's well worth getting your family involved. (Photo credit Jeffrey Coit)*

Note: Parents, read this chapter and decide if you want to read it to your kids or if they're old enough to read it themselves. I'm going to write it to them, but that decision, I'll leave to you. Know the principles are something you need to convey to them, based on their abilities and maturity.

First off, it's important to understand that a lot of kids go missing every year. Some are runaways, some are stolen, and some just get lost. Of the runaways, most are found by police sooner or later. Of those stolen, most get returned sooner or later and of those who get lost, most are found again. So, this is great news. But, some do not get returned or found. And some of them do not survive. That is why this book is important, it's why your parents are teaching you these things, and why you need to do your best to learn as much as you can.

Hopefully, getting lost never happens to you, but if it does don't panic. Instead, show your parents that you appreciate them and take survival seriously by being patient, learning skills, and practicing some of the things here. Keep in mind that every year as you get older, your parents will add to your knowledge and your skill set.

The first thing about survival is to have a good mindset. Knowing that sometimes kids get lost helps you to understand, if you get lost, you are not the only one and shouldn't beat yourself up about it. Instead, just focus on surviving and most of the time that will be enough to see you through.

The next thing about survival mindset is to understand is that it may take some time to get there. So, do not panic, and do not rush. Be prepared to sleep alone outside for a night or two. If the thought scares you, try to think of it as an adventure.

Further, once you're lost, you have to make a key decision: whether to stay put or go. Hopefully, your parents will have given you a good plan in case there is a "break in contact" or you get separated from them.

Often, the best plan is to stay put, whereever you are.

The very first thing to do once you realize you are lost or separated is to try and call out for help. If a few yells do not get an answer, then hopefully, you will have a family radio to use to call for help. If that doesn't work, try using a cell phone if you have that.

If those options aren't available or don't work, then try other survival signals such as a whistle, a pen flare or laser flare, or some other signal device.

Now your family or group will likely realize soon that they lost track of you and will begin immediately by backtracking until they find you. So if you can, try to stay put. However, if your location is not an easy place for them to find, then it may be smart to move, but only just a little bit. DO NOT GO TOO FAR.

Maybe move a little bit into an open field or to higher ground. Try to stay out of thick bushes unless you need shelter or are hiding from a danger like a predator. It may be smart to climb a tree, but always go slow and be safe. If you do decide to climb a tree, try to climb one where you can see and be seen, meaning the leaves and such aren't so bushy no one would see you.

Also, try to tie yourself to a branch so you don't fall out, but if you do fall, the tie will not hurt you, it's just there to help you to grab a close branch and not fall and get hurt.

If for some unique reason, you decide there is no way that anyone can find you or know where to look for you, then you might decide to move a little farther. For example, if you are in a deep valley, usually going up will help.

Sometimes, you might get lost high up and there may not be trees or rocks for cover from the cold and rain. Then, you might want to move down. If you do, move slowly and safely. You don't want to fall and hurt yourself. Also, if you walk slowly, you are less likely to walk on a snake or run into a wild animal.

No matter whether you decide to stay or go, you need to start thinking about making signals to get found. If you have a whistle, blow it three times every ten minutes. A whistle is a distance sound that lets everyone know a person needs help. Whistles are good for both day and night.

If it is daytime and you are staying put, consider using signals, like a bright orange trash bag or a silver space blanket. If you don't have anything man-made, start breaking branches and laying them on the ground so the lighter colors show. Always try to lay them down in a series of three, like three circles, squares, triangles, or arrows. Those show distinct human made patterns and catch the eye of people looking for you or anyone passing by.

Next, now that you have tried everything to signal help and then decided to stay or go, you need to make a quick inventory and plan.

First, check all your pockets in your backpack so you know exactly how much you have and what you have. Check all your clothes pockets, too, as sometimes, when camping we stuff things in our coats or cargo pockets and forget that we have things there.

Once you do an inventory, make a plan. If you are going to stay put, try to make a good shelter in case you are stuck for a day or two. Don't work too hard but make it as safe as you can. Plan to make signals the whole time you are working.

If you are walking, think carefully about where you are going. Are you going to walk back to camp, to the last road you saw, to where the car was parked? Think about the easiest place to go where people might find you or something bigger than you or your tent so that searchers can find you. A car is easier to find than a tent and a cabin is easier to find than a car.

Next decide how much time you have to get there. If it is going to be dark soon, unless the weather is going to kill you, it might be better to spend the night and not risk getting caught in the dark without a shelter built.

Also, shelters take some time to build, so make sure you give yourself a lot of time to do it alone. You don't want to rush and break it or hurt yourself. Also, you'll want to have enough time to rest, look around, think about how things will look in the dark so you don't get scared and have time to get your mind ready for the rest of the night.

Try to eat a little food and drink some water, but save some of both for the morning. Make sure you go to the bathroom while it is still light outside so you don't wake up afraid to go out and not getting sleep or you wake up to go to the bathroom and then get hurt or lost.

Finally, try to clean yourself up a little, as that makes you feel better, look better, and keeps you healthier. Then make your last tries for signaling help, and then get some sleep.

If you have a flashlight, you might consider leaving that on where folks will most likely be looking.

We have tiny flashlights on our son's backpack for this purpose as they last a long time and it doesn't use up his working flashlight battery. Other options are strobe lights or flashing lights, like for bicycles, are very cheap and lightweight these days and make for a great all night signal device while you sleep.

Now, depending on your age and where you are, you may have a weapon to use. For any age, I recommend having a good walking stick and that makes a great tool to help you walk and defend in case any predators come along. There are many ways to protect yourself and we'll speak more about that later in the chapter on tools. But if you have nothing, try to break or find a good strong stick to help you. It should be almost as big as your wrist and just a little bit taller than you.

Finally, some thoughts about fire. If you can't make one, consider keeping your flashlight on all night. If you are old enough to make one and have the fire-starting supplies, then don't make it too big, as it can get out of control very easily. Not matter what, be sure to gather a lot of firewood before dark and before you sit down for the night, and always be super careful collecting firewood—you never know what sort of creatures are out there. Then just rest and wait for daylight—it will and you will be okay—and then keep doing your survival plan until rescued.

So, think about this worst case scenario, and be sure to ask your folks lots of questions. The more you ask, the better prepared you will be. And no complaints when it's training time and no whining when your pack is a little heavier. You are training to be a survivor—be strong, do your best!

*Climbing and rappelling is a fantastic way to get kids into the outdoors and enjoying exciting adventure. This is also excellent training for potential survival situations, both by increasing physical strength and stamina and by teaching children that they can succeed when tasks are difficult, frightening, and unfamiliar. (Photo credit Jeffrey Coit)*

# CHAPTER THREE

# FOOD

In regards to family survival, food is even more important than it is for soldiers or professional athletes as they have the discipline to suffer for their craft or to endure some discomfort. But when it comes to children, those rules simply do not apply.

*Bugs are full of protein and nutrients and form a vital component in the diets of millions of people around the world. They are great survival food as they're plentiful and they're found everywhere. If you want to gently introduce your family to the concept of eating insects you can order precooked, seasoned, FDA-approved bugs online. The BBQ mealworms in this bowl were particularly tasty. (Photo credit Ruth England Hawke)*

Likewise, there's a saying in Green Beret training that no one has to practice at being miserable, since that happens plenty on its own. So, you hardcore parents, don't even think about making kids go hungry for survival training. But you should absolutely make them try some unusual foods.

Ruth and I are keen on the bug snacks. We've both eaten bugs as delicacies and for survival. Many places around the world eat them as a staple. So, it's easy these days to obtain some bugs as snacks and take them along camping trips to expose your kids to new things and get them in the mindset that when outside, eating new items is just a part of the experience.

Hopefully, kids will actually enjoy it, but if not, at least insist they try. Many people perish each year from starvation and it's usually from refusing to eat an edible item and not for lack of knowledge. Don't let that story become your kids' story.

As a parent, you already know about things your kids food preferences. You're also be aware of any allergies. So, one thing to do is make sure your kids have a stash of food on them at all times that you know they will for sure eat.

We always keep our son loaded with some "sweets and salties," meaning some beef, turkey, or vegan jerky. It's good to have something salty and full of protein for when you are really hungry. These items are also great because they are nonperishable, with a long shelf life and a lot of durability.

We also have some sweet snacks that are healthy, like breakfast bars. These are good because they contain fiber, vitamins, and carbs, but are also tough to keep in a backpack without being turned into powder.

Then we put a few children's vitamins in a Ziploc baggy. If your child has allergies, or is responsible enough to take a tablet for headache, nausea, diarrhea, or the like by themselves, then add those as well. In short, everything in the survival pack should be easy to store, long lasting, ready to eat, easy to open, filling, and provide energy and nutrients.

(I'll go off on a slight tangent here. Normally, I teach that you should only leave footprints when out in the wild or if trying to be found, leaving signs. But for the specific purpose of finding a lost child, I recommend littering—yes, littering. Getting rid of smelly trash may prevent animals from following your child. The important part of this specific littering is that your child is leaving a sign that might be picked up by persons and a trail that can be followed by scent hounds. So, for increasing chances of the child being found, litter.)

Obviously we need food to live. But when you find yourself in a survival situation, hunting for food usually won't be one of your first priorities. Often, finding water or shelter is more pressing. But once you have greater priorities sorted out, then start thinking about food.

*FEMA recommends that you keep an emergency food supply at home that will last at least two weeks. Here, Millie is checking the use-by dates on the cans in her family's survival supplies to make sure they're still good. It's important to rotate stock in your survival stash. Always place the newest items at the back of the storage area and pull the old ones to the front. If you have long-life dehydrated survival foods, make sure that your children know how to mix them up and let them taste them so that in the event of an emergency, the flavors are familiar to them. (Photo credit Jo Wilson)*

Once you have food, the first step is obvious—save it, since you just don't know how long you might have to go. But let's qualify that a bit. If you are in a scenario like a sinking ship, you might want to throw all food overboard or into your life raft in order to slow down the sinking.

But when you're on land and have to move and you just can't store or carry all available food. In such cases, soldiers have a simple saying: "Better to carry it in you, than on you!" So, try and eat all you can.

If you have to make a long journey and everything is perishable, you might just take a day or more and consume all you can before you begin your trek.

So, if you are in a safe location and you have food to eat that you just can't take, you might decide to stay or to stay a bit longer.

But, if you have food and you have the wherewithal to keep it for a while, you absolutely must make a plan for rationing it.

## Rationing

When rationing, there's a bit of math involved but it's fairly simple. Take the amount of food you have, divided by how many people there are, then divided by how many days you expect to be in survival mode. That's the amount that every person gets per day.

$$\text{Amount} \div \text{Number of People} \div \text{Duration}$$

But you don't for sure know how long you'll be out there. You may get rescued the next day or you may be out there for a very long time. So, for this "infinite" potential, you'll need to assign an arbitrary number of days based on the law of averages.

Let's look at averages. Survival situations that arise from crashes or getting lost in a vehicle tend to last three days. Survival situations for people lost camping or at sea tend to be around seven days. People lost in the jungles or mountains could face survival situations as long as thirty days. Consider your situation, take into account the laws of averages, and then make that your baseline planning figure.

So, you can be out there for a long time. So for my purposes, I use thirty days when planning. This gives me stronger mental preparation in case the rescue or return takes longer. Setting that figure keeps everyone hanging on longer and in better spirits than when using shorter day counts. It's a classic "better to under-promise and over-deliver" situation.

Moving on to the next factor, the number of people is simple if you're alone. But if not, then you have to be realistic in your rationing concepts. If there are kids or elderly folks in your group, they might not require as much. You might also consider weight as a factor—to give a three-hundred-pound, thirty-year-old athletic male the same rations as you'd give a petite eighteen-year-old female of ninety pounds wouldn't make sense.

You might also have some unconscious people present. Do you save their food for three days while they're out of it? What about family members who are seriously injured and whose chances of surviving aren't very good in the first place? It's not as clear-cut as just dividing equally per person. You must take into account the other factors.

The more concepts you can wrestle with during the planning phase, the better you'll handle them in reality. A key aspect of this book—much like training for combat—is that the harder you train and the more you sweat to prepare now, the less blood and loss of life there will likely be later.

## Some Guidelines

Humans will likely die if they go more than:

- Three minutes without air
- Three hours of extreme exposure (extreme heat or cold, desert or arctic conditions, or in freezing water)
- Three days without water
- Three weeks without food

There are lots of things that can impact these estimations, and one is willpower. Positive attitude from parents is key since its contagious for kids. Keeping positive and keeping busy keeps hope alive, sets a good example, and keeps will strong. If willpower is strong, you can prove all these limits wrong. They are, however, good guidelines for planning, assessing any situation, and making decisions.

## Phases of Starvation

I don't want to dwell on anything negative but this is survival and harsh realities must be confronted, especially by parents. If things are bad, you have to keep a positive attitude but make decisions accordingly. One of the realities might be a slow starvation. If you are the parents and are giving up food for your kids, then it's key to know these signs for yourselves and if you see your kids going through them, you can adjust what you're doing and saying to make allowances.

Everyone's patience will be pushed and tested and occasionally people will snap. The key is to know it, expect it, be loving and forgiving, keep moving on, and stay positive. For environmental factors, if it's freezing cold or scorching hot and your exposure to these extreme temperatures is high—or your physical demands from your surrounding elements are high—your timeframe of survival without food decreases significantly.

But it's important to remember that you can go about thirty days without food in almost any situation. And your chances of rescue or return within a month are very good. Humans can lose around 50 percent of their total weight and then make a full recovery, so keep the faith. Now, let's take a look at the signs of starvation.

### Hungry and Angry: Week 1

The first phase is hunger. Irritability and tiredness may result from lack of food and lower blood-sugar levels. There is an initial drop in weight from losing water the first twenty-four hours, and then the body begins to hold onto that water for the next twenty-four hours. After that, it starts to consume the stores of fat.

**Key:** This is the anger phase, when people are very grumpy and irritable. Be kind, be forgiving, and be understanding.

### Hungry and Angry: Week 2

In the next phase of starvation there is the obvious loss of weight, but muscle mass is also diminishing as the body begins to consume itself as a source of energy. During this phase, most people no longer experience normal hunger.

**Key:** This is when people begin to suffer deep depression and self-doubt.

### Starving and Crazy: Week 3

In the latter phases of starvation, there could be swelling from fluid under the skin, anemia, immune deficiency, chronic diarrhea, and decreased ability of the body to digest food because the digestive-acid production has been reduced. In this phase, go easy on eating food should you find some. And when you first commence to chow down, start by taking small bites, then wait for several minutes, and repeat.

**Key:** This is when people start acting crazy and extreme; in short, they begin getting desperate, go into rages, get suicidal or plain give up and quit. Keep them busy!

### Starved Properly

During the last stages of starvation, humans experience hallucinations, convulsions, and severe muscle pains, as well as irregular heartbeat and shallow breathing and they may just die.

**Key:** At this point, there is no extra energy for fighting or even crying, so it is mostly a hanging-on phase, trying to sustain and maintain and hope.

The best method for surviving while starving is a slow but constant pace of working towards some practical goal that can keep the mind occupied and not tax the body. Slowly improving your shelter or signals, collecting firewood, working on an escape vessel, or preparing for a journey by gathering supplies are all worthwhile jobs. The key is to keep busy, but not burdened. Stick together if in a group or keep it together if alone. To make sure your kids understand this, give them the "starvation/separation/survival" talk.

One thing I am big on teaching is surviving with honor. Remind yourselves and your kids that one day, this will end. You want everyone to still have their dignity when normal life resumes. Keeping this as a theme with the kids will make them love, admire, and respect you more during the situation and after.

And heaven forbid, you don't make it or others don't, those who survive will already suffer an emotional pain for life, so try not to make it a psychological pain from having done something you'd be ashamed of back home.

I also teach about cannibalism in my survival teachings but I won't here. I will mention it as something each family, particularly the parents, must discuss at some point, especially if a survival situation happens and food is scarce.

*Conch. Anyone who has eaten conch chowder knows how tasty these little buggers are. They're very handy survival food and are often just found wandering along the shoreline and in shallow seas. When foraging with small children check that everything that they gather is alive when they pick it up. When foraging in non-emergency situations, check that it's legal to remove your bounty. (Photo credit Ruth England Hawke)*

# Calorie Intake and Food Output

I'm not a big proponent of calorie count in survival. But it's good to look at some considerations when planning. We all need calories to live—but in moderation. Eat too many and you get fat, eat too little and you lose weight.

The three main components of food that contribute to caloric intake are carbohydrates (starches and sugars as found in fruits, veggies, sweets, cereals, and the like), proteins (meats, legumes, dairy), and fat (animal fats, oils, nuts).

You need all three to maintain a balanced diet and maximum health. If you're going to be surviving for a while, after the initial period of stabilization you will really need to do the best you can to cover all three areas. But the goal is always to get out and get home safe as quickly as possible, so this is more of a long-term plan.

## Calorie Facts for Average Human

* Men need about 2,500 calories per day.
* Women need about 2,000 calories per day.
* Children and the elderly may use less, as little as 1,500 but if they are in puberty, they may burn as much as a grown man, and more if they are very active.
* We only burn about 20 percent of daily calories through activity and exercise.
* Seventy percent of these calories are actually spent on all the organs working all day.
* Ten percent are burned off while processing the food from which you're getting the calories.

So, let's say you didn't eat at all for twenty-four hours. You'd still have to burn calories for your organs to keep functioning. Even if you just laid there and slept, your body would still be burning calories. This is called a "basal metabolism rate," or the base amount of calories your body is burning while you do nothing.

Though studies vary, most folks will expend about 1,800 calories just sitting there for a day.

A good rule of thumb is my "dirty dozen" calorie rule—twelve calories are used up by every one pound of your flesh every day. So a two-hundred-pound man uses up 2,400 calories a day just by existing.

What it means in true survival terms is threefold—how much food you need, how much you give each person, and what you prioritize in the first place.

It is likely that any food you have on hand is pre-packaged and labelled with nutritional values. Use that info to factor into your equation when figuring out how much each person needs.

If you don't have packaged food, it's good to have some rough ideas of what wild foods will do for you, so here are some guidelines.

## Calories from Food in the Wild

- One pound of fat is worth about 3,500 calories.
- Wild meats tend to be about five hundred calories per pound (rabbit, deer, boar, etc.).
- Fish are around 750 calories per pound on average (the range is wide).
- Plants come in way low at around one hundred to two hundred calories per pound (the range is wide—roots and tubers provide more calories than other veggies).
- Fruits are about double the veggie value at three hundred to four hundred calories per pound.
- Eggs offer about one hundred calories per egg.
- Nuts are great for pure survival energy, with 2,500 calories per pound.

*Seashore foraging can be bountiful, safe, and very tasty. With a little guidance it's easy for kids to do. This samphire was harvested from a field in an estuary's flood plain. Be sure to boil seashore succulents like samphire in plenty of fresh water to reduce the salt. (Photo credit Ruth England Hawke)*

# Sometimes Taking Life Preserves Life

## Meat! It Does a Body Good

Animals and insects can meet about 90 percent of all your nutritional needs in a survival situation, and it's an easier and safer bet to catch and kill animals than trying to subsist off of plants alone. Ounce for ounce, you will always get the most calories from meat over any other food source out there, and in survival, it's calories that count most. The brain needs glucose to function and the human body can get this from animal fat, as the liver breaks it down to its chemical components. Also, that glucose is a simple carbohydrate the body can use for energy, so you can get carbs from meat. The difference is that these are not the complex carbs you get from roots and grains, so they don't give that longer-lasting energy like breads and pastas do, but they do give you all you need to survive.

Almost everything out there moving around is edible in one way or another, whereas it's the opposite with plants—most plants are not edible for humans. So, make meat part of your family survival strategy. Further, be it fishing, hunting, or trapping, you should consider giving your kids at least one meat-based survival skill as part of your strategy for them to survive without you.

### Having Meat Means Getting It and That Means Killing It

It's never pleasant and I take no joy in it, but killing animals is a survival necessity. There are many ways to kill. I assure the non-hunters there is no real *nice* way to kill.

You never know if you're going to end up killing a baby critter or a mama critter with hungry mouths to feed. It happens. You have to look at it in the bigger picture—that animal is on the food chain for something to consume, so it might as well be you. Heck, if you died out there, it might the other way around and that critter would be nibbling on your flesh. So, you're only doing what you need to do, and that animal's end is its fate.

All you can do is dispatch it as quickly and humanely as possible, and be thankful for the nutrition it is providing you. At the end of the day it is the law of nature, and it is a natural way for an animal to go, being eaten by a larger predator. It just happens to be you as the predator today.

### Hit Fast, Hit Hard

The safest and most humane way to kill is to be the meanest and most brutal you can in the offing of the critter. Like with first aid, sometimes you must be cruel to be kind. Don't try to "beat it to death gently."

*Morgan caught three of these chipmunks, cleaned them, and then fried them up with onion and garlic. It's a hard lesson for some children to learn but there is no difference between eating a cute furry animal and a hamburger, and in a survival situation you're unlikely to come across a burger joint. (Photo credit Kim Serigne)*

For survival hunting, simple is always best. It is usually a two-part process: first, disable or hurt it enough so that it stops moving, at least for a moment, and second, kill it the second you get the chance to finish it off.

Try to kill outright whenever possible. Adopt the mindset that you need to try to seriously injure your prey with the first blow, and then close for the kill. If you need to, throw a rock, sharpened stick, or weighted club to distract or disable it long enough for you to close the distance. Once committed to the kill, is must be fast, furious, and final.

*Play is an oft undervalued part of learning. If your kids are playing at survival, then they're developing skills. There was no sharpened end on this spear, but Gabe still learned how to walk on a riverbed without slipping, how difficult it is to see through the glare of the water, how quickly fish move and where they hide, how to get underwater when insects bother him, and how long he can stay in the water before getting too cold. All of this was learnt through play, without him even realizing it. (Photo credit Ruth England Hawke)*

## Catching Animals

Before you can kill an animal and eat it, you have to catch it. Too bad it's not as simple as walking into the butcher shop and pointing at what you want. In the wild, you have to use all your wits and resources to catch these critters. So you'll use tracking, hunting, snares, and various traps in your efforts to find, catch, kill, eat, and live.

*Bub (aged eleven here) and his brothers and sister eat their alligators in red gravy. Bub actually caught this alligator with a rotten chicken and a hook and just jumped into the water with it for fun. (Photo credit Kim Serigne)*

## Tracking

There is an art to tracking but the real deal is that when you are hungry, you'll track animals for food. Once you find signs that animals have been present, make two key determinations: Are the tracks of something too big for you to bother with? If they are not too big, are they fresh enough to be worth pursuing?

Tracks usually lead to one of three places: home, food source, or water source. And the finding of any one of these is a good thing.

It might not sound so nice, but feces are a natural part of life and are usually found somewhere around tracks, making it easier to track the animal. I recommend gathering information on animals in your area that includes their tracks and scat markings.

By learning these things together with your kids, both you and they will have a greater understanding of your environment. Many rodents and small game like weasels, raccoons, and squirrels have paw pads with or without claws. If there are claws evident, the tracks are likely from the feisty critters; conversely, tracks lacking clawed pads are mostly from the class of the easier "prey" animals.

To guesstimate an animal's weight by their tracks, just step beside their tracks and see what kind of impression your foot leaves in relation to the track. The depth will give you an idea of their weight.

Fresh tracks will have crisp edges; look at the soil and see how dry or crumbled it looks. Take into account what the weather has been lately and you can guesstimate the freshness of the tracks.

As for droppings, the wetter and more scent they have, they fresher they are. Even if they're dried out, check around to see if there is a home nearby.

Further develop your tracking skills by looking for signs of feeding and foraging. Things that have been chewed on, scratched at, dug up, turned over, and in any other way disturbed and/or modified from their natural condition are all signs that critters are about. Once you see these things, keep looking for more signs until you find tracks.

## Hunting

This is the simple act of looking for, finding, and then engaging the animal either by stealth or direct confrontation, usually with a weapon. Hunting is my preferred method for finding chow, but it isn't always the desired technique as it requires time, plus not all the critters in your environment might be best acquired by hunting.

Now, while you're out "hunting" for tracks and drops, whether it be for small or big, you're still looking for birds' nests for eggs to raid, as well as anything you can whack on the head along the way such as lizards, snakes, bugs, etc. Everything that moves is a food source. So keep your eyes open at all times, and keep several weapons handy at all times as well.

### Be Safe and Consider the Time of Day

Start in the morning, at first light or just before. This is when many critters are most active. Night dwellers will be headed for home and day dwellers will be looking for breakfast. No matter what, do not hunt at night! And try not to risk hunting at dusk, either, because the predators come out at night, and they can see in the dark while you can't. Also, it is very easy to get disoriented in the dark and you could easily end up spending a miserable night away from your camp.

If you must hunt at dusk, keep a fire lit, keep it in sight, and hunt only for the things that might come to check out your fire's light. Surprisingly, while big things tend to stay away from fires, smaller, more inquisitive critters often come for a peek.

### Finishing

Everything fights for its life, and as such, everything can hurt you in its own self-defense. Always exercise extreme caution with teeth, claws, horns, and anything like stinging tails, spitting, etc. If the animal has it, it will use it, so always be cautious and safe.

## Snares and Traps

Outside of hunting, the other way to get food is to capture it in a snare or trap. I recommend using these techniques for smaller creatures, as these don't provide much food and so don't justify using a lot of time and energy to hunt them. Also, they can be very difficult to catch, so best to let trickery and technique do the work for you.

The basic principles of traps and snares fall in line with those of hunting, except hunting is all about mobility operations, and "snaps" (snares and traps) are about static operations. It's important that you choose your location carefully. To do this, you apply the same techniques for hunting—looking for drops and tracks and then finding a home, hole, or feed spot—and set up your "snap."

Snaps take a lot of time and work to initially set up. After that, they just require vigilance to check regularly to either get your catch or re-set your trap or improve it, as often a first-time snap setter will find they need to tweak their technique. Just be patient.

### Snares

If you have wire, twine, string, rope, or cordage of any kind, you can make a simple and effective snare. The cordage provides the mechanism for tension, which is the basis for a snare's spring action. The trigger is what causes the release of the tension energy, by the animal's movement. Remember it this way: snare the hare. Hares have springy legs, so the spring of the snare will make him hop right off the ground.

The spring snare is just what it sounds like. When it is triggered, it will pop like a spring under tension and snare your prey. The best way to make a spring snare is to take a small sapling tree and bend it over to look like an upside down "U." Then tie a small piece of string to its top, and tie the other end of that string to a little wooden hook, which is then hooked onto a small stake in the ground. Then tie another piece of string in a circle with a loosely fitted slip knot, and hold it open using two small twiglets.

Choose a sapling on the side of a game trail and add bait to lure the critter. The animal will put its head into the loop to get at the bait, and in doing so, will disturb and inadvertently tug on the looped string. This causes the string to pull the wooden hook out of the stake, releasing the tension on the little sapling tree which then springs back up to its original upright position. In the process, it snatches the noose tight around the critter's neck, snatches its body off the ground, and holds it dangling off the ground with the noose choking the life out of it.

If you don't have bait, the concept is such that the snare will be on a pathway that the creature will need to pass, and in doing so, will be caught. Snaps sometimes fail, spring too early or not at all, so be ready for failures and just re-set and try again.

**Bait and Place**

Now both snares and traps can be used with bait or place techniques. "Bait" involves food or other form of attraction to lure an animal into the snap. "Place" simply means that you situate the snap on a well-used animal trail or lair. Ideally, you'd want to employ both bait and place combined to enhance your chances. Choke points are the key. It's just like setting up an ambush for soldiers—use the terrain to channel them in, then use a ruse as bait to lure them into the channel.

So, choose a good location, right outside of the animal's home, hole, lair, etc. Or choose a spot near the feeding grounds or watering hole that looks well used. The principle to these is that, no matter which route the critter takes, it will always come home, need water, and go to feed. So, these are ideal sites for laying your ambush.

Now, if you don't find such obvious sites, but you're onto a good game trail, as many critters will use a trail like a veritable highway, then use the game trail for your location. But when you do this, be sure to "channel or funnel" the critters into your newly made love-nest of hate, by laying logs, rocks, sticks and brush in a way so that it funnels them into your trap *both ways*! This important point is often overlooked by newbie snap layers. Picture an hourglass angle from above, so that a "V" focuses them into your trap from either direction of approach.

## Traps

If you don't have cordage, then you have no capacity for tension to make a snare and must use a different principle of physics to create a trap. Basically, traps use leverage or gravity as the mechanism of tension. The trigger is the loss of balance cause by the animal's movement, allowing gravity to apply the energy to execute your trap. Remember it like this: slap the trap. Just like you'd slap your hand down to catch a mouse trying to escape, your trap will slap down on your prey.

### Deadfall

The deadfall is the most basic of traps. You need a weight that can fall like a dead weight and kill the creature dead. You'll need bait most of the time on the tip of your trigger or you can put the trigger on a path and let the creature bump it to set it off. The key is to use a stick to hold the weight up and balanced in a position so that it's strong enough to hold the weight, but delicately placed enough so that a little nibble of the bait on the trigger will make the stick move causing the weight to fall.

It takes some time and finesse to make traps and snares, and there are no guarantees that the right-sized critter will come along or that the trap will work perfectly. So the real key to success is the "P for Plenty" method, also known as the "Shotgun Hunting" style. In contrast to the "one shot, one kill" motto of the sniper, you need to set out lots of snaps all over the place in hopes that you'll get something, much like a hunter with a shotgun who shoots into the bush somewhat blindly, or at a flock of birds hoping something will get hit. So, instead of spray and pray, spread the dread so all the critters live in fear of you.

### Nets

If you have a net, you can use the snare method replacing the noose with the net. You can also use a net with the basic deadfall method, and instead of getting crushed, the animal will get ensnared in the net after it triggers the net to fall upon it. You can also use a net to hunt with, by hiding and then throwing it onto your prey as it comes near unawares. You can also use nets to catch birds and fish.

### Holes

When all else fails, start digging holes. It is hard work to dig holes, so this method is not to be undertaken unless you have energy to expend. But know that digging a simple hole is surprisingly effective for catching things. Snakes and small critters just seem to fall into them when placed in the right spot. Dig your holes (size and placement) based on the type of animal you believe is nearby and hope to catch. Regardless of size, try to loosely cover the hole with light twigs and leaves, making sure that an animal can break through this cover and that the hole is deep enough to contain them once they do. If you have bait, place some in the middle of the cover above the hole.

### Boxes

Another technique is making cages or boxes with a small hole for the critter to stick its head in and inverted spikes to hold the animal's head from pulling out. It's sort of like a Chinese finger trap. The animal will press its head through the opening to nibble at the bait, but they won't be able to get their head out.

### Fishing and Techniques

If you're anywhere near water, going fishing is always a smart option. Tackle is not that difficult to make in the wild, the techniques of catching fish are varied and achievable, and almost all fish are safe to eat.

There are lots of ways to improvise when fishing but that is beyond the scope of this book. What I do suggest, is that everyone in the family have a mini fishing kit as part of their bag so everyone can do some form of fishing to survive if they're alone and if the family is together, all of you can stay busy fishing together!

For those who may have lost their bags or not packed a fishing kit, here is a quick overview of what you can do to create a fishing system.

*Daddy and baby fishing in California. Mykel is practicing primitive fishing using a stick, filaments from some 550-cord, and a bent pin. There's no way that that method would hold a three-year-old's attention for long but a dipping net is the perfect introduction to fishing; there is always something to catch, even if it's just water bugs and algae. (Photo credit Ruth England Hawke)*

Again, fishing is fairly easy in terms of physical exertion so it's a good activity for survivors, and it can take time, so when you need to pass time, it is a good way to feel productive and stay focused.

Finally, fishing provides easy-to-make meals, and most folks, especially kids, are averse to cleaning fish.

So try taking the family on a fishing trip and go to the types of water that are in your area, or where you might normally go camping. Remember that rivers, ponds, and oceans all require slightly different techniques.

## Poles

Pole are very helpful if you need to get your hook out farther into the water than you could without it. It also helps for taking some of the tension off your hand from pulling in the fish. If you have to put a lot of line on the pole to get it out farther, once you get a fish on the line, place the pole on the ground and your foot on the pole and then work the fish in by the string. I find two sticks or crudely-fashioned gloves will help me work the string without hurting my hands.

## Weights

Weights are sometimes needed either to cast out or to get your baited hook down to the bottom if that's where you think the fish are. For survival fishing, I find the best way is to tie a rock or other weight to the end of the string and then tie the hook with an additional piece of string onto the line six to twelve inches above the weight. Look for rocks that will be easily secured to your line—for example, a smooth round rock won't work as well as a rock with natural grooves to hold the line better.

## Bait

Bait is anything that you think will make the fish bite the hook. Bugs and animal guts are usually the best bait. You might consider "chumming" the water by spreading extra guts on its surface to attract numerous fish into a feeding frenzy, and then whack them with sticks as they feed. You can use insects, worms, berries, or even fish eggs from other fish. When you use bait in the traditional way, make sure you fasten the bait onto the hook or barb as securely as possible—you don't want to be giving those fish a free meal. If you can hook a live insect onto your hook, all the better.

*Bub with some lovely fat shrimp. Bub knows how to drive his dad's shrimp boat, catch shrimp, and cook them. Kids can achieve a lot when they're not stifled by helicopter parenting. (Photo credit Kim Serigne)*

## Lures

Lures are a good substitute for when you don't have bait. Anything like feathers or light pieces of cloth can be used to mimic a fly. Anything shiny can be used as a "spoon" to get the underwater biters—tops of soda cans, small pieces of plastic, metal, or anything shiny that you can trim to a small piece and tie off to your string. Tie it just above your hook so it moves around right in front of but won't stop the fish from getting a bite on your hook.

## Floats

Floats are useful in two ways. If you're after mid-depth feeders or just-under-the-surface feeders, then you want to mount to your line a piece of stick or plastic that will float on the water so your eye can see it, but will hold your baited hook suspended underwater and off the bottom, at the depth you set. Once in the water, simply watch the float or "bob" for any motion—when fish bite at the baited hook, the float will bob up and down telling you that it's time to pull in the fish.

The other way to use a float is just to let it get your hook out into the water where you want it. It will still function as a "bobber," but you're also using it to help in your placement by letting it float over to where you want, either with current or wind. In this manner, tie the bob just a couple inches above the hook.

## Spears

Spears are good to make and use for fishing, though they take some skill to master. The real trick is that the points have to be very small and very sharp, and to include several points on the end. The best kind are long thin spears with small nails at the end filed very sharp and positioned in a circular pattern, as opposed to horizontal like a dinner fork.

## Sticks

Sticks can be used with some success in shallow waters like ponds, slow streams, and shallow bays. In such settings, it may not be a bad idea to try this method first before spending time on the more time-consuming methods—at least for a few minutes. Stand in the shallow water and position yourself perfectly still, then wait. If you see fish swimming by and close to the surface, swing hard and directly at the fish's head. Often this will only stun a fish, so be ready to finish with several quick and hard whacks, or simply grab them and chuck them onto shore.

## Nets

Nets are great tools if you have them.

*A cast net is a great survival tool and is more interesting for a child to use than sitting still with a fishing pole. It takes a little while for a little one to master the technique required but it's worth persevering. Buy the smallest net when your child is learning. (Photo credit Ruth England Hawke)*

String the net across the stream or river in a manner known as a "gill net," placing it close to the inside bank of a river bend and going as far out into the stream as its length allows. In the ocean or on a deep lake, if you have a vessel from which to fish, you can fasten weights to the corners of the net to hold it down just below the surface, then pull it up quickly to try to catch anything that may be in it.

You can also use a net by standing on the bank of a river or lake and casting it on top of fish that swim by—just make sure the perimeter of the netting has enough weights tied to it to hold the fish down in the water long enough for you to quickly approach and club. You can also use the simple scooping-type nets to catch fish. If you have a smaller net or one with finer mesh, use that for catching small fish like minnows. Or use the big net to try and head them off or divert them into the net, and then swing them onto shore or your raft.

### Light

Light is actually an effective tool for hunting lots of things— you just need a flashlight or a little pocket laser or even something reflective that you can divert the sunlight with. Laser lights and flashlights that you point and maneuver on the

*Morgan, Joe, Logan (Bub), and Avery with redfish, black drum, and a gaspargou. Their dad believes that if some catastrophe befell him they could survive on their own by hunting, trapping, and fishing. I think he may well be right. (Photo Credit Kim Serigne)*

surface can lure freshwater fish as they are attracted to the light and may check it out, allowing you to club or spear the fish. You can also hunt crayfish and frogs and lots of other critters with a flashlight until they are stunned or scared enough to be killed.

### The Rules for Eating Fish Are Simple

Eat them soon after you catch them—anything from the water spoils quickly in the air. If they look ill or deformed in any way, don't eat them, but don't throw them away either—instead, use them as bait. Use all fish guts for bait—don't eat any fish guts. If they look okay, clean fish by gutting. Also, skin creatures like eels or catfish, and scale any fish that has them. Use the heads and eyeballs to make soups.

And some fish, like catfish or eels, can be tricky to skin, so try and stake them to a tree and use a pliers to pull their skin off.

There are plenty more fishing tricks like making tidal traps or fish baskets or using plant poisons, but those are advanced techniques and at this point, you just want the kids to be able to be fed, so a pole or net will usually do the trick.

## How to Prepare Animals for Consumption

- **Birds** can be peeled out of their skins, but you lose all the fat that way. So pluck them as best you can, save the feathers for other uses, and then burn the rest of the feather stubble off by rolling the birds in the fire before cooking. All birds are safe to consume. There are rare birds with poisonous feathers, but they're generally not a concern.
- **Mammals** are universally safe to eat. Some have poisonous sacks, teeth, claws, spikes, and many other types of defenses you should be wary of, but once killed, skinned, and cooked, they are all safe to eat.
- **Reptiles** are mostly safe to eat. All snakes are safe to eat once killed, beheaded, skinned, and cooked. So, too, are turtles, tortoises, lizards, and gators. Frogs get a little dicey, as some have poisonous skins. In general, the amount of meat on frogs is not worth the effort to catch, cook, and clean, but some big giant frogs might be worth the trouble, and all those big ones are safe to munch. Of course, if you can come by small frogs with little effort, them grab them and eat them if they're not of the poisonous persuasion. The general rule for poisonous frogs and toads is that the very brightly colored ones are no good. The general rule for all reptiles is to skin, gut, and behead them. Then cook or boil them. If you are unsure what kind of critter you've got, try to skin it with sticks instead of using your hands as their skin might be poisonous. But once the skin is off, they're good to cook.

*For most children, helping to prepare a meal might mean peeling potatoes or scrambling some eggs, but not for Kim Serigne's kids. Bub, Joe, and Avery are skinning and cleaning frogs for dinner. Most days when they're not in school, they're out catching dinner too. Their dad has taught them how to live off the land and hunt and trap according to the season. This is vital knowledge in a survival situation. (Photo credit Kim Serigne)*

- **To Skin or Not to Skin:** Skin all reptiles. Skin most mammals (except pigs, as they cook better in the skin). Don't skin birds; pluck them instead to get the fat. Scale and/or skin fish.
- **Guts** are to be put to their best use, not necessarily their full use. I teach that it's good to eat the key organs—heart, liver, and maybe the kidneys if large enough, but usually they're not. The rest gets a bit iffy and are best used as bait for traps and fishing.
- **Bones:** If you can't use them for tools, or dry them by the fire for chalky anti-diarrheals, then try eating the marrow out of the big bones and boiling the small bones to get the marrow nutrition out of them and into a broth for drinking.
- **Cooking** is best done by boiling, if possible, as it allows you to get good, clean fluids into your body and add some flavor to it. On a practical level, it is easy to drop everything in pot and let it stew while you do other things rather than have to tend the fire and turn the meat so it doesn't burn.

If you don't have a pot or pan to cook in, then you can use sticks and cook them over the fire but be careful of the sticks, make sure they don't have any white sap or bad smells. You can also cook by laying meat on stones by or in the fire; just make sure you don't use river rocks as those can explode when heated.

Also, when cooking meat, it helps to throw bugs and plants in for flavor and texture. If for some reason you can't boil, just cook the meat over your fire, rotating it often to cook it all the way through. You can also cook meat by placing it on a flat board close to the fire, or turning it to cook through (this is called "planking"). Or use sticks and lashings to build a spit on which to place the meat above the fire.

## Bugs

Eating bugs is a super way to survive as they are easy to find, catch, and cook, but it's the hardest for our mindset.

Bugs are everywhere on the planet, and since they are often at the bottom of the food chain, that means there are more of them than anything else. They are more plentiful than the animals and a whole lot easier to catch. They are also more plentiful than edible plants and provide a whole lot more energy and nourishment than the plants.

So bugs are one of your best survival food resources, period. That said, let's look at some basic bug nutrition to help you get your head around the fact that you're going to need to be eating them. I'll also focus on which ones pack the most nutrients, so you know which ones to go for.

*Avery loves frogs. She caught these frogs with her dad and her brothers by taking a boat out into the bayou at night and shining a light into the frogs' eyes, then grabbing them by hand. Avery skinned the frogs while her dad fried them. Notice that Avery has a whole frog on her fork, not just the legs. There is very little waste this way, making it more respectful to the animal and best practice in terms of survival. (Photo credit Kim Serigne)*

**Bug Nutrition Facts**

I am not one of those folks who likes to eat bugs, but I have eaten giant cockroaches, huge maggots, big fat grubs, spiky crickets, biting praying mantis, and many other assorted flavors of creepy, crawly critters. At home, we occasionally buy dried bug snacks as a fun change of pace. By doing so, we introduce the kids to new flavors and convince them that it's okay to eat bugs in the case of an emergency.

My first option in survival is always to kill bigger animals to live, but if I were to be wounded or ill, then I might have to eat whatever I can get my hands on within crawling distance, and it is certainly far easier for children to find and catch bugs than it is to hunt or fish.

I also teach that it would be pure foolishness to ignore the insects as a food source and a good supplement to any diet out in the wild. So if you see them, eat them! As a matter of fact, many people eat these things daily or as a delicacy in various cultures. That said, let's look at the real value of eating some insects—you might be surprised how they stack up.

Let's use two well-known forms of meat, pure beef and cod fish, as a standard.

- For 100 grams of lean ground beef, you get about 28 grams of protein and no fat.
- For 100 grams of broiled cod fish, you get about 27 grams of protein and no fat.

Now look at comparable protein and fat statistics per 100 grams of the following insects:

| CREATURE | PROTEIN | FAT |
|---|---|---|
| Beef | 28 | 0 |
| Fish | 27 | 0 |
| Grasshoppers | 20 | 6 |
| Termites | 14 | 0 |
| Crickets | 12 | 5 |
| Beetles | 19 | 8 |
| Ants | 13 | 3 |
| Worms | 9 | 5 |
| Caterpillars | 28 | 0 |

*Compiled from studies done in Africa, Mexico, and the US.

In short, bugs are probably one of the best survival foods if you can get enough of them. If the quantities are lacking, then use them as you catch them to supplement your diet.

## Bug Dining Rules

*   **Beetles, Caterpillars, Ants, Crickets, Grasshoppers, Cockroaches, Etc:** The general rule is if they are brightly colored, smell foul, have spikes or barbs, or bite, then you might want to avoid them, but that doesn't necessarily rule them out as a food source. Remember, everything has exceptions! It's almost always better to boil them or roast them. Remove anything hard like shells, legs, wings, pincher heads, and stinger tails.
*   **Hairy Insects** should be squashed and the guts thrown into broth for boiling. Burn the hairs off with the flames.
*   **Spiders** are edible, but they're really not worth the time or risk as you usually only get one at a time. However if you find a huge tarantula, chuck him into a stew.
*   **Scorpions** also can be scarfed. Just be careful, remove the stinger, and cook well.
*   **Bees** are very nutritious and often come in bunches. There are two tricks to eating bees. One, you must kill them before they kill you. And two, you must remove their stingers before eating them. However, to kill bees or get them to leave or at least remain calm, you'll need to use smoke, and it's simply far too risky a venture for a parent and certainly for a child. However, if you want to make this part of your survival skills, definitely do your homework and be ready to get stung.
*   **Slugs and Worms** are all edible, but they require an extra step. Soak them for a day or so in water to get them to purge their guts, then cook them up well. Again, anything brightly colored, especially around the sea, is likely dangerous and is better to leave well enough alone.

That's about it on the bottom of the food chain, and for food in general. The good thing is, there's lots out there to eat! It takes some doing, thinking, and getting used to, but mostly, know that there is food out there and you'll be okay in that regard.

# Eating Plants

This is important: Eating unknown plants can be deadly! So the best rule is to avoid eating plants unless you are 100 percent certain of the plants. But, for those plants you do know, it's best to start teaching the kids and treating them to snacks of those plants, while safe at home.

The bottom line is that it's just plain dangerous to rely on plants as a food source if you do not know the plants you're trying to eat. And if you're going to do it, practice at home so kids can get used to it so if they have a bad reaction, you can safely get them to advanced medical care.

Another harsh fact is that plants simply don't give you enough bang for the buck nutrition-wise. They do have nutrients in terms of vitamins, minerals, fiber, and some carbohydrates.

Such nutrition for the survivor is a secondary concern, whereas real energy in the form of calories is critical and that comes best in the form of meat, plain and simple. But, if you find a lot of something, and it looks like it might yield a large amount of food, then the taste test comes into play.

Of course this might warrant the ultimate risk—death. Use all of your experience and common sense in trying to assess not only the quantity and quality of the potential food source plant, but also its potential danger. Use what you know to be good.

### Ask Yourself These Questions

- Does it look like anything you've seen in the store or restaurant before?
- Does it look like any food source you've heard of or seen pictures of?

Now let's talk about the real deal with the Universal Edibility Test (UET). With that, let's dig into the Universal Edibility Test (UET). I'll include the official *US Army Survival Manual* procedure and my own comments and observations based on experience and application. Ultimately, it will be up to you to decide what you do and how you do it.

## Edibility Tests

### The Military Version

- Test only one part of the plant at a time.
- Smell for strong or acid odors. This alone cannot be relied upon.
- During this time, test for any contact reactions by placing the part to be tasted against your inner wrist or elbow for about fifteen minutes.
- During the test, eat nothing except the part being tested and purified water.

### Hawke Taste Test

The above is absolutely correct, but also neglects common sense. Most folks aren't going to arbitrarily take a plant, mix it up, and make a salad. The Hawke Taste Test is adjusted for the everyday person.

*The first cucumber to be harvested! Our son's vegetable consumption rocketed with his first garden. When kids are involved with food production they're much more likely to eat the end results, be that plants or animals. Getting them used to a variety of flavors now makes them much more receptive to any unusual food that they may have to eat in a survival situation. (Photo credit Ruth England Hawke)*

First, there are some good foods that are stinky, but smell will tell you if you're on the right track or not. Touch it to the outer part of your forearm and, if no reaction there, then try the inner part. This way, if it does flame up, the outer hurts a whole lot less. Nothing wrong with waiting fifteen minutes, but really, five will give you a good enough indicator if it's going to burn or not.

Next, if you have purified water, you're already doing okay. Furthermore, if you have other food, stay off it while testing so as to not mix or dilute your test results.

Next, separate all the components—leaves, stalk, roots, flowers, fruit, buds, etc. This too, tends to overlook the obvious. Most survivors who are starving aren't looking for all the parts to eat; they want that one thing they think they know that might be edible.

Now, do not eat for eight hours before the test since, if you are starving, you probably haven't eaten for much longer than eight hours. The point is to have an empty stomach for the best "thorough" analysis of the potential food source as viable or not. Most people will surely be here by the time they're ready to risk their life by eating unknown plants.

You can also choose to add a scratch test. Scratch a piece of your flesh with your nail and see if rubbing the potential food on that causes a reaction or irritation. Not scratching yourself is an option to be extra safe; especially if you have dirty fingernails and you're in the tropics, I don't recommend tearing holes into your only layer of protection from infection.

Next, take a portion of the part of the plant you plan to eat and prepare it the way you plan to eat it. If you have fire, cook or boil everything. There is no reason not to do so. Yes, cooking or boiling might take away some nutrients, but it will also take away more bacteria and toxins, which will hurt you a lot more. Boil if you can as that makes a broth you can drink to stay hydrated and still get some of those nutrients. But if you have no fire, then this test will be done in the "raw." But do rinse or peel whenever possible.

Before tasting the prepared plant part, touch a small portion to your lip and see if it burns or itches. If there is no reaction, chew it thoroughly for fifteen minutes, but do not swallow.

If anything goes wrong or there is any negative reaction at all, induce vomiting and drink lots of water.

If after three minutes there is no reaction, place a pinch on your tongue and hold it there fifteen minutes. However, you'll probably know sooner than three minutes. One minute is likely okay for the first touch, but the prescribed fifteen minutes on the tongue is a bit much. I say five minutes is good. You'll know if it's not right pretty quickly as you'll be so hungry and your juices will be flowing, so reactions will be much more concentrated and quicker. If there is no burning, itching, stinging, inflammation or other reaction, then swallow and wait eight hours.

If so far so good, swallow and wait. But I'd say, based on your sense of the food closely resembling a plant you know or think you know, wait up to two hours, though most of the time you'll know in the first hour or so. However, the Military Test says to wait eight hours; if nothing happens, the plant part as prepared is safe to eat.

While waiting, take a nap, get up, and move around a bit to see if activity induces nausea. But if all seems good, it's likely okay to consume.

If nothing happens, then start with a quarter cups' worth. Eat a decent amount but don't gorge yourself. If it's not good, it would be worse to have a belly full of it.

In short, the Military says the UET takes twenty-four hours. Hawke says it takes eight hours.

## A Primer on Universal Edibles

### Fruits, Nuts, and Berries

These are found all over the planet. Even in the arctic it is possible to dig up berries from under the snow. The problem is that they come in so many shapes, sizes, and colors. So be sure to apply the rules of the UET:

**Amount:** Are there lots to eat, or are they big enough to make a real meal from a few?

**About:** Do they look like something you know or have seen before?

**In Doubt:** Do any warning signs—smell, touch, taste, look—call it into doubt?

If in doubt, throw it out!

Also keep an eye out for the critters around you. Are they nibbling on something? Could be a nut or berry. Are there lots of insects about? They could be attracted to some fruit either in the trees or on the ground.

### An Easy Way to Remember the Berry Rules

- PB&B: Purple, Black, and Blue Are Good for You (90 percent good to go!)
- Yellow, Green, and White Mean Death by Night (90 percent deadly to you.)
- Red can be good for the head, or . . .
- Red can mean you'll soon be dead (it's a fifty-fifty chance, so be cautious.)

## Roots and Tubers

Anything you dig up should be cooked if at all possible. Not only is there concern about ground bacteria, fungi, and other evil spores, but the real deal is that roots are a concentrate of everything that's in the plant's storage facility. Boiling or cooking can neutralize any toxins or otherwise strong concentrations that could harm you.

It's quite hard to arbitrarily dig up food. It takes time and energy. So, try to have an idea what to look or smell for, and only commence to digging if you're pretty sure that the edibles you've found will keep you in stock for a while.

Again, look at the ground for signs of disturbance to see if any animals have been rooting around. Chances are that if they dug, they got it, so study the plant stalk left behind.

I sometimes teach adults about eating trees and grasses but this is far too difficult to teach kids. So with the little ones, focus on identifying fruits and nuts in their area.

## Regional Factors

I like to break a lot of these survival things down into regions, as some facts are quite location specific. For example, there is little use in teaching arctic knowledge to desert dwellers. Also, concentrating on a specific region helps parents focus on what to teach their kids.

With that, let's take a general look at some of the most common plant food found in abundance in each of the different regional climates.

### Dry and Desert Areas

- **Cacti** are all over most deserts and they're mostly edible. If you chop into them and they're green, they're good to go! If they have a white sap, don't rule them out right away—smell, finger-touch, lip-touch, and/or tongue-touch the sap. If no bad smell or burn, go easy at first; but figure its likely ok. But if it doesn't look right, forget it.
- **Agave and yucca flower stalks** are good to eat and provide a decent meal. Cut off about three feet of the bud and stalk (which looks like a huge asparagus tip), peel the hard outside part, and eat raw. The flowers of both are edible when raw, but cooked tastes better. The fruit of both can be eaten as well, and it's best to eat while white inside. You can cut the agave down to its middle section and dig a hole that fills with water. After drinking, cut it off and cook it for a few hours— the agave is like a big potato, and the yucca roots are also just like potatoes.
- **Date palm** is a good food find. It looks like a normal palm tree but instead of large nuts, you'll see clusters of small round fruit. The best way to get at them

is to cut the tree down. If you should happen upon these fruits—which are like coconuts and bananas—in the jungle, you'll know what to do and enjoy.

- **Acacia** are little trees with the thorny spines and yellow flowers. They can be found worldwide in good quantities. Just one tree can provide a whole meal as the flowers, the buds, and the young leaves are all good to eat.
- **Amaranth** is found all over the world as well. It is full of vitamins and minerals, and when found, it is usually in abundance. It can be eaten raw or cooked. It is also known in:
  - Africa: Vegetable for all, or yoruba
  - Asia: Different names all over, but the Chinese call it yin choi
  - Latin America and Caribbean: Here it's called callalou
  - US: Chinese spinach

I'm a fan because it is easy to identify, plentiful, and has lots of protein in the seeds. It grows in any areas where it is drier in climate.

### Oceans and Seashores

Seaweed, kelp, samphire, and pretty much anything green from the sea or near the sea can be eaten. We have samphire all over South Florida and we harvest it for dinner often when we go for hikes.

The seaweeds and kelps can be eaten raw in a pinch, but only take small amounts unless or until you can cook or boil them. Many of the harder shoreline plants are also edible, but best boiled. In general, most sea greens are fairly safe to munch, just make sure they're healthy and still anchored in somewhere. The only poisonous one you might encounter looks feathery, not leafy. Do not eat any sea plants that are colorful.

Ideally you'll want to boil your sea greens to reduce the salt, kill any bacteria and parasites, and make them more palatable. If you don't have fire, try rinsing well in fresh water if available and letting it dry in the sun. They can cause a laxative effect if too much is eaten on an empty stomach.

### Cold and Arctic-like Areas

- **Green stuff** here is generally hard to come by, but it is there. Most of the mosses that you find on trees or the ground, and the lichens you find growing on rock, are all edible. In a pinch, these can be eaten raw, but are best boiled—a few times, in fact—to get out the bitterness, and rinse them clean. These have been used in hard times as a food source by Eskimos. They even dry them out after boiling, and then beat them into a powder to make a nice starchy flour for bread.

- **Arctic Willow** is a plant that you pretty much will only get to chow on its tender little sprouts in spring. If you're there in spring, enjoy!
- All **pine and spruce** are edible, and the same rules for eating apply to both. The needles are edible and make fine, nutritious tea. The inner bark is edible, as are the baby cones and pine nut seeds from young cones in spring. Most parts are almost always better boiled because you need the warmth and the liquids. These too have been used by Native American Northern Tribes, who found hunting difficult after some longer harsh winters. Like the Eskimos, they would also eat these raw, boiled, or roasted, or dry the bark out to crush and use as a flour to make a nice carbohydrate bread source.
- **Ferns** are a fine plant for eating. But only eat the freshly sprouted tips that look like their nickname: "fiddle heads." These can be eaten raw, but are also better and safer to eat any quantity after boiling. They often grow in batches, so chances are you'll be able to get a whole meal out of them. They are starchy and high in vitamin C. The roots can be dried, then boiled and mashed to get the more than 50 percent starchy pulp out so as to be able to separate from the fibers that are also in the root.

### General Woodlands, Forest, and Mountainous Areas

Lots of green stuff is out there, in volume, easy to identify, and safe to eat.

- **Oaks, pine, and beech** all have edible inner bark and edible raw needles, baby cones, and seeds from the cones. The deal for eating bark is to peel off the brown stuff from the tree, then find a thin layer of slightly slimy but meaty bark, kind of like an inner skin—this is what you peel and eat. Not the dry outer bark, and not the hard wood inside. It will always taste funny, it's a tree! But it is edible and nutritious and filling. It is harsh on the trees, but that is survival.
- **Burdock, plantain, cattail, arrowroot, sorrel,** and **sassafras** are all good finds as food sources.
- **Pokeweed** is poisonous when raw, but one plant provides a lot of food after its boiled.
- **Purslane** grows everywhere, often in open sunny areas. It is a thick, fleshy-leaf plant with all parts being edible raw or cooked.
- **Chicory** is great for making field coffee. To do this, roast the roots until dry and dark brown, then crush and use like coffee. Just look for the sky-blue dandelion-like flower on the base of the stem with milky juice. It grows all over the world and all parts are edible too.

- **Thistle** is good when you peel and boil the stalk, and eat the roots raw or cooked. It can usually be found in dry woods.
- **Wild onion, garlic, wild rose, and water lily** are good for starters. These are found most anywhere in such regions.
- **Cattails** are my favorite as they are near almost all swamps, ponds, and small stream areas, and they offer so much food in that all of it is edible.
- **Dandelion roots, heads, and leaves** are good to eat—just discard the stems with their milky white sap (which makes a decent glue). They're good to eat raw or cooked. But try not to eat a lot at one go just because you found a field of them—tummy upset is likely to result if you do.

### Swamps and Jungles

- **Palms** are just wonderful things to find in the jungle. They mean life. Not only in terms of shelters and cordage, but they are a good food source. Cut the tops off and eat the tips, soft parts, flowers, seeds, and heart. This is high in fat energy.
- **Nuts** are not only a great source of food, but they are excellent travel food as they'll last for months in their shells. So save these up for any journeys being planned. If you do find a lot of nuts, you can squeeze the oils out of them by wrapping them in a strong cloth, beating them, and then using something to "press" the oils out. You can use the oils for your skin, cooking, candles, etc. Also, use the oil cloth as a wick for your oil candle.
- **Coconuts** are simply the gift of the gods in the jungle. They're easy to identify, but not so easy to get. Chop the tree down if you can't climb it, as that will be less risky than trying to climb and taking a fall. If you must climb the tree, coconut trees usually grow on an angle and you can get up it fairly easily. Use bare feet, and wrap a strong cloth or towel around the back of the tree and hold it on either side to create pressure; then walk up the tree by scooting the towel up after each few steps. They're not easy to get into, either, but worth the effort. If you don't have a knife, take a sharp rock and just start jabbing into it. Brace the coconut between some other rocks or logs to keep it in place while cutting. Do not use your feet to hold it in place—it's too risky. Many cultures call the coconut tree the "tree of life" as they have so many uses.
- **Bananas** are another great food source. Easy to access and plenty filling, they'll last a week or so depending on their condition, and the banana tree itself is a fantastic source of water as well. Papayas are super to find because they are so huge that one will fill you up. But like any of the soft fruits in the tropics, they will go bad quickly, so consider slicing them very thinly and drying them in the sun for longer use.

- **Bamboo** is also awesome to find for the absolute all-purpose utility of it. The baby shoots can be eaten raw, although they can be bitter. Boil with a few changes of water to make them a lot nicer tasting.
- **Sugar Cane** is not a likely find, but it is all over the tropics as remnants from failed plantations. Peel the outer hard layer and enjoy, as these are very nutritional.
- **Taro** is found all over in the tropics, and again, it has to be boiled to neutralize the oxalates. Once that's done, the leaves and the roots provide super tasty greens and starches, and one plant can make a whole meal.
- **Water lilies** are plentiful and actually tasty, but it's real hard to get out there and actually pull up their tuber roots. Once done, boil or roast and enjoy.
- **Sops** are some crazy-looking fruit to most Americans. They are mainly in the tropics of Asia and there are two kinds— sweet and sour. They are tasty and plentiful.

## The Universal Edibility Test

The first thing to understand is that there is no failsafe universal test to see if something is edible or not. For example, there are plants that are fine when raw but can kill if cooked, and vice versa. Likewise, there are exceptions for every rule out there for plants that are safe.

It is important to understand that the Universal Edibility Test (UET) really should be called the "Edibility Test Universally Applied." That is its intended purpose and why it was designed by the military. They recognized that it was not uncommon for soldiers, sailors, and airmen to get separated during the course of warfare and become isolated in remote regions where they might need to rely on the land for food.

So the military designed a "universal edibility test" as a guide for soldiers to use to test the safety of unfamiliar local plant life. It's not infallible, nor is it the only way to go about testing safeness. Remember, humans have been trying foods since the beginning of time, and it all comes down to observation, common sense, and calculated risk.

Understand that many people die every year from eating poisonous plants, and that animals should always be your first choice in a survival situation. But if there aren't animals around, start eyeballing plants right away.

First, look for anything familiar. If you know what something is for sure, or you find a plant that looks a whole lot like something you know is edible, then there is a chance it might be of the same family or a local variation of that edible plant.

Next, make sure there's lots of it. This is really important! No point in taking all that risk, and making all that effort to get a handful of nibbles. If there aren't a whole lot of little things, or a few really big things, then it might not be worth the risk.

**In general:** things that stink, sting, burn, or are barbed are usually not good candidates for the taste test.

**Exception:** prickly pears on cacti have mighty mean tiny spines but taste great and are very nutritious.

Thistles are tricky though, as are some of the crazier tropical fruits which have heavy "hornage" but juicy innards.

## Plants to Avoid

- **Mushrooms:** These are tasty and they do have some nutritional value. But, eating any mushroom out in the wild is borderline suicidal! There are experts with years of study who still die from eating the wrong mushroom every year. For the survivor, mushrooms are simply avoided no matter what.

  Now, I know some edible mushrooms well, and when I've found them, I've eaten them because I could identify them. But I never teach mushrooms to my basic survival students, because it doesn't pass the common sense test. You'll usually simply not find enough, and even if you do, they have hardly any nutritional value.

  And here's the kicker for mushrooms: They can taste fine, you think you're good to go, then they kill you twenty-four hours later. If you're going to try and eat the things anyway, then do try and cook them. But know that many fungal toxins are resistant even to high heat, and so cooking mushrooms will not always kill toxins. So, teach your kids not to eat mushrooms in the wild.

- **Shiny-leaved plants** are generally taboo, but not shiny like banana leaves—we mean shiny when they look like they have a sheen from a light coat of oil.

- **Yellow and white berries** are almost always bad, though there are exceptions. But in short, if it's yellow, white, or green, stay off it!

- **Red berries** can be tricky: We all know strawberries and cherries are edible, as are cranberries, raspberries, salmonberries, and lingonberries. However, many red berries are poisonous, so the guide here is like for mushrooms—if you don't know it, don't eat it. Holly berries are red and juicy but are toxic, whereas Hawthorn berries are dry but healthy. In general, if the critters can eat it, so can you. But this is not a hard rule because some animals have immunities to these toxins.

- **Umbrella-shaped flowers** are bad.

- **Plants with three-leafed growth patterns** are bad. Some of these are also poisonous to the touch, such as poison ivy.

- **Milky or discolored sap** is usually bad. One of the notable exceptions is coconut milk.
- **Beans, seeds, and pods** are generally best avoided unless you know them.
- **Grains** are tricky because often it involves too much work for them to be worthwhile nutritionally speaking, but if you find any heads with a pink, purple, or black spur leave them alone.
- **Plants with a soapy taste** are best left alone. Yucca is an exception.
- **Fine hairs, spines, or thorns** are signs of plants to avoid.
- Plants that look like **dill, parsley, carrot,** and **parsnip** are often very poisonous. If you're truly desperate and have many of these roots staring at you as a potential food source, then risk the taste test at your own peril as the poison in the plant resembles deadly hemlock—which can kill you in a hurry. Don't go there.
- **Almond smell** in plants in general almost always indicates it's poisonous. Some chemical and biological weapons, like cyanide, also smell like almonds. So unless it's an almond, anything almond-smelling should be considered poisonous. Even if the almond smell is on the leaves and/or woody parts—skip it! (The counter to this is the general rule that plants smelling of onions and garlic are usually safe to try.)
- Avoid **mangoes** and **cashew** if you're highly sensitive to poison ivy and sumacs, as these have similar properties on their surfaces that can cause a bad reaction.
- Don't eat plants with worms as they are decayed—instead, eat the worms!

The last thing I want to touch on regarding food is waste.

Try not to waste any food. Eat everything you make and save anything you can't eat. If you have to throw some food away, then try to use it as bait in traps or as lure for fishing.

If you can't do that, then consider burning it if possible or bury it if you have to do so. It's more work and it may lead other creatures to the burial site, so, be sure to bury it far enough from your camp so as to not let any animals pose a threat to you, your family, or camp site.

Then there is human waste. If you are on the move, then go to the bathroom a short distance off your path and make sure it's safe. Have one family member serve as a lookout. You don't need to dig a cat hole for urine, but you always should for feces. Even if you just flip a rock and then kick up some dirt with the heel of your shoe, attempt to make a hole for feces and then cover it up. Again, you don't need or want to go too far off the trail when you are moving.

But when you are making a camp, for an overnight or longer, it is very important to dig a hole for the latrine. The longer you intend to stay, and/or the more folks you have, the deeper the hole should be. Save the extra dirt to cover up a bit each time after someone goes.

Also, make sure that the latrine is downwind, so the smells don't drift into your campsite. You might lay some sticks down to outline the trail or path to it or have a string that leads from the camp to the latrine that the kids can hold on to at night. If you have chemlights, these are useful to help make it safer.

So now that most of the key stuff is addressed, let's dig into some thoughts on how best to do and teach foraging with your family.

## Family Foraging Practice and Eating Weird Stuff

I've eaten all manner of weird things, during both my survival training and on trips around the world. For example, I've consumed slugs on a boot lace, boiled in a geothermal puddle in Iceland; fermented pig guts, tadpole, and water snail soup in Borneo; seaweed, milk thistle, tree bark, tarantula, scorpion, centipede, armadillo, possum, and rattlesnake in the US; raw sea urchin and jellyfish in Japan; boa constrictor in Peru; crocodile in Botswana; nettles in Bulgaria, live hairy maggots with pincers in Colombia . . . the list goes on.

*A good way to get kids into the notion of wild food is to have them involved in the process and to eat your catch immediately so no excitement or interest is lost. Plus all food tastes better outside. This eel was a family affair: Myke hooked it in Devon, England, Gabe scooped it into the net, and Grandpa cooked it up right there on the beach. Eels are good survival food because they're full of fat. (Photo credit Ruth England Hawke)*

Most of these meals look worse than they actually taste. The slugs were a bit gritty and sulfurous but they were essentially the same as eating escargot in a French bistro, minus the garlic and nice wine. The fermented guts were sharp and strong in flavor and I only went off them a bit when I saw the striations in the flesh and worked out what they were. The tadpole and water snail soup was great, like a mild fish broth. The seaweed and milk thistle were as pleasant as any salad, while the tree bark was a bit tough and chewy but wasn't offensive. The tarantula and scorpion tasted like seafood. Eating the spider was a bit of a challenge to get my head around; I was quite tired at the time and I couldn't quite bring myself to bite down on it, so I squeezed its abdomen instead and ate the gunk that oozed out like a string of toothpaste. It tasted good. The armadillo was delicious, like the dark meat of pork. The possum and rattlesnake tasted surprisingly similar, the flavor was a little like the smell of raw chicken, but still was palatable. I loved the sea urchin and jellyfish, which were just like sloppy sushi. I had a little difficulty eating the boa as, like a lot of meat sourced from the wild, it was riddled with worms, but we cooked it until it was almost jerky to kill the cysts and it tasted quite good. Crocodile tail was amazing, like monkfish or lobster crossed with roasted chicken thighs. The nettles were wonderful, reminiscent of spinach.

The Colombian maggots took a few attempts to swallow. First I had to remove the pincers so they didn't nip a hole in my throat on the way down, but the most difficult part was that they wriggled in my mouth when I chewed them. However, the flavor was actually pleasant, like butter and smoke. They are considered to be a delicacy in that part of the Amazon and one of our local guides asked to take the spare maggots home with him so he could have them for dinner.

The only thing from that list that I didn't like eating was the centipede. It didn't help that the thing was as big as my face but the main problem was its acrid favor. Even so, if it were the difference between life and death, I'd still scarf it down.

Eating strange foods just requires mind over matter. It's about overcoming fear of the unknown. Once you've tried a few unusual dishes it becomes much less of a problem and can become something to look forward to. When I stayed with tribes in Borneo in my twenties, I often had no idea what I was eating. The tribal people ate amazing fruits and jungle stalks that I had never seen before or since, and there was bush meat that I couldn't identify at all. I dined on a succession of exciting mystery meals.

I credit my willingness to try new foods down to my upbringing. I grew up in an era where parents made the rules, so when food was on the dinner table you ate it, whether you liked it or not. Fortunately my mother is a good cook, but there were still plenty of childhood instances where I was left alone at the table until I forced down whatever it was that I was trying to avoid, now cold and congealed, and a lot less pleasant than when it was first served.

I've tried to instill the same discipline in my son, primarily because I don't believe in wasting food and I want to train his palate so he eats a healthy diet. Additionally, in a survival situation he may have no choice and I want him attuned to that idea from the outset. I don't want him to waste away because he's revolted by the concept of eating food that doesn't look like "food."

However, as a parent I know that getting kids to eat what they should is often easier said than done. The earlier in life that you can start that process, the better. When my son was a toddler I had a policy of "I won't make you eat everything on your plate but you must TRY everything on your plate." That is, take a proper mouthful and swallow it. There were wars of will, tears, and bribery but little-by-little he became accepting of new foods. My friend Perky started expanding her children's palates even earlier, when they were newborns. Perky is from Cameroon and her husband is from neighboring Nigeria and when their first baby was born, both her mother and her mother-in-law advised her to dip her finger into her adult food whenever she was eating and dab it on to her baby's tongue so she would be used to the flavors by the time she was ready for solid food. Perky says this is standard practice in that part of Africa.

In addition to early introduction to varied flavors, old-fashioned discipline and perseverance, getting your child involved in making or sourcing the strange food, and making the process fun definitely helps. My dad once grew a batch of kohlrabi when I was young. Kohlrabi is a kind of bulbous cabbage-flavored vegetable. Not the most appetizing thing for a seven-year-old but because I'd watched them grow and then I'd helped my dad harvest them, when I came to eat them I did it almost as a matter of pride because I felt some kind of ownership over the strange thing on my plate. I watched Gabe's vegetable consumption almost double when we had our first garden. Like me, he prepared the soil, planted the crops, watered them, harvested them, and ate them because he had made it all happen.

We of course took things way beyond kohlrabi and radishes when giving Gabe survival food training. At four years old, we had Gabe picking conches from the ocean and eating them right on the shoreline. On another occasion, my son dined on a raw iguana tail that the poor animal had shed when he tried to catch it. I nearly hit the roof about the latter because of the hygiene issues but thankfully there were no ill effects and Gabriel, bolstered by the adventure of it all, became more open to the idea of eating food from the wild.

That brings me to hunting. Hunting is a contentious issue but unless you're a vegetarian, there should be no moral dilemma if you're killing in order to eat.

Those sausages you might have fried for breakfast came from a pig and those chicken breasts neatly packed in plastic in the grocery store were once part of a bird. It's easy to put these thoughts aside when things are handed to us when the dirty work already done but I believe if you eat it, you should be able to kill it as humanely as possible, and know how to prepare it too. In a survival situation, you would have to.

Here I want to talk about our friend Kimmie Serigne. Kimmie is pretty much the poster child for getting kids to eat unusual wild food with enthusiasm because he involves them in every aspect of the process. Kimmie is a single dad and a fireman in southern Louisiana and when he's not dragging people from burning buildings he's teaching his four children to catch, kill, prepare, cook, and eat food from the land, water, and air.

As well as being a fireman, Kim's a sixth generation commercial fisherman whose family settled in the marshes in the late 1700s and have been trapping and fishing ever since, with each generation of his family passing on the knowledge and skills to the next. They live season to season—not spring, summer, fall and winter like most of us—but shrimp season, deer season, duck season, trapping season and so on, living in tune with the land and off the land.

Kim's kids, Morgan, Logan (Bub), Joe, and Avery eat frogs, squirrels, porcupines, turtles, blackbirds, doves, alligators, crawfish, crabs, and plenty of more conventional foods like wild boar, deer, ducks, and just about every type of fish local to their area.

The Serigne clan seems utterly impervious to the weather, and come hell or high water they'll be outside catching lunch. This lifestyle is not without some risk, as anyone who spends time outside knows. Boars, alligators, and snakes can kill you before you kill them. There have been cuts, bites, and more than a few stitches in the Serigne family but Kim has trained his children well. They know how to read the environment, how to shoot a gun, make a hook, mend a net, and sharpen a knife. They also know how to gut and clean their catch and the eldest two know how to cook.

Passing on his Creole culture is important to Kimmie, but he's also teaching his children the skills that they need to survive in an emergency situation. He's also passing down the confidence that comes from self-sufficiency, the knowledge that they don't need to lean on others to succeed.

Now most of us don't have the benefit of generations worth of hunting and fishing knowledge to pass on and many of us don't have ready access to wild lands where we can hunt and forage while teaching our children to do the same; but that doesn't mean that we can't introduce our kids to the concepts of hunting, gathering, and eating wild food. There are lots of courses nationwide that specialize in teaching hunting, fishing, or survival foraging and some are designed specifically for kids.

It also makes sense to learn a few edible wild plants local to the area that you live and to go out as a family to forage from time to time, even if it's just for berries and nuts. It introduces your kids to the idea that food doesn't just come from the store—it's outside for the taking if you know what you're looking for.

If you decide to be more adventurous with your foraging, there are many, many tasty and nutritious plants out there. However make sure that you know what you're picking. If you're not completely sure of a plant's identification, it's not worth the risks.

Germs are easy to deal with—just wash your bounty before eating. It's important to (repeatedly) explain this to ages two to six years as their natural foraging reach is within what I call The Dog Pee Zone. I'm talking male dogs here.

In terms of pollutants, avoid busy roads, industrial areas, and hedgerows around crop fields that may have been sprayed with pesticides.

If you have a backyard or access to one, you can also forage for insects or larvae. Entomophagy, or the practice of eating insects, is something that many in the western world find pretty abhorrent. Yet it's a practice that's being going on for centuries and even now, millions of people around the world rely upon it as an essential part of their diet. Having eaten many myself I can confirm that it just takes some getting used to the idea. The flavors of insects are varied and often pleasant and they are packed full of protein and nutrients.

Crickets and grasshoppers are good backyard snacks although you should check first that none of your neighbors are using chemical pesticides. It is also very important to cook your insects before eating them, because even bugs have bugs. Crickets and grasshoppers can carry tapeworm cysts. Thorough cooking kills these horrors outright but eating them raw could put your family at risk of tapeworms. There are lots of different ways to cook bugs but always remember to remove the legs and wings for young children as they are a choke hazard. If you don't fancy catching insects yourself but you want the kids to try eating some you can order cooked, FDA-approved creepy crawlies online.

The seashore is a great place to forage for food and a fun place to practice foraging. Also if it's your child's first time catching and eating a wild animal it's most likely easier for them to deal with from a psychological perspective because, unlike a fluffy bunny, the invertebrates that you find on a beach aren't typically called "cute."

Tropical seashores are my favorite places to forage. There, everything seems bigger and more abundant, and of course there are generally coconuts nearby with their lifesaving combo of fats, protein, and electrolyte-packed water, but all beaches the world over contain edible life.

At the top of the beach near the dunes or in the mud of an estuary you can find delicious succulent plants that have salt inside them. There are lots of different varieties depending on your location. Marsh samphire and sea purslane are Hawke family favorites. In the US I've heard samphire called glasswort or sea beans, although it has neither pods nor beans. Samphire is very salty so you need to wash it in fresh water and then boil it for a few minutes to try and reduce the sodium content. Kids love it with lemon juice and butter.

Sea purslane is very nice raw; again, it's salty, and its texture is a little bit like cactus, though not as slimy. We tend to just nibble on it when we're at the beach, it's works very well in tandem with a boiled egg and the shear novelty value of tearing off a leaf from the wild plant and poking it into an egg seems to really appeal to children. Our eggs sometimes end up with purslane hair or horns!

Samphire, sea purslane, and other succulents that grow in that no man's land between the sea shore and dry land proper play a vital role in preventing coastal erosion, so when harvesting children should remove leaves or cut stems and not pull up the plant itself. Unless you're in a real survival situation of course—then feel free to tear the whole thing out with your teeth.

Down on the beach itself we're into the seaweed section. A great many seaweeds—which are actually marine algae—are edible. In terms of plants it's far safer to plunder the shoreline than it is to forage on dry land. As in most things, moderation is best, as some of the brown seaweeds, like the big thick bull kelp can upset stomachs and all seaweeds can absorb pollutants from the water. Arsenic and mercury have both been found in high levels in seaweeds. In a survival situation you take what you can get but when you're in practice mode be sure to forage away from built-up areas, marinas, and roads. And look out for drainpipes or streams that might be transporting bacteria-laden debris into your beach garden.

As the tide is going out, when fresh rock pools and rocks that are normally under water are exposed, is the best time to pick. That way everything is fresh and hasn't been baking in the sun. Avoid stagnant pools higher up the beach and make sure that everything you pick is alive. A good way of doing that is by only taking plants that are attached to rocks by their roots. During foraging training teach your children to cut a portion of the seaweed and leave the part of the plant that anchors it to the rock so it can re-grow. Obviously as the tide goes out rocks will be slippery so watch the little ones. Wearing water shoes is a good idea to avoid feet getting cut on barnacles and the like.

*Chitons are delicious shellfish that are easy to forage. You can lever them off a rock with a knife. I like them raw, cut into strips, but cooking survival food is always the safer option. And apparently they feel quite nice when you stick them to your arms.*
*(Photo credit Ruth England Hawke)*

It's worth repeating that seashore succulents and seaweed are extremely salty. This is okay if you're just having a taste to expand your children's palate, but in a survival situation you must ensure that you have good supply of drinking water to combat the dehydration that the salt can cause, otherwise instead of prolonging your lives your seashore smorgasbord could end up killing you. Repeated boiling in fresh water helps reduce the salt content.

Low tide rock pools and rocks are also full of meat protein in the form of mollusks and crustaceans ready to be harvested, and anyone who has seen a small child with a bucket and a net at the beach knows that they are natural seashore foragers!. Mollusks and crustaceans are great food for kids as they are invertebrates, meaning there are no bones to contend with.

A lot of survival food that I've eaten out in the wilds is okay flavor-wise, particularly when you're starving, but you generally wouldn't choose to stock your fridge with it. However, fish and survival seafood absolutely don't fall into that category. Amongst other delights, I've eaten Scottish limpets and Costa Rican sea snails, which as far as I'm concerned, rival the fare of fine seafood restaurants. The grand prizes for gastronomic delight would have to go to the huge gastropods like conch and abalone, and also to the gargantuan crustacean, the coconut crab. Abalone is particularly good in this respect. If you've never had one, it's as satisfying as eating a slab of steak.

The main difference between crustaceans and mollusks is that you hunt one and gather the other. Crustaceans are swimming, scuttling things like crabs, lobsters, and shrimp. The tasty crawfish is also a crustacean but is usually found near the samphire in brackish creeks or inland in freshwater. Crabs can be found in or near salt, brackish, and fresh water. Crustaceans have to be hunted and like most hunted creatures, they will fight back if they feel threatened. The point here is, those with small fingers should only hunt using a net. Most crustaceans have their fighting parts up front so teach older children to grab them from behind.

I've speared larger crustaceans with a sharpened stick but kids with spears on slippery rocks is clearly not a clever combination. If you do choose to let your child use a spear, make sure that the spear is taller than the child so if they fall on it, it's much, much less likely to impale them. This holds true for all spears, staffs, and walking sticks with sharp points.

Most decent-sized crabs will be in deeper water rather than in rock pools and it's pretty easy to catch them using a net and a bit of cut bait (slice of raw fish) or piece of raw chicken tied to a piece of string. Hunt for them on a jetty, dock, or the bank of a tidal river. Then just sit and wait—you'll catch something pretty quickly. Little kids and those with a shorter attention span are better suited to the rock pools as the hunt is more interactive.

Keep your crustaceans alive until you're ready to cook them. I always boil shrimp and crawfish since they're small. With larger crabs and lobsters, there are more cooking options.

Mollusks are easy picking—literally—for all age groups. Mussels, oysters, whelks, and limpets stick to rocks or roots and are ready to be plucked. Clams and razors burrow along the shoreline. You can buy special shovels for digging mollusks, but it's easy enough to do with your hands,—just look for the air bubbles and dig a few inches down!

Mussels are easy to collect, as they have a sort of hairy root that's easy to snip through with scissors or to break by twisting. Oysters are tricky because their shells can be very sharp and you'll need something like a knife or a rock to lever them off whatever they're attached to. Limpets can be a real challenge to remove from rocks because they clamp down as soon as they sense any vibrations. The trick is to catch them by surprise—just sit still for a couple of minutes and then whack them with a rock or, if you're wearing shoes, just kick them off. Chitons can be removed in the same way, while whelks and other forms of sea snails are by far the easiest to collect. Little children must be very carefully supervised when collecting mollusks not only for not only for the obvious drowning and falling risks but also to ensure that every mollusk they collect is alive. It can be extremely dangerous or even fatal to eat shellfish that are already dead when you harvest them.

A lot of seafood can be eaten raw, but cooking food is always the less risky option, particularly when you might not have ready access to working medical facilities. Also when you're eating bivalves, the type of shellfish with a hinged shell such as scallop, oyster, or clam, heating them up causes them to conveniently open their shells for you. If any don't open, don't eat them—they were probably dead before they were harvested.

I tend to prefer the gastropods, like limpets and sea snails, and you can harvest them without a knife, which definitely reduces the stress factor when children are involved. The easiest way to cook sea snails and many bivalves is to boil them for a few minutes. I've used both sea water and fresh water to do this, the latter being preferable as you're able to drink the broth as well. The best way to remove small snails from their curly homes is with a sharpened stick or toothpick. Another way to cook mollusks is directly in the embers of a fire, which works well for larger snails, limpets, and abalone. Obviously, shells thrust into a fire will be hot so allow sufficient cooling time before dining.

As with seaweed foraging, check that there are no obvious signs of pollution in the areas that you are gathering your seafood. This also includes creeks and rivers spilling onto the beach that may look clean enough but who knows if they've passed through farmland or areas of human habitation further upstream where they could have become polluted. Some mollusks feed by grazing on algae, while others are carnivores that bore through the shells of other shellfish to devour them. But a great many mollusks are filter feeders, meaning they suck water into their bodies and strain out particles, nutrients, and toxins if they are in the water, making them hazardous to eat. The worst of these are produced by algae blooms and can cause a deadly neurotoxin to accumulate in the flesh of the shellfish. Therefore, always check coastal reports before seashore foraging. During a real survival situation you probably won't have this option but a good rule of thumb is never to harvest shellfish during a heat wave as water that is warmer than usual is favorable to algae blooms. Cooking well does not remove these toxins.

Although fishing is a time-honored and pretty humane method of hunting, some youngsters can find fishing with a pole to be intolerably boring. Although fast-flowing rivers full of trout and salmon can be fun as can some back bay fishing, fishing from land is often an exercise in endurance. Patience is a vital trait when you're out surviving but when you're teaching little ones a skill it's good to keep things interesting. That said, I find it's best for kids starting out in fishing to just "top and tail" the activity. Teach them to bait the hook, cast out, and then stand still until they start to get twitchy. At that point release them to play for a bit and then get them back again when it's time to reel in a fish. If it's a big fish or one that requires a bit of play, have them help with a scoop net.

I strongly believe nets are the best way to get children into fishing. Fishing with nets can be exciting and the child is constantly active while using one. There's always something that you can catch with a net even if it's not technically a fish—a little water louse or a shrimp can help ignite the interest. For ages six and under a dipping net is definitely the way to go, and in my experience older children still really enjoy using them too.

The next level up is using a cast net, which are great because even though they are typically used to catch bait fish, you can actually catch fish large enough to eat and plenty of them. A cast net is a large circular net with weights around the edge and a rope attached to the middle which you throw a bit like a Frisbee. They're really good fun and quite addictive once you've mastered the throwing technique and the best part for kids is you never know what you're going to pull out of the water with them. They come in various sizes in terms of diameter and with different types of netting. Buy the smallest that you can for a child and have them work their way up to a larger net as their skill level and physical height increases. Recreational cast nets generally range between three feet and twelve feet and are sold by radius size (not diameter) so, for example, a three-foot cast net will open to six feet across when unfurled.

There are lots of techniques for throwing a cast net, but the gist of it is that you hold the rope and most of the net in your strongest hand and a bit more of the net in your other hand and cast sideways. If you can't get a friendly fisherman/woman to teach you how to do it there are plenty of examples online. The one technique that I would warn you against is the surprisingly popular method of putting part of the net in your mouth in order to spread it out as there is the potential for children to catch infections and possibly lose some teeth!

Once you catch them, gutting fish is easy, even for children. If your child is proficient with a knife and used to holding slippery fish, have them slice the underside of the fish from its anus towards its head and stop at the gills. Then, they should shove their fingers inside the fish, grab the guts, and yank them out. Then rinse the cavity with water.

Some fish have scales, which need to be removed by scraping. A blunt knife, fork, or even spoon can work. Make a series of raking motions from the tail to the head against the grain of the scales, and they'll lift off. Fins on certain fish can be sharp enough to stab and slice your hands so watch out.

*Fishing is an excellent survival skill to have. Standing with a rod can be boring for young children, so at first just call them in for the fun parts so they get interested in learning more. Myke and Gabe caught this shark in south Florida and had it for lunch. (Photo credit Ruth England Hawke)*

*Cleaning a fish is an easy skill to learn. Slice it from its anus to its gills, pull out its guts, and then rinse the cavity. Kids should be wary of the fins as on some fish they're sharp enough to cut your hands. If you're still fishing you can use the bits to chum the water. (Photo credit Ruth England Hawke)*

The way to get the most flesh off a fish is to cook it whole and then slide the meat from the bones. In a survival situation where food is scarce, every mouthful counts so this is undoubtedly the best way to go about things. If your children are young, palpate every square inch of their portion for bones. It's a real drag and takes forever but is an essential precaution.

Fish cooks very quickly so keep an eye on it if you're cooking over a fire. In fact it's a good idea to cook the fish next to the fire, either on hot rocks or a damp piece of wood. You can also steam it by wrapping it in leaves.

*Shark 'n' Pepper! Gabe caught the shark, gutted it, and decided exactly how it should be cooked. Getting your kids involved in the whole process builds confidence and self-sufficiency. (Photo credit Ruth England Hawke)*

If you're not in a life or death situation and have small kids in your family, you might want to fillet your fish prior to cooking so there is no risk of bones getting stuck in little throats. Filleting is pretty straightforward so with practice a child can definitely accomplish it. An effective fillet knife needs to be super sharp and wet fish are slippery buggers so close supervision is required. I like to start at the head and work towards the tail. Place the fish on its side and cut downwards behind the fin next to the head, and when you feel your knife graze the backbone stop cutting and change the angle of your knife so its pointing towards the tail. Next, work your way towards the tail with a back-and-forth slicing motion; you should feel the ribs under the flat side of your knife as you're doing this. Once you've removed one fillet, turn the fish over and repeat.

With a large fish you can skip the scale scraping session by removing the skin and scales entirely with the knife once you've removed the fillet.

Larger fish can also be cooked in steaks. Simply place your fish on its side and slice all the way through the flesh and the backbone in the same manner that you might chop a carrot. Make the chunks about an inch wide. This is Gabe's preferred method as it is easier (and safer) than removing a fillet and the little barbarian enjoys hacking through the flesh. You can also "cook" your fish by curing chunks of it with lime or lemon juice, ceviche style.

We're not quite at the stage where I'm happy to let my son alone with the oven and his catch, but he is absolutely in charge of seasoning and he likes to dictate the method of cooking and help. I encourage this, in spite of the mess everywhere, as these life skills are important.

When training your family in hunting, gathering, and foraging, safety is the primary issue. Always make sure that you know what you're doing or that you're with someone who knows what they're doing. There are a couple of other things to bear in mind too—never take more than you need and always leave some of the wild animals and plants in place to reproduce. It's also wise to check local laws.

*Shark steaks! From ocean to table, thanks to a ten-year-old. Midsized fish like this one work well cut into steaks and, as cutting fish into chunks requires less skill than carving a fillet, it's easier for a child to do. Obviously, supervise kids with sharp knives and slippery fish extremely closely. (Photo credit Ruth England Hawke)*

*Kimmie Serigne, his son Morgan, and a nice trout. Kimmie is the king of getting kids to eat unusual food. Kim's four children will eat everything from porcupines to frogs and goodness knows what else in between. What's more, they know how to catch it all themselves and clean it. Their dad has trained them in all aspects of hunting, fishing, and trapping. True survivors! (Photo courtesy of Kimmie Serigne)*

# CHAPTER FOUR

# WATER

It's always better to have water on you, but water has weight and it's often too heavy to have a lot with you or to have your kids carry a lot in their pack.

It is important that everyone have some water on them at all times. My family carries a spare bottle that never gets opened that lives in our packs. I get the stronger bottles, for this long-term storage plan as the cheaper water bottle will rupture or leak as the backpack gets tossed around. Then I make sure I have some zippered bags rolled up in the backpack as a back-up canteen in case the water bottles get lost. The ability to carry water is very important if the family is to make any kind of movement to civilization unless you're following a water source like a river, but more on that in the chapter on navigation.

A really great idea is to have an in-line filter for every person so that you can drink water straight from the source and it's safely filtered as you drink it.

It's important to note here that you should not put dirty water in your clean canteen to use with the straw unless that is all you have. Also, you should not put clean water in it until you can boil it and clean it out before using it as a clean water receptacle again.

I also keep some water purification tablets on hand so I have the ability to purify water if the straws are lost or become unserviceable. Tablets are also good when it's rainy and a fire is difficult to start. I prefer the chlorine-based tablets for look, smell, and taste, but they are not as effective as iodine tablets, and iodine can be used as an antibiotic too. However, some people have an allergy to shellfish and iodine can cause the same reaction. Also, iodine tablets can quickly lose their effectiveness once opened as they're more sensitive to moisture in the air.

So, you'll need to research the best tablets for you to carry but the main factors to keep in mind when planning echo the principles listed in the beginning of the book.

P: Have a working canteen to drink from and refill regularly; keep on hand at all times.

A: Have a backup bottle of water (or small bottle or pouch of pure water) in bag.

C: Have a life straw or UV light for purifying water on the go (mechanical).

E: Have some treatment tablets or drops for emergencies (chemical).

WCS: Boiling is the safest method but takes the longest and is the most work.

No matter where you go, make sure everyone is carrying a bottle of water on them. Also have a backup bottle.

Now, I like to break down the basics of water into a few simple rules.

1.  Keep it in you.
2.  Get it in you and keep it flowing in.
3.  If you have it, ration it. If not, prioritize getting it.
4.  Scan around for water sources such as flows, holes, cracks, and traps.
5.  Use plants, animals, bugs, and birds before working for it yourself.
6.  Scout hard before walking for long, and look hard before digging. Never dig too deep, and consider digging more than one hole.
7.  Combine digging, plants, and other options and tricks when there is no obvious answer.
8.  Use all your wits when you have nothing else to go on.
9.  Break all the rules when all else fails.
10.  Consider the extremes, if necessary.

## What You Really Need, and How to Use It

You don't need as much as you think and you certainly don't need as much as you drink back home. Whether you're a health nut who drinks gallons a day or only drink sodas, humans can survive with a lot less water than ideal.

In fact, humans have lived throughout most of time at a very low level of hydration; yet, as a species, we're still here. So we don't need as much as is proscribed by modern conventional wisdom. However, you must get some fluids in you or you will die.

Humans have about five liters of blood in their body. The heart pushes this amount from any start point to the same finish point in one minute. This is about sixty to a hundred beats per minute and about twelve to sixteen breaths per minute.

Each minute, you lose a certain amount of fluid just by being, and on each pass, organs and tissue take a little water out of the bloodstream to maintain their functioning.

On average about one liter of water can be lost each day, even through no activity whatsoever. Any complications such as high heat, high humidity, extreme cold, and loss of blood through trauma, all cause less than optimal functioning and therefore inefficient use of water in the body already due to illness or fatigue, which is to be expected in the stress of any survival scenario. It is easy to see how dehydration can set in very quickly.

The human body starts to lose effectiveness with a simple decrease of only a half liter of blood volume since the average total body composition is about 60 percent water.

A mere loss of only 2 percent causes overall performance to deteriorate; four percent loss leads to muscle capacity decreasing; 6 percent leads to heat exhaustion; 8 percent leads to hallucinations; and loss of 10 percent of body fluid can cause circulatory collapse, stroke, and death.

Granted, these are guidelines, not hard and fast rules. But when laid out in small incremental doses like this, it clearly demonstrates how important water is and how quickly even small losses can impact our overall performance. Most people do not drink enough water daily to begin with, so they are already operating at a deficit when the survival scenario commences.

Unless you happen to have plenty of water, then it needs to be one of your very first priorities. Right after life-saving first aid and shelter, water is always a crucial early issue that must be addressed.

It's easy to become complacent because it is too hot or cold, etc. You have to be very aggressive in your pursuit of water while you can, and make sure your kids are drinking, or you'll quickly be in trouble. Hydration is no joke and cannot be emphasized enough, especially with children. Heat stroke and dehydration can jump their bones before you realize it.

So, let's look at what happens when you don't have water so you'll know what to be looking for and how to track your progress and status. However . . . I want you to remember that this is only a guide. You'll have to use your experience and knowledge of your family to gauge their real status when it comes to hydration.

## The First Signs and Symptoms of Dehydration

- Thirst
- Headache
- Decreased urinary output. Dark, strong-smelling urine and pain when urinating
- Light-headedness, dizziness, seeing stars or fainting when standing up from a sitting or squatting position

## Advanced Signs of Dehydration

- Lack of tears if crying
- Rapidly fatigued (lethargy)
- Constipation and loss of appetite
- Rapid heart rate
- Elevated body temperature
- Nausea and vomiting
- Tingling in the limbs
- Skin that's shriveled and wrinkly; pinching it may reveal reduced elasticity.
- Visual disturbances, hallucinations, delirium, unconsciousness and death

You should be aware of these things so that you will know what they mean if you experience them when surviving. Don't get caught up in the moment and forget to pay attention to your and your kids' health.

By knowing these signs and symptoms of dehydration as a check system for yourself, you can gauge how you're doing and what you need to be doing. Human beings have survived weeks with very little water, and if necessary so can you!

Ideally, one would drink 500 ml every hour when it's hot or when doing strenuous exercise or very laborious work. That's one of the standard individual drinking water bottle sizes. It works out to about ten hours of work a day, drinking five liters of water total, which is completely replenishing the full amount of blood volume. This is a good standard to strive for but by no means is it practical, so do not stress about hitting it.

The reality is that we lose about three to fours liters of water a day and we get most of that back every day, about 20 percent from our food and the other from the thirst generated by the food we ate and then slaked by quenching that thirst.

However, in extreme circumstances, if you can get just 500 ml of fluid in you each day you can survive. Even if you only get 100 ml, that is something, and can help keep you hanging in there.

By using what you have—and keeping it inside you—you'll stay hydrated and that's the key to success when you don't have enough water. So, working smarter is the way ahead. If it's hot, work by night, if there is enough light from the moon. If not, then work at dawn and dusk, but rest in the middle of the day. If you're in the cold, rest at night and work during the day. Keep dry if it's cold, as best you can, and pace your work so you don't sweat. You try to pace yourself in all survival situations so that you don't rush and make mistakes, but also so you don't sweat and lose water.

Sweat happens when you push the machine and it needs to cool down. It's a mechanism that allows the body to push hard and still keep cool. But sweat is precious when it drains your very chance of survival drop by drop. Try to work at a comfortable pace so that the work is still being accomplished but the sweat is not wasted. Best to keep it in you is the golden rule.

## How Much Time You Have

Now here are the harsh facts. If you're seriously dehydrated, have terrible diarrhea, have lost lots of blood, or you're in the middle of the desert in the summer time . . . realistically, you only have about twenty-four hours to live. Even if you're feeling none of these symptoms, if you're in the desert in summer, without water, you realistically only have about three days left to live. In an ideal situation, equipped with water and know-how, you might have about seven days, but even that is pushing it.

These are your approximate timelines for survival in a desert region. They essentially apply when at sea as well, since that is also one of the harshest environments to survive without water. They don't really apply to the arctic as you can eat the snow when there. Guidelines recommend not to do so, but that is a recommendation that has some truth but also some flexibility. The main reason not to eat snow in the cold is because it reduces your core temperature, which is true. But if you have dry clothes, shelter, and can maintain warmth without a fire, then there is no reason to die of dehydration when surrounded by good water in the form of snow.

The key is to eat small amounts to wet your whistle and hydrate. Let your body warm back up before you consume more snow. When people are near death from hypothermia, and then eat snow, that is when core temperature drops. But if you are working hard, or walking in the snow and thirsty, then grab a handful of the cleanest snow you can find and eat. It will hydrate you and help prevent hypothermia in the right circumstances.

Now, these are only approximations to help you make the best strategies for how you work, build a shelter, and maneuver yourself in your environment. If you factor these in and operate accordingly, you can extend these timelines indefinitely.

Knowing you may have seven days in the desert with a small amount of water will help dictate to you if you need to risk a movement or if you can afford to hold and wait for rescue.

But all the hope and willpower in the world will not change the fact that you will need some water sooner or later, so plan on getting it or using what you have to get you out.

## First Priority: Finding Water

The first place to start looking is where you are and in what you have.

Is there water around you? Look for a river, stream, lake, creek, pond, water fountain, fish tank, toilet, flower pot, kettle, water tank, and anywhere else around you. Next, look at the environment's indirect potential water sources: snow, ice, rain, fog, morning dew, puddles, etc.

If nothing directly or indirectly water-producing is available, start by looking right where you are as many folks end up in a survival situation while in transit on some form of transportation. Is there any water in your craft, vessel, or vehicle? Look first in all the obvious places—storage, emergency compartments—as maybe things were left behind, stowed away, or forgotten.

When all the immediate ideas do not produce or stop producing, start to think outside the box. Look in the engine compartment of the vehicle—is there a water reservoir or anything that can be used as a source of water? The key is look everywhere as you might even find it, even places you couldn't imagine . . . you might get lucky.

If your natural and man-made resources are lacking, it's time to start looking at the alternatives and techniques that can get you water without digging. The reason to avoid digging if you can is that you will burn energy, and therefore water, while digging, and you might not find any water or might not get enough to replace what you've lost.

The next step is to start looking at the environment for anything that might serve as a receptacle for water. Rock crevices , holes, cracks, plants with pockets or pools of water that might be trapped at joints, the base of stalks, the splits in trees, or anything around you that may contain small pools of water. Look everywhere! And when you find any water, act quickly to prepare it for drinking.

# Making Water Safe to Consume

There are many ways to make water safe to drink, and water from any unknown source, natural or man-made, should be made safe to drink always before consumption.

Of course, if there is simply no way to make found water safe, and if you can find no other source, then the choice is simple: drink it and maybe die, or don't drink it and surely die.

The nastiest water-borne bugs are *giardia lamblia*, which cause giardiasis, or basically terrible diarrhea. The other most significant cause of water-borne disease is the harder-to-kill bug called *cryptosporidium*.

Falling victim to either of these or other bacteria by drinking untreated water can cause a world of pain, and the inevitable weakening of your body can start you down a slippery slope to death. So take water purifying seriously and, for the most part, never drink untreated water in the wild if you can help it.

But also, know this: lots of people have drunk from many streams out in nature and as long as the general environment is healthy, there is a reasonable chance your water from a river will be mostly safe too.

### Boil It

The best way to make sure your water is completely safe is to boil it. That's great if you happen to have enough firewood for sustaining the fire that long but it's also time consuming, as it takes a while to get the fire going, boil the water, drain it, and let it cool so you can drink it.

In general, a full one minute at a rolling boil will do the trick most of the time. In fact, this is all I ever do. But in a real bind for a heat source or time, just get it hot enough to hit a boil and most likely it will be okay, and for sure will be safer than before.

The science behind boiling water is very simple, bur I'll review it here so parents can make the safest assessments of water preparation for the kids.

Water hits a boil at 212 degrees Fahrenheit and 100 degrees Celsius. The fact is that almost ALL things in water that can make humans sick are killed long before the water hits that temperature. Therefore, once you hit a rolling boil, YOU ARE SAFE.

Letting it boil for one minute, three minutes, five minutes, ten minutes, or fifteen minutes, won't hurt you, but doesn't help you either. And it may even hurt a bit as it uses more fuel, more wood, and more time, which means longer waits to cool down the water and longer intervals between drinks. So, get water to hit a rolling boil, let it cool, and drink safely.

**Note:** At higher elevations, water boils at a lower temperature so it is recommended to boil for a minute when above one mile in elevation, but the reality is, most water from sources that high, are usually pretty clean to begin with.

A fun piece of information: Mount Everest is the highest point on earth, at just over 29,000 feet and most of us will never be that high up, but at that altitude, water will boil at just under 160 degrees Fahrenheit. Again, the water will likely be very clean, as most pathogens are killed before that temperature is reached. The general recommendation for drinking water this high up is to give it a little longer on the fire.

*Blake is purifying water by boiling it. This kettle whistles when it reaches a rolling boil so he can just sit back and listen instead of having to watch for bubbles. This is a safe option for small children around campfires. (Photo credit Ruth England Hawke)*

## Treat it with Chemicals

Ideally, one can use any of the multitude of fancy chemical tablets and liquids out there that are designed to make the water safe to drink—that is, if these are available when you find yourself surviving.

Many bacteria are in water and they are fairly easy to kill with heat or chemicals. But some other organisms are not so easily killed. The survivor may not have access to store-bought chemicals specifically designed to kill bacteria in water. Luckily, there are some improvised ways to treat water chemically.

Bleach is great as it's found all over the world and it's easy to use. There are many formulas out there for how much to use, but a spoonful per gallon won't hurt you.

### Rules for Adding Bleach to Cleanse Water

- One drop of 10 percent strength for a liter
- Ten drops of 1 percent strength per liter
- Five drops of 10 percent strength for a gallon
- Ten drops of 1 percent strength for a gallon
- Double all amounts above if the water is especially dirty
- Add the bleach, shake vigorously, let set for fifteen to thirty minutes, then drink up. Most people drink some chlorine in their tap water every day, so it is safe.

Bleach will kill a lot, and though it won't kill all giardia, it sure will put a hurt on it and if it's all you've got, go with it.

Iodine is also a great way to treat your drinking water. I keep liquid iodine drops in my first-aid kit. It not only can treat a minor cut when you don't have water to wash it out, but it also doubles as a way to treat water and make it safer to drink. Most tincture of iodine comes at 2 percent strength. Place a few drops into your water and shake, then let stand for thirty minutes before consuming.

### Rules for Cleansing Water with 2 Percent Strength Iodine

- Two drops per one liter
- Ten drops per gallon

There are other chemicals available for this purpose, but these two are by far the safest, most commonly used, and most commonly found out and about.

## Filter It

There are many store-bought filters which can be used and should be used whenever possible and available.

## Sun It

When you have no way to boil, layer, filter, or otherwise treat your water, you can let the sun do the work for you. That is, if you have sun. The light from the sun comes in the form of UV rays, and can actually help you to make your water safe.

If you have a clear plastic bottle, this is ideal, but anything that is clear can be used, even a zippered bag or piece of plastic. Ideally, you only want to use about four inches of water, as any more than that makes it harder for the UV rays to penetrate that far, so it takes longer.

The concept is simple. Take the water you have, and filter it as best you can to get the sun-blocking particles out. Put the water in the cleanest, clear plastic or glass container you have, nearly fill it, shake it well to oxygenate it, then top it off so that no air space is left. Then, leave it in the sun for as long as you can. Lay it on something black or hot like a dark rock or metal surface to help increase the heat. The hotter it gets, the better. The longer in the sun it remains, the better.

**Basic Guidlines for Sunning Water**

- On a hot day, the water can get over 120 degrees Fahrenheit (the target temperature) in about an hour.
- If it's sunny and warm but not hot, it will take about six hours. If it's not that hot, but bright and sunny, it can take twelve hours.
- If it's consistently cloudy, then let it sit for two full days.

The one problem with this technique is that the bacteria will build back up after a while, unlike when you boil water which makes it safe for storage. So, in all sun conditions, it's best to set your bottle(s) out in the morning and drink the water when the time is right. In other words, you should drink what you treat each day.

Bottom line, you can make your water safer to drink just by putting it in the sun. As a last resort for sunning water, even a bucket or other container with the water exposed to the sun can do some good; just sip the water off the top after it's been exposed for a period of time.

If you don't have a traditional water source, you can try catching rain water. Make sure whatever you're using is as clean as can be as well as the receptacle and be ready to treat it if necessary based on the cleanliness of the catchment tools being used. If everything is clean, know that rain water is pure and you can drink it straight without having to treat it. You can also try soaking water off the grass if there is no way to catch rain water, or absorbing the dew off the plants if there is no rain.

# Keys to Finding Water

Water is usually not hard to find if it's available. The secret is to use your wits and look around thoroughly, using all your senses. Can you hear it running? Can you smell it? Sometimes you can smell rain coming, or smell a pond or stream if you're downwind and paying attention. Look at the flow of the land, and key in on all things sloping downward that might lead to water. Look at the terrain and think about where water might be naturally occurring in that environment. Draw on your experiences from parks, gardens, local forests, or any similar environment you've been in before.

If all else fails, try to get to a high point for a better vantage point—climb a tree, walk up a small hill, or climb a bit up a mountainside to see if the enhanced viewing position will show you the way to water. But take care to conserve your energy in these endeavors.

Sometimes you'll notice an area that is a bit greener than the rest, which may indicate water is near. Or you may notice a game trail which may lead to a water-hole. Bottom line is always look at the environment and pay attention, as it will tell you many things.

## Clouds

These can sometimes help you to find water as well. Heavy-looking, low-hanging black clouds say rain is coming. If the winds are medium to high, chances are good that you're about to have a drink. So, when it does rain, *stop everything* and *use everything* to catch all the water you can.

When the rain does come, take off your clothes and get a wash (hygiene is still important when you're surviving). Use your clothes to catch water and wring it into a container or your mouth if you have nothing else. Catch, drink, and repeat as long as it's pouring down.

# Seeking Water in Specific Environments

## Dry Places

The desert is the classic worst-case scenario for survival. However, most deserts are not barren wastelands, as many people may wrongly believe. Most deserts do have plenty of life, and all life depends on water. The key is to know where to look and what to use.

*Bamboo is a lifesaver when it comes to water. You can tap water from young, green bamboo by cutting the top, bending it over and then catching the watery juice in a container. Older, larger bamboo often has water trapped in its segments, so just cut a notch and drain it out. Bamboo can also be used to help sterilize unclean water from a river or puddle. In this picture Myke is holding a bamboo water boiler. He cut a hole in a single segment which can now be filled with water and boiled over a fire like a pot. (Photo credit Jeffrey Coit)*

## Scout About

First, follow the basic rules for locating water: scan the area, look for low-lying areas where water would converge and collect if it where flowing. Follow the natural lines of the terrain for the lowest points. Then look and see if there are plants and, if so, notice how green and healthy they appear. The greener the plant life, the more plentiful the water.

If you do find these low points with greenery, they are likely in a dry stream bed. Look for water first just to see if it's sitting there on the surface, then look at any walls of the gullies to see if there is some seepage of water on the face of the rocks. If there is no open source, or no obviously wet or moist areas, then look for bends in a dry river bed. The outsides of these bends will be where the water would have been the most recently, as it would have lasted there longest. Therefore, you might find some water there if you dig a bit.

But before you start digging, make sure to take a good look. If it looks bone dry, chances are there isn't any water there. So, calculate how much time, energy, and water you have on and in you, *before* you start digging for water in the desert. Save digging in the desert until you're sure, or you're desperate.

If the ground looks a bit moist, find the lowest point and dig about one foot down to start. If you dig two feet down and don't hit water, you're not likely to find it. Don't give up yet; come back and check your holes later, maybe some water will have seeped in, or if it rains, it may become a reservoir for you.

## Cacti

The cactus is an okay source of moisture in the desert. Notice I said moisture, not water. To get at the wet stuff, you have to cut off the outside of flat cacti; or lop the top and chop up the insides of barrel cacti. If they are highly corrugated then they are likely dry and waiting for water just like you are.

The prickly pear is a fruit that grows on the tops of the flat cactus. They are tricky to de-skin as their spines are much finer than the cactus itself, but they are deliciously sweet. I don't count them as a good source of water due to their sugar content, but if you're down to sucking cacti, suck them too.

The big agave plants that are common in most deserts sometimes have water trapped at the base of their meaty and pointy leaves, although they're strong and their water is hard to get to. Again, a sip of water is not to be turned down wherever you can find it. Check most plants for such deposits.

## Make a Solar Still

Save all the ejected pre-sucked cacti bits and pieces and then use them to make a solar still. The solar still is one of the best friends of anyone surviving in the desert. To make one, you'll need a poncho, tarp, or some sort of plastic. If you have none of these to begin with, keep your eyes open for them as you make your way around.

Unfortunately in this day and age (though fortunately for survivors in such situations), you can find human trash and debris in every corner of the planet, including all kinds of plastics, containers, and so on.

Making a solar still is simple. Dig a hole about one to two feet deep, or a bit deeper if you can do so without putting yourself in jeopardy by sweating too much. Make the hole as wide as your tarp, poncho, or plastic sheet so the hole will be covered completely. In essence, you want a cone-shaped hole dug into the ground.

Next place a bunch of vegetation, spit-out cacti, bad water, and anything green in the hole. Place a cup or something to catch water in the center of the hole. Lay your tarp over the hole and use rocks or sand to secure its edges on the surface above the hole so that it's as air tight as possible. Then place a nice-sized, smooth, and round rock in the middle of the tarp outside the hole. This rock should force the tarp to droop slightly down into the hole above the water catch that's inside.

Here's how it works. The heat from the desert sun will draw all the moisture from all your materials inside the hole and condense on the inside of the tarp. Then, gravity from the rock on the outside of your tarp will cause the water to trickle downward and drop into your cup. Make as many of these stills as you have time and supplies.

Put all your spat-out cacti inside the still, adding any leafy green stuff you can find—just don't let it touch the edges of the poncho. Keep it flat and step on the plants a bit to bruise and crush them so they leak any moisture they have. And as gross as it may sound, make that hole the place where the family goes to urinate (any impurities from the urine will be distilled in the solar process).

Be aware that a solar still won't give you a full day's worth of hydration. You may get 200 to 300 ml of water from it, which is about maybe half a normal bottle of drinking water. But in the harsh desert, that is a wonderful amount to have.

If you have an abundance of plastic bags, you can try the evaporation method of placing the bag around as much foliage and vegetation as possible, tying it off on one end and placing a small pebble in a corner to weigh it down so all the water converges there.

You can poke a hole in it and drink that water, or, if bags are sparse, untie it carefully to keep as much water as you can in the corner, then tilt it and drink that way. I find in the desert, there is a tendency for pointy plants to poke holes in the bag.

Note that in most other environments, this method produces more water than in the desert—typically a small cup of water in a few hours, depending on how leafy the plants and how hot it gets.

If you have a handful of bags, tie them over many branches at once to produce a good quantity of water. The trick is to find leaves that appear light and green and not too thick or dark, and certainly not any that ooze white stuff when broken. The water will be greenish in color, but it is fine.

Don't leave the bags on too long as the leaves will start to wilt and make the water less tasteful.

The bottom line for desert drinking: cracks, crevices, cacti, and solar stills are your best bet for desert hydration.

*Brennan and Grandma Jocelyn are making a transpiration trap to collect water. Plants release water through tiny pores in their leaves called stomata. This water can be collected and drunk without purification. Take a bag and secure it tightly around the branch of a non-poisonous, leafy tree or bush, getting as many leaves inside as possible. Leave it for twenty-four hours or as long as you can. A thick bag is best so it doesn't get punctured. The amount of water that you will collect will vary according to the size of the bag, the type of leaves, the temperature, and time of year. (Photo credit Ruth England Hawke)*

## Cold-Weather Places

The arctic environment has plenty of water in the form of snow and ice, but its forms can kill you if you're not careful because consuming ice or snow will decrease your core body temperature, which will cause your body to shiver more to stay warm, which in turn will cause further dehydration. This is why it is strongly advisable to always melt snow or ice with fire before consuming it in water form. However, if you have absolutely no means of melting snow or ice, it is better to take small amounts and let it melt slowly in your mouth than to die of dehydration.

Yes, eating a lot of snow will eventually kill you. But, if you're nearly dead already, refusing to take in some icy cold water is just like laying down to die. You either have options that you can try when all else fails, no matter how extreme, or you don't have the options or refuse to take them.

### Rules for Hydrating in Arctic Regions

Snow and ice should be melted and boiled before drinking. The best and most effective way to melt it is in a pot over a fire. If you have no pot, wrap a ball of ice or snow in a t-shirt or other material, hang near fire, and let it drip into a container.

If you have no cloth, pot, or cup, try heating a rock in the fire and then melting snow or ice with it. First, dig a small hole and pack the inside walls of it tightly. Then drop in a soft pile of snow, and drop the heated rock on it. Once the snow has melted, quickly and safely remove the rock and sip out all the water.

If you need to draw water from sea ice, use the blue stuff—the bluer the better as it has less salt.

Make a hard-packed snowball and place it on a stick (like a marshmallow over a fire). Make sure to have something to catch the water as it drips. If you don't have a catch, clean the stick as well as you can, and then let the water from the melting snowball drip down the stick into your mouth.

## Seashore

The seashore can be a very formidable place to find water indeed. If you're stranded on a small island with no dune break, then try to drop back past the highest watermark you can see and start digging a hole there. It's a good sign if

*Rather than increasing his risk of hypothermia by eating snow, Dean is melting the snow first, having placed it in a sock to filter out any debris. He can sterilize the melted snow on the fire afterwards. (Photo credit Morgan LaPlonge)*

you find vegetation, as plants usually won't grow where the tide reaches. If there are dunes, then drop back behind the first row of dunes and start digging. In both cases, the holes you dig will fill with water and this water will be safe enough to drink. It takes some work, as the holes need to be a bit deeper than the freshwater filter holes discussed earlier. Be prepared to dig a two- to three-feet-deep hole, and just as wide as the sand tends to fall back in. The upside is that digging sand is a lot easier than digging dirt.

Often seashore in the tropics will have coconuts. Coconut is a great source of water and food. The greener the nut, the better the water; the browner the nut, the more meat and white milk present, which can cause diarrhea if too much is drunk. But if that's the first nut you crack, drink up. There are likely more green ones around, so go for them next and don't drink more than one white-milk coconut a day if you can help it.

A word of caution: a coconut is a truly tough nut to crack without a blade. The best method I have seen is to shave down to the nut with a shell or rock, unless you know a stick technique to de-husk a coconut. Next use the outer shell as a way to hold the nut up so you can crack into it without spilling juice everywhere. Ideally, you can get in with a stick or knife. Alternatively, crack it along the circumference with a few whacks of a rock and it will usually come right open. This is tricky, so be extremely careful that you do not injure yourself while doing so.

A final way to make water potable if on the shore without a pot, is to make a fire, dig a hole, let it fill in with water, drop hot rocks from the fire into the hole, and drink.

If you have some way to boil salt water and then catch the steam, this distillation process could be the best method for you but it requires a lot of time and fuel.

When push comes to shove and your water resources are extremely low, you may be tempted to drink from the bountiful sea water. Of course, sea water is extremely salty and drinking a certain amount of it will lead to death. But with everything else, if it's your last resort, take it, but only if you can add it to some other fresh water.

## Hawke's Rules for Drinking Salt Water

Don't drink salt water unless you are sure you will die from dehydration otherwise. Wait until you are absolutely desperate, and there is no hope for finding water via fish, rain, or other means.

Start early if you know it's inevitable. If you are in the middle of the ocean and have no water at all, and there's no real hope of immediate rescue, begin after your first twenty-four hours without water. Don't wait until it's too late, as you may start to go crazy from delirium caused by dehydration, and the salt will push you over the edge.

Dilute the sea water if you can with any fresh water you may have, or take sips here and there in between rinses or swallows of your fresh water.

If you have the materials and are on a small vessel or floating device, make a solar still (as described above). Scoop some seawater into a container, place a smaller cup or catch in the middle of the container (you may need to place something in it to hold it down), then cover the container tightly with plastic or similar material, and place a weight on top of the cover to sink it slightly into the container. Any condensation that collects on the inside of the cover and drips into the cup will be fresh water.

Never, ever drink more than a few gulps of seawater at a time, and then never more than a cup over a twenty-four-hour period. Ration small amounts of fresh water and space out the timing of consumption.

The bottom line is that drinking sea water is a bad idea, and should only be a last resort. But it can be done and should only be done when death seems very probable.

*Water vines are miracle plants. They are ubiquitous in the tropics but I've seen them all over the South. This photo was taken in the Atchafalaya Basin in southern Louisiana. When you're cutting a section of water vine, cut high before you cut low because the plant sucks its water upwards when it's cut. Drinking from a water vine is sometimes like sucking a wet wash cloth, other times water floods out like a faucet! The best part is that you don't have to sterilize it; the water is fresh and potable. Never drink from a vine that produces white sap. Water vines are fairly easy to cut but ideally you need to cut them in one hit to avoid losing water. This is a job for an adult or teenager. (Photo credit Jeffrey Coit)*

## At Sea

The sea is one of the most desolate places for finding drinking water.

If you don't have a fresh store of water, a desalinization kit, or a reverse-osmosis pump, you're starting off at a serious disadvantage. In this case, you might consider drinking urine or seawater.

Otherwise, the best source of water when surviving at sea will come from the atmosphere. If it rains, drink, catch, and store all you can, for as long as you can. You don't know how long it will be before you are rescued, make landfall, or get another rain. Catch and use any and all precipitation sent your way very judiciously. If there is fog, then use all the cloth you can to capture that and squeeze its moisture into a container or your mouth. Don't let any fresh water go by un-drunk!

If you have the equipment and some sort of vessel or float, you can try to make a solar still. Obviously this is impossible if you're simply floating in the water trying to survive.

## Jungle

The jungle is one of my favorite regions for surviving, especially because of the abundance of water sources. Not only do you often have rain, and usually plenty of water in the form of rivers and streams, but there are many plants that offer a source of water if you know what to look for. A key element here is to always take the time to ask locals, whenever possible, about what plants are good for water. If you don't have the luxury of getting local knowledge, rely on the basic concepts and information provided here.

### Water Vines

There are many vines in the jungle. Not all provide water, but many do. It takes a bit of practice at first to identify them. Usually their bark is a bit lighter and fluffier than the non-water vines, and when you tap them, they sound hollower than the white-sap-producing varieties.

To get to the water, cut high then low. They suck the water up from the ground at the first cut (called "capillary action") so that if you cut low first, the water will be sucked up already by the time you cut high and you'll have less water to drink.

Hold the vine like a long canteen and let the water drain into your mouth. If you can get your fill and also have a container, fill up on all the water from vines you can find. The water tastes great, it's safe, and the vines are easy to cut. If without a knife, try to break it open high with a heavy stick, then break it low with your hands, and/or with leverage over a branch and drink it that way.

*When it's raining, use large leaves to funnel the drops into your mouth as Brennan is doing here. I've seen people who live in jungles snap a banana leaf off during a storm and drink from it as naturally as a cup. First thing in the morning you can also shake the dew from leaves or lick them if you have to. Large leaves can be fashioned into cups and left on the roof of your shelter to collect water if you think it may rain overnight. (Photo credit Ruth England Hawke)*

## Bananas and Plantains

This is a wonderful plant to find. It can be felled right across the base just like chopping a head of cabbage in half, and then, watch it fill. The water is good, though it's strong-tasting at first and mellows after a few bowlfuls. This plant will also generate water for a while, so you might even camp there for a day or two if you find one.

## Fig Trees

It can give up a lot of water but needs to be tapped into. Use a piece of pipe, or tube, or some small bamboo fashioned into a tube, then cut a hole into the tree and wedge the tube in. Let the water drain, but make a reservoir catch for it.

## Palms

These include nipa, buri, coconut, and sugar. You can get water from many of these fruits, and even the little ones will yield a nice lemonade-flavored water. Additionally, you can draw water from the tree itself. It is best to use the smaller ones that are less than twelve feet, so you can reach the top, chop it off, and keep it bent over so it will "bleed" water for you. This can be a repeated a few times to stimulate more water production.

### Leaves

There are many plants that can catch and hold water for you, but the water will need to be treated. Big leaves, like elephant ears, should catch your attention because these large leaves make excellent devices for catching rain water.

### Bamboo

As stated before, bamboo is a gift in respect to water. To obtain water from it, green bamboo can be bent over and the top cut off to produce water; older, browner bamboo usually have water trapped inside their segments. Tap or shake them and listen for the water swishing and splashing. If you hear that, cut a little notch at the base and drain the water. Usually, you can do this with each segment above and below as bamboo shoots are compartmentalized.

## Mountainous Areas

Getting water in the mountains can be a challenge, but there is often plenty of water to be found and one distinct advantage is that you have better visibility than, say, the jungle or forest. That visibility greatly increases your chances of finding water.

Look for land sloping down, but don't drop down until you're certain you see a source of water. Stay on the high ground, preferably the ridge line, so you can look both ways on your hunt for water.

If the weather is too rough to walk the ridgeline, drop on the safe side of the wind, but every kilometer or so, go back to the ridge top and look over the other side, both behind and ahead of your direction of travel.

Once you have spotted water, then and only then, start dropping down and mind how you go so you don't end up in a false valley and have to make another water-draining ascent before you can get to the valley with your spotted water source.

Secret: Walls and cliffs are the best places for looking for water in mountainous areas. If you spot any of these, and the trek to them is within reason and your ability, try to scope them out. Often these breaks in the integrity of the mountain range will have a leak from some small underground spring as it pushes through the mountain. It might only be a wet little trickle, but you can lick that trickle all day.

## Forested Areas

Finding water in the forest usually isn't too difficult, but sometimes you can come upon a long stretch of land before you do find a water source. Scope out your surroundings and follow the land to where it looks like it would naturally produce water. If all else fails, dig, but dig wisely.

Find the lowest point you can in what looks like the nicest ravine you can find. Usually, the higher and steeper the two hills are that create the ravine, the better the chances are of finding water. And, just like in the desert, find the greenest, wettest, lowest point you can and dig a hole one- to two-feet deep. Wait and see if any water seeps in.

If not, try the condensation method described above using a poncho (or natural materials like leaves) to cover the hole, so your effort in digging it doesn't go to waste, then keep looking. If you're hunting for little trickles of water, the opposite holds true—a good, long, wide slope of a hill basically means there is more surface area to catch water and channel it down, so if you see a great expanse of field sloping down, try walking to the bottom of it.

I do not teach a lot of technical items like names of plants and trees and that sort of thing. Occasionally, it is very helpful to know a bit of technical information. For instance, know what a willow tree looks like and remember that these are always near water. Cottonwoods share that quality.

Further, be ever aware that underground springs are all over in the forest, so anytime you step on some soggy soil, you're likely there. So look for these darker patches of soil as you walk through the forests.

## Swampy Areas

Swamps are filled with water, but that doesn't necessarily mean that your problems are solved. The problem is making that water safe to drink.

Fires can be a challenge to make in the swamp, especially if you're in mangrove-type swamps. So the strategies here are much like in the jungle—i.e., dig a filter hole, use your clothes and charcoal/sand if you can find some, and in the worst case, scoop up some water into a shallow container and let the sun work on it for the day, then sip the top water off at night. It's not ideal, but it'll make you feel like you've attempted to make it as safe as possible.

### Resorting to Desperate Measures

People can drink urine! Now that I have your attention. . . . The rules for urine drinking are pretty straightforward: drink it as soon after you urinate as possible; the first time you urinate is usually fine to drink; and you can drink the second pass in dire circumstances, but after that, it gets dicey. After the second pass, chances are that you won't be urinating again anyway if there is no more fluid going in. There simply won't be any fluid left to be passed.

**Fact:** Urine drinking has been around for literally thousands of years. It has been considered a medicinal practice for health by nearly every major civilization at one point or another throughout time. So, contrary to survival manuals by both the US Army and the British SAS, you can drink urine safely, if done correctly.

**Myth:** You will not die or get sick if you drink urine. It is not poisonous. It is actually mostly sterile the moment it leaves your body, and only contact with the air allows for bacteria to grow.

This is why you shouldn't urinate and then store it for later.

# CHAPTER FIVE

# FIRE

Let's start this section by saying that you should always carry a lighter. We can't stress this enough.

The real decisions for parents shouldn't be whether or not to have their kids carry some sort of fire starter for emergencies, but rather, which ones to let them carry. And a lot of those answers will depend on the age and abilities of your children.

Fire is one of the key elements in any survival situation. It provides warmth, light, and heat for cooking. It can sterilize knives for first aid and help make cooking utensils. It boils water clean. It protects against predators. You can use it to signal. It's a major necessity in survival situations.

There are a lot of good tools out there to help get a fire started. We review a few in this chapter, and also provide basic fire-starting principles and primitive fire-starting methods. I recommend that every member of the family learn a few methods.

## Fire-Starting Tools

### Lighters

First and foremost of the fire-starting tools is the lighter. I love Zippos©, but they require maintenance, so I recommend the disposable types for survival situations. I prefer Bics© for this purpose and carry the tiniest ones they make.

For your kids, give them the lighter that fits in their hands best. The bigger the lighter, the more fuel it has, which means more fuel to burn.

### Matches

If you think the lighter may be a bit too much for your child or too difficult to manage, then consider matches. I don't recommend the packet types, as those get beat up too easily and go bad with even a little bit of moisture. A better kind are box matches but they are usually not really rugged enough either.

I recommend water-proof, light-anywhere stick matches. These come with a tip that is called a "strike anywhere" match and are very helpful if your flint striker has become moist and unusable. They also have more burning material on the length of the match which makes them last longer and even re-ignite if a drop of rain hits it or the wind mostly blows it out. These come in water-proof containers so they float, they're easy to find, and they have a strike surface on the side to give you the best chance at getting a fire lit. I recommend keeping these in every child's outdoor backpack as children of almost any age can light them.

## Magnesium Bars

These are great tools but they do require work and skill. They're great as they can be submerged completely underwater and still create a fire. But they often require a knife and some skill with the blade as well.

They work by scrapping some of the magnesium off the bar, and then forming those shavings into a tiny pile. Then you run the knife or the small metal saw-like tool they often come with, across the striker (usually a ferrous rod) to make sparks and those ignite the shavings. In essence, this gives you the same result as the lighter flick or the match strike.

If you're going to give these to your kids, consider larger ones that have a handle so the kid is not scraping the knife on the magnesium anywhere near their hands.

Also, get the kind that have a high-grade ferrous rods embedded in them. These make insanely good sparks that make igniting much easier and faster. The little metal shavings of magnesium will burn even when wet. These temperatures are quite hot, in between 2,000 to 4,000 degrees Fahrenheit, so make sure the kids are aware of that when they light them. The bright white burning is great for getting anything lit, but it happens quickly, so the tinder must already be assembled and ready to go.

For now, patience is key when shaving. It's hard. It takes some finesse, as you're slightly dragging and scraping the magnesium with the sharp back edge of the blade of your knife. It's easy to slip and slice. And you need a decent-sized pile, about a thumb nail's worth, to spark.

Once you have your pile, the safest method for kids is to put the knife safely back in the sheath or fold it and stow it. Then use the scraper to make the sparks.

I recommend kids practice throwing the sparks first, so they get the hang of it before they try lighting their pile of shavings, as it is easy to knock the pile and

*There are lots of firelighters available but when it comes to preventing singed baby fingers it's hard to beat long handled matches. (Photo credit Ruth England Hawke)*

lose the work. After a two to three strikes and sparks, they are ready to ignite their pile of shavings.

Often, the safest way is to hold the larger item steady by the pile. Place it into position so that it is braced on start point, with the key being to place it so it doesn't move when striking sparks. If the striker is long and the kids have a good control of the technique, they can strike towards the pile.

However, if you don't have a scraper and must use a knife, we suggest putting the point of the knife slightly into the ground near the pile, helping to hold the knife steady. I prefer the blade pointing down towards ground so you can pull the rod up and towards yourself while the sparks land straight on the pile. But depending on knife, rod, and hand size, blade up may be easier.

Try to make it as safe as possible for kids to strike sparks and ignite fire without getting sliced. I make them practice with throwing sparks and rehearse what to do afterwards two to three times.

Kids often get so excited when they throw sparks and ignite fire, they just stop and stare. But then flame goes out, work is wasted, and they lose enthusiasm. They have to practice the steps of strike, spark fire, put knife/scraper and bar down safely, and grab tinder ball quickly but not sloppily, and place on top of burning fire.

As it burns hot and upwards, it will ignite the tinder ball and then all the other principles of fire making come into play. Platform, fuel, structure, air, time, and build all have to be done the same way for any and all fires. These principles never change, only techniques do. See more on the principles of fire later in this chapter.

*Myke teaching scouts in New Orleans to start a fire using a magnesium bar, ferro rod, and a flint, with cotton wool for tinder. Everything is contained in a baking tray for safety while they learn. (Photo credit Ruth England Hawke)*

**Note:** Test your magnesium bar before using, as some simply don't work. I can't express how sad I was one day, during a group event, when a student couldn't light their fire with their mag bar. I tried and tried and finally got it. Then I found half the class couldn't do it. We discovered that day that some brands light, and some simply don't.

## Magnifying Glass

Starting a fire with a magnifying glass is great practice for kids and it takes some finesse, but once learned, they really do have a great back-up technique for starting a fire. For parents who have kids with glasses, you might see if their glasses can be used to start a fire. That will make them feel a lot cooler about having to wear glasses!

The trick here is that it really needs to be a sunny day. Hotter is better, but even in winter, magnifying glass can start fires.

Nonetheless, this is a fun skill you can take thirty minutes to teach your kids and instill them with confidence along the way.

*Abbie is using a magnifying glass to start a fire in this shot. She has made a tinder nest, built her fire teepee, and is focusing the sun's beam so it is a small dot. The bigger the magnifying glass the easier this is. Strong sunlight works best, in some climates this method will only work in summer. Abbie had the benefit of midsummer, midday sun in Louisiana here, but it often helps to be just a few inches above your tinder bundle.*
*(Photo credit Jeffrey Coit)*

## More on Lighters

I'm not keen on rubbing sticks together, even though it is very cool to make fire that way. Although I don't smoke, I keep a lighter on my person at all times because having to start a fire with friction for survival is a lot of hard work.

Always have a lighter! Stash them all over your backpacks, house, vehicle, and on your person whether you're in the wilderness or on the streets of a city.

There are lots of different types of lighters. You might think it's worth it to have expensive wind-proof kinds, especially if you spend time up on mountains or in generally open areas. And they're not bad for some purposes. But in fact, the jet-propulsion of the flame can blow out your fledgling fire. No matter where you are, you should seek out a sheltered area to start your fire, so you won't need a wind-proof lighter. Besides, they're expensive.

Not only are disposable lighters great, they are also cheap, and easy to come by. Even after the fuel runs out, you can get a spark out of them, which is still good for getting a fire going in a pinch. You can get tiny-sized ones which are great for stashing everywhere.

Sometimes, though, you need a lighter for actual "light." In these cases, lighters really earn their keep, especially Zippos©. They be lit and set down and used as a lamp. I've even used it a tight spot as a mini stove or fireplace.

You can also refill them. When you're away from civilization, you can use alternative fuels like moonshine alcohol, alcohol in first-aid kits, or vehicle fuel to refill one. For these reasons, lighters are very diverse. So, if they work for your situation, then they are a great tool to have.

**Caution:** Some fuels are dangerous as they have fumes and vapors that will create a fireball when ignited. Before you load up your Zippo© with an alternative to lighter fuel, give a test light of a small puddle. If it gives off a great ball of flame when sparked, it's likely too combustible to use in your lighter. In these cases, just load it in a container and carry it with the Zippo© for the spark. But when the liquid fuel source candidate just gives a nice, smooth burn, then it's usually safe to use. The general rule with fuel, as with anything in survival situations, is always to use common sense and try things first.

**Tip:** It's a good habit to test all gear in your survival kit regularly. It doesn't need to be daily, but it should be looked at every once in a while.

**Tip:** Always carry a lighter. Everything else that follows in this chapter involved what you would have to do if you didn't carry a lighter. Carrying a lighter can be the thing that saves your kids' lives, so, think about how you want to approach the subject of fire with your kids and what skills you want to teach them.

Following are a few ways to make sure your fire survives the conditions.

# Preparations

### Fire Platform

In general it is good to make a simple platform to give your fire lift so air flow can come under it, helping it burn upwards, give better light and heat, and burn more fuel, faster. The easiest way to do this is to make a square of similar-sized branches or logs that are fairly straight and lay them down side by side in the general area for the fire. It should be about a two feet by two feet square. Then lay another layer of sticks of the same size and width across the base layer, but perpendicular to them. This will form a simple platform that is especially good for low wind days.

### Fire Pit

This is a good technique for when you have high wind. Make a shallow hole in the ground that is about two feet by two feet, so you have a decent working area for your fire. It doesn't need to be too deep, just low enough so the wind doesn't blow all the smoke and ashes everywhere. Sometimes, placing rocks or logs around the fire can serve this same purpose.

### Fire Wall

Fire walls are a great supplement to get the most out of your fire. Whether you're sleeping in the open or in a shelter, it's good to make a wall of some fashion on the opposite side of the fire. This will reflect more heat and light your way and deflect more wind and cold as well. It also keeps the smoke flow down so your face doesn't get smoked out—and you always want to avoid any drain on your physical condition, such as smoke in your eyes.

You can make a fire wall with sticks and logs, dirt, rocks, tarp, or other man-made materials if you have any. The concept is simple—just fashion a wall about a foot behind the fire, extending a couple feet to either side of the fire and at least three feet high.

Make sure it's as wind-proof as you can make it, often by packing the holes with dirt. The specifics of what you build will be dictated by time, terrain, and need.

But do give consideration to a fire wall and use one whenever possible. It's simple, easy, works, and makes a world of difference. And in survival, it's all about the little victories.

## Making the Fire

The main two ways man has made primitive fire in the past has been percussion and friction. Percussion involves striking steel and/or stone to get sparks. Friction involves rubbing sticks together to get coal. The main difference in the friction methods are driven by logistics. If you have cordage, make a bow drill. If not, then use a fire plow for fat wood or a hand drill for skinny wood.

The most common image that comes to mind for primitive fires is that of someone rubbing sticks together. It can be done, but it is extremely hard work, even after you perfect your technique. Once you get a fire started, try to keep it going. But, if you fall asleep or are gone too long, most of the time, you can re-kindle it with some tinder and air.

It is also very time consuming and, therefore, can take a toll on both your physical and mental well-being. If you know this and inform your kids, then everyone will be prepared for the challenge and failures.

Now, before we discuss friction fires, let's talk about wood and different types of it.

## Hard Wood vs. Soft Wood

Before we get into the various preparations and techniques, let's have a look at the kind of woods you may consider.

Most survival books—in fact, every one that I have read—state that for starting fires, use a hard wood against a soft wood. I have found this not to be true.

Both the British SAS and US Army manuals, and indeed in all the most popular survival books, promote the hard-wood-on-soft-wood theory. Now it might be a hard-wood spindle or a soft-wood base, etc., depending on the technique being applied, but they all speak to using contrasting woods.

But I have found that when it comes to rubbing sticks together to make fire, two soft woods work best. Some folks might get bothered about this, but the logic is simple. The less dense the wood, the faster it will ignite. But if it's too light, it will rub away before it ignites.

I know that some woods classified as hard woods are soft feeling, and vice versa. But I don't think it is so important to know all the wood names or classes, just the wood types. So, let's look at what is a hard and a soft wood.

Try the "nail test." If you can stick your thumbnail into a wood and leave a dent, it's a soft wood. If not, it's a hard wood. It's that simple. I don't care what its name or scientific designation is, and neither will you when you're freezing in the wild alone.

Now, rubbing any two sticks together long and hard enough will get you some friction and some heat. If you're starting with green trees and saplings, you might

*Gabe, aged six, re-starting a dormant fire from ash and embers by agitating it with a stick to allow oxygen in and adding long dry pine needles. Pine needles are fantastic tinder.*
*(Photo credit Ruth England Hawke)*

as well be starting fire with water; you're going to be there a while. Green wood simply won't ignite.

You need dry wood to start a fire and the best place to get the dry wood is not from the standing tree that is green and alive but from the fallen tree if it's dry. The best kind is that which is either in the bushes or on a broken, but still hanging tree branch. The key is to find wood that is as dry as possible.

Next, you don't want something so soft it will crumble, either. What you're looking for is some wood that will be strong enough to hold up to the pressure you're going to apply to it, but also, not so hard that it will take a lot of effort to heat it up.

The wood I have found to be best for fast fire starting is yucca or sotol.

So, I too have found that a moderately hard piece of soft wood against another piece of the same thing is the best way to go. Think of balsa wood as an example of this. When it's thinly sliced, it's very fragile, but when in a solid piece, it's still light, but sturdy. The real secret here is the friction-to-flame ratio.

If the wood is softer, it'll give way to more friction, and the more friction, the quicker the flame comes. But any way you work it, it will be work.

## Preparation

Now let's look at the things you need to consider before attempting to start your fire.

### Location

First, choose your location wisely.

Here are the key factors regarding location:

- Find a spot away from wind, rain, other elements, and harm's way (e.g., under snow-covered tree branches).
- Give yourself enough area to work around the fire—cooking, sleeping, drying clothes, etc.
- Pick a generally dry spot and clear away combustible materials from the surrounding ground surface.
- Lay some sticks, logs, leaves, rocks, etc. on the ground so your fire is elevated to allow a slight amount of air/oxygen under it, as well as to keep it off the moist ground, which tends to zap a fledgling fire.
- Look for soil, rocks, logs, snow, etc. to create a wall around your fire area.
- When camping, teach your kids that when they pick up rocks for the fire pit, be aware of bugs and snakes that may be under them. But also, teach them to

remember where they got the rocks, flip the bottom side towards the fire and when they are done, to put those rocks back where they found them, burnt side down, is it will show a fire scar for many years. It keeps a site looking natural. In survival situations, leave the camp site as is so it helps rescuers find them.

## Starter Materials

Once you've found an ideal location, begin to gather up a good supply of starter materials—tinder, kindling, and fuel.

### Tinder

Tinder is the smallest material, and includes all the little fragile things you can find and grind into a powder. After getting the initial ember from friction, combustion, heat, or another energy source, tinder is what makes the bridge from spark to flame.

There are many techniques out there, but the basic idea is to gather the driest, fluffiest little ball you can from whatever you can find for your tinder. I've seen pocket lint, a lock of hair, toilet paper, leaves, and bark all used to make a successful tinder ball. You take strips of bark and dried leaves, mix it with whatever other man-made materials you can supplement with, and then rub them together and mix them up in your hand and try to make a nice little fluffy ball. Once you have a nice wad of fibrous material, spread it a little so as to make a nice ball. Then make a dent in that ball, molding it into a nest. Then take all the loose powder, shavings, and droppings from your friction formation and sprinkle it back into the middle of your nest.

One of the best sources for tinder one can find in nature is a bird's nest. Birds usually scavenge all the light and fluffy things in the environment that one needs to make a fire. If you look around, you'll often find a nest; I've even found them in the desert when I was looking to start a fire.

### Kindling

Kindling is anything slightly larger than tinder, and includes small branches and twigs.

### Fuel

Fuel refers to any material that will combust and grow into your full-on fire. You should collect fuel of various sizes, starting with three-to-six stacks of wood branches that are just bigger than a twig, and then work your way up to a large pile of wrist- or ankle-sized logs.

*Manny has made an excellent fire starter from everyday household trash – lint from the tumble dryer inside a cut up toilet roll tube. A couple of sparks and a gentle blow is all it would take to ignite it. (Photo credit Ruth England Hawke)*

# Wet Places

If everything around you is wet, look for slanted trees and take the bark on the underside, peel it off, and underneath the outermost layers you'll find dry bark that you can crush into a fine tinder.

Cut a piece of bark off and then scrape it to make shavings. This makes an excellent source of tinder, and is often my first choice. Scrapings make flat curled pieces of wood that catch easy and burn in a circle, and so, the flame is warming the wood before it burns it and does a really nice job of keeping air circulating while preserving heat.

Now sometimes you need a little cheater or helper. For me, I find pine resin does just the trick. Pine resin makes a good food and glue, but it also burns very well. This fuel source is called "lighter knot" or "fat lighter." Often a fallen pine tree will have a lot of resin that will have oozed and concentrated in the stump. (This resin is often found in stumps where trees have been felled, and if you're near felled trees, you're likely close enough to civilization to walk out!) Pine resin is usually

*These seventh graders are engaged in a fire-lighting competition. They have to light a fire large enough to burn through the 550 cord suspended about sixteen inches above the fire pan. They are using flint and steel—no mag bar—so this is a real lesson in what type of tinder ignites easily and burns fiercely. (Photo credit Jeffrey Coit)*

orange or yellow in color and will burn even in rain. I have used this to start fires in the rain. If you have good weather, save it for the wet days.

Another great tinder in nature is the ever-useful cattails. Not only can you eat these, but if you scrape the brown heads you'll get lots of fluff, and this stuff catches pretty easily. Even if the cattail has been in the rain, the fluffy stuff is still dry.

Of course, leaves and needles are great as long as they are dry and brittle brown. Crush up some of the leaves into a powder and they'll catch the ember pretty quickly. Also, some types of dry moss will catch as well, but they don't burn well. There are other plants that will work too depending on your location.

The key to finding tinder is to look through "tinder glasses"—simply look at everything around you for its fire-catching potential. This is such an important part of making a fire, and such effort will go into creating the initial heat that you need for success.

### Kindling

Kindling is medium-sized wood, from twigs to sticks. Anything bigger should be considered fuel. The most basic rule for fire making is simple—use dry stuff. Try and gather your kindling from tree branches that are dead and brittle. Try not to use ones that are lying on the ground, as those tend to be moist. And don't use any live branches, as they're green and most definitely moist.

You *can* burn green stuff once you have a good fire going; technically, the hot fire will dry out the green stuff before burning it. However, these make a lot of noise and smoke.

### Fuel

If it burns strong, it's fuel. If you can burn it, do it. Ration your fuel supplies and use them sensibly.

There may be occasions when you want a huge fire, again, maybe to signal for help or to make a lot of coals for cooking or to make a coal bed to sleep warm through the night. In these cases, burn on! But mostly, go easy—you don't need a huge fire, and gathering materials itself can be hard work that depletes energy.

### The Teepee Method

I find the "teepee method" is the best way to prepare your tinder, kindling, and fuel to start your fire. All the rest of the so-called techniques are just flashy ways to get the same thing done.

Start by using a bunch of kindling to make a small "teepee" shape—about one to two feet tall—that rests on a bed of sticks and tinder. Leave an opening in the teepee for access to the empty space inside. Then take your soft tinder nest and place it right next to that opening.

Once you've generated your tiny coal ember, transport that ember onto a small piece of bark or leaf onto the tinder nest (which should be very close by). With the coal atop the tinder nest, begin to gently breathe air onto it, bringing it from a smoldering coal to a beautiful ember and into a fantastic little flame!

Then, place the flaming nest through the opening in the teepee and onto the bed of tinder inside, and continue to nurture it with gentle breaths as it catches the twigs of the teepee on fire. Once the teepee twigs begin to catch fire, gently lay one piece of kindling after another onto the tepee, slowly reinforcing the walls of it as each layer is consumed by your new hungry offspring of flame. After a few minutes, you'll have a nice little fire and a giant feeling of warmth inside you.

At this point, stay calm and do not rush the process. I have seen many fires killed at this critical juncture by people who are so excited that they over-stack their fire too quickly and crush it.

Since you've done all the preparation beforehand, there is no need to rush and panic, and no need for excessive moving around finding and breaking sticks. It's all there and you are ready, so enjoy the show and watch it grow.

Now, let's talk about some of the techniques of fire making, or more point-edly, "ember making." Some are very basic while others are more advanced. But as in everything else regarding survival, there are no hard and fast rules; there are only principles by which you should be guided.

## Fire-Starting Techniques

Once you've made all preparations including choosing a wise location, gathering your materials, and building a fire wall, it's time to start rubbing sticks. There are many variations on how to start fire with sticks. Each one requires a lot of hard work, many require special accessories, and most require a refined technique. But these are all variables. Fuel, air, and heat are the constants. Think: FAHre.

For this, you can use gas, wood, paper, or anything that burns as a fuel. You also must have air—not enough to blow it out, especially at the delicate start-ing stages, but enough for the fuel to combust. And finally, you'll need heat. This might be the spark from a lighter or battery. It might be from a lens of a glass, or it might be from heat generated by friction.

Here I will focus on tried-and-true methods. There are dozens of ways to start fires, but a lot of them really require advance skills and that's not our purpose here. We want to provide skills that parents can teach their kids.

## Fire Plow

I don't recommend it, but the fire plow is the best way to start a fire when you have nothing else. The fire plow requires one "plow stick" about the thickness of a broom handle and about a foot long. You also need a "base board," which should be about two to three feet long and about two inches thick.

You'll need to use a rock or other object to scrape a running rut or groove into the top face of the base board through which the plow stick will be rubbed back and forth. The technique is not complicated, but it is hard work and hard to master.

Find a comfortable kneeling position that allows you to hold the base steady either on the ground, in your lap, or wedged into your waist or tummy and the ground at an angle. Then hold your plow stick with both hands, begin rubbing it quickly back and forth into the rut of the base log, developing some friction.

I find that keeping the base flat with my foot helps a lot once I have a good groove made. The goal is to rub the plow stick quickly, with force and high friction into the base log until it produces heated shavings that eventually become ignited and a coal is generated. Then use that coal to light your gathered tinder and apply the fire-building skills.

It's important to find the right angle of pushing down. If your plow stick is pointed too sharply down, you risk digging a hole through your base-board. If your plow stick's angle too closely parallels the base log, the area of friction is too dispersed and there's no chance for a coal to develop.

So, it's essential to get the right angle to develop friction, heat, smoke, and a coal on the end of your plow stick's runway. Be prepared: this takes time. Some folks find making a split in the wood allows air in and helps get the fire going faster. Just lash the board together so it doesn't break into two pieces under pressure.

If your sticks build up too much slickness or get shiny, then there's less friction, so sprinkle a little sand or dry dirt in the base log's groove to roughen it up, or scrape it with something like a rock and get the friction increased.

Ideally, you'll do this a few times for fun, practice, and exercise before you need it. If you do find yourself in a survival situation, hopefully you'll find or make time to start working on this before you need it.

I should point out here that once you know how to do this, and have refined your technique as well as developed your sense of which types of wood work best, this can be done in fifteen to thirty minutes given good environmental factors.

And once you have your materials broken in, they can often get you a fire in only about five minutes. Of course, if you're completely new to this and in a survival situation for the first time, it could take you an hour or more of constant work to get a coal.

## Hand Drill

Another primitive friction method is using a hand drill. This is basically the same thing as the fire plow, but the difference is that your friction is pinpointed onto a particular spot on the base, as opposed to a long groove. The friction is created by quickly spinning the stick on that point instead of rubbing it lengthwise.

You'll need to make a notch in your wood base, and I find this no easy task without a knife. Not to mention, unless you happen to find some really nice, smooth, thin sticks, without a knife to whittle it down and make it smooth, this technique is not viable as it requires some modifications to the base and spindle that simply can't be done without an implement of some sort. But it can be scraped smooth with stones or bones.

If you can improvise a knife with a sharp rock or other found object, that will help you create a notch in the base that will focus the friction, and also help to smooth out the spindle stick to make it easier to work with.

To begin, find a good piece of base wood that's flat on top, and make a little notch in the middle of the flat surface that tapers down to a small hole that you can lay some tinder directly under. Then place your long spindle into the hole and sit down comfortably.

Press your hands together with the top of the spindle between them, and rub them together briskly as if you're warming them up. At the same time, apply pressure downwards to create friction and heat.

Your palms will slip down toward the base pretty quickly, so when they get to the bottom, hang onto your stick with one hand while holding pressure downward, quickly bring the other hand to the top of the spindle. Keep pushing downward, then bring your bottom hand up and resume the motion.

Keep the spindle spinning back and forth and driving down the whole time to keep up friction. If your spindle is not smooth, this activity will feel rough on your hands, so take the time to smooth out your spindle before starting.

If you don't have the strength to do the fire plow method, the hand plow will accomplish the same effect. Again, getting the coal embers to drop into the bundle of tinder below will give you what you need to start your fire.

### A Shortcut

My favorite shortcut if I make a hand drill is called the thumb loops. Take a simple piece of string anywhere from six to twelve inches long, with two loops, big enough for your thumb, one on each end. Then make a small slit at the top of your hand drill spindle like the back of an arrow. Place your string in the slit, put your thumbs through the loops, and push down. This lets you push down harder and without as much friction.

At the end of the day, the fire plow and the hand drill are primitive ways to start a fire with just two sticks. It is good to try both. Master one and you'll always be comforted with the knowledge that you can make a fire if needed. That can make all the difference between living and dying.

## Fire Bow Drill

This is the best way for children to make fires requiring the least amount of physical strength. But these methods require some practice. However, with practice and good wood, most kids ten and older can make a primitive fire this way.

This is my favorite of the primitive methods. If you have a knife and string handy, then the bow drill method is far better on your back, hands, and muscles than most of the other methods. And once your kit is made, it is tantamount to having your caveman lighter on you at all times.

Materials Needed:

- One flat baseboard (think a wooden cutting board) that's about an inch or so thick and made of dry, sturdy wood.
- One spindle stick, also about an inch thick and straight, that you will use to spin rapidly to create friction. This should be dry, sturdy wood about twelve inches in length.
- One wooden block to press down on top of the spindle. This should be a couple inches thick and wide, and should fit into your closed hand, though it can vary; just understand that the purpose of this block is to protect your hand when you're pressing down on the spindle.
- One spindle handle, or bow. This should be about an inch thick, two feet long, made of fresh wood so that it's strong yet flexible. It needs to be strong and thick enough to take your weight as you put downward pressure on the spindle.
- One long, sturdy string (when necessary, even a six-inch piece will do).

First, carve a round indentation with your blade tip less than an inch from either long end on the top face of your baseboard. Also carve the tip of your spindle to a blunt point in order to fit into the indenture. Prepare the wooden block by carving a shallow round groove in its face into which the top of the spindle can be held in place as you press down on it.

Then cut a "V" notch on the underside edge of the baseboard directly below the indent—you want to remove most of the wood here, leaving about a quarter inch of the board's thickness below the indentation above. When you're making these cuts, place the board on something like a sheet of bark or leaves to catch and hold the dust that results; it's that dust with your bit of tinder that will catch and give you a coal.

Use whatever string you have—almost any thickness will do, but a sturdy boot string will usually do the trick if it's thick and not made of synthetics. Obviously, the amount of string or cordage you have will be the best determinant for the size of your bow. This can work with even a six-inch piece of string.

Cut notches on both ends of your spindle handle about an inch from the ends, and tie either end of the string into these notches, making sure that the tautness of the string creates a bowing effect on the spindle handle.

Sit or kneel next to your prepared teepee and tinder nest, lay the base down, and put the shavings and other tinder directly under the "V" notch on the base. With the string taut and in place on the bow, loop it once around the middle of the spindle, positioning the spindle at the middle of the string. Then place the blunt point of the spindle into the base indent, and position the block on the top of the spindle. Now you're ready to begin.

The basic motion you need to employ is like using a saw. Hold the bow with one hand and press down on the block with the other keeping the spindle in place in the base indent, then begin "sawing" the bow back and forth.

As you do this, the string will cause the spindle-point to rotate quickly in the notch, creating friction. Once you get a good rhythm going, you will begin to generate significant friction, then heat, then a spark that will light your tinder.

*Myke teaching Gabriel to start a fire by friction. Friction fires can be exceptionally hard to get going and they require more physical strength than most children possess.*
*(Photo credit Ruth England Hawke)*

*The bow drill is the only friction method that works for a child because using the bow to spin the spindle reduces the physical effort, but it still requires an awful lot of work and practice. It can be accomplished by one person but it's better to share the load and have a second person push down on the spindle. (Photo credit Ruth England Hawke)*

If you prepare all your tools properly, this is one of the easiest ways for beginners to start a fire.

## Fire Piston

This is a super cool way to start a fire, but it's not recommended for kids or beginners. Parents, if you find yourself interested, then please do some research. It's an amazing way to start a fire and it's based on compression, not friction or percussion.

## Bamboo Fire Saw

This is one of my all-time favorite methods. But it is, again, far too advanced for beginners. Additionally, we don't have a plethora of bamboo here in the states.

### When It's Wet

Getting a fire going in wet conditions is particularly challenging for anyone. It's also one of the times when it's most needed. It's good to know that it can be done, but there are some tricks to making it so.

*Tools of the trade. A bow drill is made from four components, aside from strength and perseverance, you will need: a baseboard, a spindle, a bow, and a strong object to press down on top of the spindle. Gabe here is using half of a coconut shell. I've used seashells, chunks of wool, and flat pebbles. (Photo credit Ruth England Hawke)*

Look for dry stuff. Sounds like common sense, but for folks who don't spend much time in the woods, it doesn't seem likely to find dry stuff in such conditions, until you look. Many trees have a slight tilt, or the rain might be coming down at a bit of an angle—look for the dry parts of trees where they're not exposed to the rain. Look for the branches and leaves in these dry areas and scrape some bark off the dry part of the tree as well.

Sometimes you can find dry wood inside the bark: pick up a few branches, peel off the bark, and see if it's dry inside. Sometimes leaves will cover the ground well enough that twigs underneath might still be dry—so look under piles of leaves. There are some tree barks that are very good for finding a dry layer under a wet outer layer, but I don't want to play the name game—just use your common sense and search.

Look for dry nooks and crannies and little spaces that might have avoided wetness. If you find dry items, and they are not the right size, shave them down into kindling and tinder.

Prepare your surroundings for a fire and make it as dry as possible. But first bear in mind you'll need enough area around you to stay dry, dry your clothes, and rest safely and comfortably.

### When It's Cold

Any snow covered terrain is a harsh environment. For these, it's best to make a fire wall on all sides to retain as much heat as possible. It does diminish your fire's ability as a signal, but staying warm is the priority in icy cold places. And be very careful with kids near the fires in these environmental conditions; they often want to get too close, and end up burning boots, bags, and sometimes, themselves.

## Fire Extenders, Helpers, and Enhancers

When it comes to making fire, in addition to a good location, a lot of preparation and the usual work to make it and build it, you might run into challenges and there are some tricks than can help you get over the hurdle. So, review this list and keep as many extra helpers as part of your operational plan as possible.

### Tricks and Treats

### Hand Sanitizers

Commercially available hand sanitizers are very good for helping to start a fire. We sometimes call them fire extenders. You will still need to get the spark or coal and light the tinder bundle but the alcohol in these does burn and if you have a small tinder bundle or it is a bit moist, once you have the flame, hand sanitizers can help it burn long enough to dry you tiny tinder and get the fire going.

And it's great to have this in your kids' bags at all times anyway, since they will use their hands when surviving, and eating or drinking with dirty hands is the fastest way to get sick.

### Vaseline

Many soldiers carry Vaseline gauze dressings in their first aid kit. These are great for your hands and lips when they get chapped; they're awesome for sealing a sucking chest wound; and they're super for starting a fire as the petroleum-jelly-covered gauze catches easily. Campers and outdoorsman for years have used cotton balls soaked in Vaseline as a reliable fire starter.

### Perfume

Depending on your situation, check in your inventory of supplies and see if anyone has any perfume, aftershave, or other astringents. If the first ingredient in any of these products is water, it likely won't work. But if the main ingredient is ETOH or alcohol, you have a good fire-starting enhancement.

## Alcohol

Some of the higher-proof drinking alcohols will also help start a fire.

## Batteries

If you have batteries with enough juice left in them and two small wires, it's easy to start a fire. Just connect one wire each to the positive and negative on the battery. Then touch them together on top of your fine tinder to make a spark.

*Aaron is using a quick and easy trick to make fire without matches or a lighter. He's using wire wool and a 9-volt battery. It's a simple method to learn and children like it because it's instant. First, fluff up your wire wool because all fire needs oxygen and then simply place the terminal end of the battery into the wire, making sure both terminals are touching it. Electricity is conducted through the wire causing it to become hot enough to ignite your fire! Narrow grade wire works best. A note of caution: the molten wire can stick to your hands if you're holding it. (Photo credit Jeffrey Coit)*

## Steel Wool

Note that some forms of steel wool work better than others, and I have run across steel wool that simply wouldn't burn. Fluff it up like a nest and it will burn at a high heat that will be good for setting your tinder alight. The cool thing about steel wool is that you can simply touch it to your batteries to get a spark and start your fire.

## Pine Sap

This has already been mentioned, but it is great to use in helping to get a flame. Always look for it.

*In some environments it's really difficult to get a fire going even if you have a lighter or matches; jungles during the wet season are especially challenging. That's when a fire extender comes in handy. A fire extender makes a small fire burn for longer, allowing it to ignite the kindling around it. Cotton wool or dryer lint soaked in petroleum jelly works well but so does snack food with a high fat content. The fire extender in the picture above was carefully crafted from a smear of peanut butter and some Cheetos, much to the delight of the children watching. (Photo credit Jeffrey Coit)*

### Flint and Other Rocks

These take a little practice at finding and identifying, but I always say try anything. If you happen to have rocks lying around, time on your hands, and need for a fire, just start grabbing rocks and striking them against one another to see if you get sparks. If you do, that's all you need to know.

A piece of steel or a knife is preferable, but flint and rock can work, too. Now even with a nice piece of flint and a good strong steel knife blade, it takes a little practice to get the angle strike right for creating sparks.

This is the principle for modern lighters—flint and steel make a spark, which ignites the gas, which in turn results in a flame. Flint is found all over, but more so in some locations more than others.

### Rubber

Rubber is a great fire enhancer. Many survivalists cut up small pieces from an old inner tube and throw these into their survival kits. Rubber never rusts or decays, and it can even get wet and still burn. It won't catch a spark, but rubber will help a tiny fire get big in a hurry.

### Any Fuel or Lubricant

Take a creative and thorough approach to making an inventory of your stock in a survival situation. Look for new ways of using all that you have available. Even cooking oil or tanning oil might come in handy for making a fire, or keeping one going in foul weather.

### Processed Food

Foods like Cheetos and Pringles are known to burn well as fire starters, due to their high fat content and being processed. Most processed foods have a layered structure that permits air to let them burn well. Peanut butter often burns well, too.

### Tampons

If these are available, they're great as tinder—be sure to fluff it up first.

### First Aid Dressings

These are also great for starting fires as they are perfectly dry and light so they take a spark readily. But only use them if you have no immediately pressing first aid requirements for a bandage. If so, evaluate the benefits of using improvised dressings if they would not start fires as well.

### Fire as Trash

The principle of the magnifying glass reflector can be applied to anything highly shiny and bendable enough to focus the sun's light. I've heard of everything from dark chocolate to toothpaste being used to scour and polish the bottom of an aluminum can. Because cans are of a convex shape, they naturally capture and focus all the sun's light in one direction. Research different ways to start fire and let your kids practice with you.

### Candles

Store-bought and improvised candles won't necessarily help you get a fire started, but they're very handy to have as they keep a flame with little effort or oversight—as long as you keep them protected from the elements.

I can't recommend this enough: let your kids have a candle. There are strong, safe, and protected options available. One match and one candle, and you get light to see, to help start fires to cook, and to be a signal to help you get rescued.

Teach them all the basics of fire making and the principles of fire building with a little bit of time management for collecting and resource management for getting them through the night with enough fire wood. You'll have a kid whose chances of survival just tripled, or more.

It's important to teach your kids some cooking skills. BBQs are a great chance to get kids learning about fire and cooking on a grill with open fire or gas fire and heat. Make sure they have a metal cup to cook and boil in and a spork to eat with.

### Camp Stoves

These come in all shapes and sizes and we don't recommend them for kids in general. For teens, with some skill and practice, they can be perfectly fine with a hiking stove. In general, these are best left to the parents to carry and operate.

### Fuel Tabs

These are fantastic for kids to have and we highly recommend these. Some good types are the small cans of sterno as they can be opened easily, lit with one match, used to cook a meal or boil a cup, then put the lid on, the fire goes out, let it cool while eating or drinking, pack it up again and go. They are light, small, safe, and easy to handle.

You can also try fuel tabs. There are many brands. Find the ones best for your needs and your kids, but test them first as I have found some of these products do not burn at all. These are single use items.

Always teach your kids to be safe, prepared for emergencies, have an extinguisher, hose, or bucket of water, or in the worst case, be ready to urinate on the fire to put it out. Teach them to make sure the fire is completely out before break-ing camp. Turn the entire pit into a muddy slushy wet pool with no coals or smoke left to risk re-igniting in a wind and starting a fire.

*Thea and Gabe learning the importance of fully extinguishing a fire, with water pistols for fun! Tasha has placed logs around the perimeter of the fire bed as markers that mustn't be crossed, since the embers are still hot. (Photo credit Ruth England Hawke)*

# CHAPTER SIX

# SHELTER

Kids are naturals at building shelters but it's important to teach them how to build shelters during survival situations.

One of the biggest factors for shelter building is location. Often, the easiest shelters to build are hidden from view and out in the open. This is where you want to be so you can be easily seen and found. Constantly remind kids that the biggest part of survival is getting out and that means building signals or using navigation to get home. However, if you're caught out in a storm or darkness falls on you quickly, then you may want to make the most of whatever is available and reinforce this concept with your kids.

For location selection, you have to make sure there are no things that could fall on you. And make sure you're not in a flash flood area or that you're not on a game trail between animals and their food, water, or home.

After a danger assessment, you want the kids to consider visibility in regards to their shelter location selection. Can they be seen from the air? Can they be seen from hills or mountains? Try to make a guess as to where rescuers would be coming from and make your site visible to that approach.

Next, assess weather and winds. If you're on a hill, you might notice there is a strong wind, and from that direction, a storm could blow in during the night. So, you might want to build your shelter just a little off the top of the hill and more on the side out of the wind. These are the things to teach your kids, but are great points for parents always.

Make sure that your kids are informed about the importance of time. Teach your kids that a good shelter takes two hours to build. Sometimes you can get it done in an hour, but kids move slower when parents aren't there or when they are scared and uncertain what to do. So, they will often not estimate the time correctly and may find themselves in the dark before they've finished their shelter. So, instill in them that it takes a long time and hopefully, they will start sooner rather than later should they find themselves alone and in need of a shelter.

Once the basic principles of location and time are covered, discuss at shelters themselves. In an ideal situation, they would have a tent. A tiny, light-weight, self-pop-up for a single person to sleep in is ideal, but they are expensive.

The second best kind of shelter is the modern jungle hammock. They get them off the ground, have a rain tarp/rain fly and mosquito netting in between the top and bottom, and the bottoms are solid material, not netting. These are a lot cheaper than a ground bivouac tent but harder for a kids to set up, as there is some art to hammock stringing. So, figure out the best tent for your environment then have them practice without help.

Simple divvy sacs are also easy. They are light-weight sleeping bags, consisting of a water-proof, wind-proof sac. To use it, just pull it out, slide in, and lay on a flat piece of ground in a good location. These are cheap and light so, they will be the best bet for most budgets.

An additional shelter for your kids is a tarp, poncho, or even just a large, heavy-duty trash bag. Again, these are cheap, light, tiny, and have a lot of uses. Teach your kids based on whatever tools you're giving them and that they are carrying.

*A single tarp makes a great quick shelter and if you're "bugging out" it's much, much lighter than a tent to carry. Alex and his dad Jeff erected this shelter in Big Bend National Park quickly and easily by using their hiking sticks as tent poles. Tarps are very versatile. You can tie them to trees and bushes or just drape them over the supports of any shelter you have made. (Photo credit Jeff Coit)*

Even if you have nothing, there are other ways to make shelters in the wilds and survive. In regards to shelters, the rule is easiest first. Look around you and make what you have work for you. If you have a broken-down vehicle, aircraft, sea vessel, or any wreckage or building debris, then use it.

Be aware that building a shelter takes time, and a good one takes some work and therefore energy—especially to make it windproof and waterproof. If you are lucky enough to have all that sorted out for you, or if you're in such a pleasant climate that you can do without, then maybe you can consider not even making a shelter. But we don't recommend teaching that to your kids. Even in the best of conditions, we still recommend using something for cover. Weather can change quickly, and night temperatures may be very different than daytime temperatures.

So, don't risk it. Just make time and make a shelter first unless you're just completely wiped out by illness, injury, or fatigue. Preserve health and energy and it just might be what saves you. Guard health, and let common sense and concern for unnecessary risk be a major factor in all your decision making.

When teaching your kids, focus on asking them what could go wrong at every step and let them see the potential risks and provide solutions, even if it's just slowing down. It's vital that they learn how to keep healthy and avoid injury whenever possible.

## The Time Factor

Give yourself at least one hour to make a minimal shelter if you have good stuff around you. If there's not much around, give yourself two hours. Shelters take time to build. Build time into your plan. If it's early morning, great, you have time; if it's afternoon or evening, move shelter higher on the priority list. Even if you have something for shelter already, get in it and test it before dark.

I have taken all day to make a very good shelter, but only after I had food and water sorted out. In some shelters I have slept as well as I ever have in any bed. In these I took the time to get it off the ground and protect it from wind, rain, and animals, and made sure that I was well padded and covered while inside. With every shelter, be sure to gather lots of cushion for sleeping and lots of leaves and foliage for warmth.

The focus on the first day is to just do what you need and only to create a shelter that's just good enough. Otherwise, hydrate, eat, keep dry, tend wounds, make fire, make tools, make signals, or do anything productive if there is plenty of daylight once you've made the shelter.

## Teach Sleep

Sleep as much and as long as you can the first night of a survival situation. You have likely just gone through hell. You are more tired and scared than you know.

*Gabe and Gran practicing sleeping in their wickiup shelter. They didn't spend the night as there were still one or two gaps in the walls! This type of shelter is made from thin supple green branches woven through each other, with foliage covering the walls for insulation. If you use willow for the verticals, your shelter may actually take root and grow! The only downside to the woven walls is sometimes the horizontal sticks poke out at eye level. Place potatoes on the ends for safety if you're at home.*
*(Photo credit Ruth England Hawke)*

This is normal. Everyone is concerned when they are not in control. But you can control yourself.

Start by getting rest, or "recovery." It is necessary for your body to have down time to recover its strength and maintain its health. Do not underestimate the power of sleep and do not neglect it as a mandatory part of your planning in all phases.

Additionally, do not let yourself or your kids become demoralized, and instead, focus on remedying the situation by making your shelter good enough to ensure you get a good night's sleep the second night. The whole world will seem better to you after that.

## Stay or Go

After resting, you can make a more informed decision whether to stay or go. If you decide to go, then having spent too much time on a shelter would have been a waste of time and energy, one that could cost you dearly later. This is another reason why you should only make a simple shelter for the first night. Even if you do decide to stay at your location, you might find your actual shelter site might not be the best one available in your immediate vicinity. You might be in an opening to the prevailing winds, or be open to a trickle of water if the rains pour.

## Scout

If you're staying put, scout around and see what you have available. I call it shelter shopping. It can save your precious time and energy.

I've found lots of natural holes, indentures, or concave pieces of terrain suitable for building a nice low-level shelter. I've found many nicely leaning trees, large-rooted trees, and well-placed boulders, which are all good for turning into a nice shelter.

If you decide you need to go, as you walk, always be on the lookout for a good deal, that bargain shelter waiting for you to pay a visit. I have stopped a long trip short simply to exploit a nice opportunity when it comes to shelters. If you're making a movement, you have no real idea how long you'll be going. I always plan for a long time, so I get my head around the fact that "I'm here until I'm not."

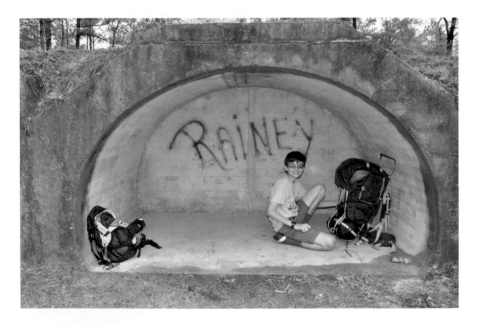

*It takes time to build a shelter. A good one takes hours to construct and you expend valuable energy doing it, so it's always best to use what is already there if you can. Alex had just hiked for ten miles through Mississippi carrying a twenty-five-pound pack when he came across this bunker in an old POW camp, a perfect ready-made home for the night. (Photo credit Jeffrey Coit)*

Bottom line, the function of a shelter is to protect you from the elements when necessary, and to protect you while vulnerable during sleep. Its quality level will affect your sleep, which in turn will affect all your decisions, judgment, and reaction time.

## Considerations for Shelters: Basics Must be Reviewed and Reinforced

There is no exact "right way" to build a survival shelter. You will be making your shelter out of the materials available to you, and so each shelter you build will look different.

However, there *are* basic principles that you should know and practice that will enable you to make fine protective shelters in practically any environment, regardless of what tools or resources you may or may not have.

Some terms describing the most basic shelters include: A-frame (a stick frame shaped like the letter "A"); teepee (shaped like a common Native American teepee made from sticks and foliage); and lean-to (basically, a wall of sticks built on a leaning angle to protect from elements). You can also burrow out a shelter, make a shelter from rocks or logs, dig into snow, and so on. Let's get into the details.

### Rocks

Rocks are generally not good for shelter-making. Sleeping on them will zap all heat out of your body, unless you have a sleeping bag and/or pad. And rocks sometimes fall for no reason. So, basically, don't sleep on big rocks unless that's all you have and always check to make sure no big ones are in danger of falling on you or rolling down a hill onto you.

### Get Off the Ground

The first rule in all cases is to get off the ground. I always look to the trees for shelter first when I need shelter fast. It gets me off the ground and keeps me safe from most things—flash floods, animals, and bad bugs.

No shelter is perfect, and there is always risk of something like a snake or insect, but rarely is this more likely in a tree than on the ground.

In a worst-case scenario where you have no tools or little time, simply find two good branches—one to sit on, straddle, or otherwise hold you up, with another one close enough to wedge yourself in so you won't fall out. And then let the rest of your body lean against the base of the tree. I call this "airplane sleeping." You're high up, and you can almost sleep, but not quite, like in the economy seats on airplanes.

But it will get you off the ground, provide you some shelter (if it's bushy enough, and not too windy or rainy), and it is safer than nothing unless you're so high that a fall could be harmful. In any case, it's wise to use a belt or shoe strings or an extra item of clothing to "tie in" so you don't fall completely. For one example, you can tie your arms or legs together and, if you should fall, the tug will hold you up while you quickly respond.

## Immediate Action Drills

I always rehearse my "immediate action drills," or IADs, before I go to sleep when I am away from home, whether camping or sleeping in a hotel. Teach these principles to your kids, as well.

If in a tree, I practice a few times, preferably before dark, by reaching and seeing where I'd grab if I fell. So if something happens or gives way, my response will be rehearsed enough that I'll react appropriately and immediately, even from a dead sleep.

I practice IADs everywhere and anywhere. I imagine what could happen, make a plan, rehearse it in my head, and practice it if it's something that requires a physical response. It's a good starting point for any exigency.

I also always have some sort of weapon for defense, whether it's a stick or rock or something else, and I rehearse reaching for and using it.

So, tie in and rehearse IADs before going to sleep and make sure you always brief your kids on a link-up plan in case something happens in the night. Do this religiously.

## Tree Shelter

When picking a tree or trees, I first look to see if it is easy in and out, or in this case up or down. All things considered, I try to find an easily climbable tree with a nice fork of two very strong branches so I can lay some other branches between them as a platform—and now I have a pretty good starting point for a shelter. It helps to lash these branches down before building up on them. I also look for a nice third branch as my roof. The height of your shelter off the ground will be dictated by the trees you find, but ideally you'll be at least shoulder height, and not so high that a fall would be fatal.

## Tree Bed

If I'm among trees that are simply too big, too high, or just not right for a shelter, I look for groves of smaller trees, ideally three or four close enough together that I can, again, lay some other small log-like branches across their branch joints near the base to give me a platform off the ground.

Think of these strong branches as your bed frame. Try to make them as level as possible. Using the trees' forks in this way will save you from having to make and apply lashings, which is especially handy if you don't have any.

Also, don't be self-restricting in your preconceived ideas about how things should look. If you can't make a square bed like back home, maybe because you only have three trees close together, then make a triangular bed and sleep curled up. Or if you have many trees, but they can be linked together by your branch poles, then make that situation work. Getting yourself off the ground and onto a fairly flat platform where you can rest safely is the key. Outside of those two criteria, there are no limits to what you might make and no number of drawings can cover all the possibilities.

Once I build my bed frame, whatever its shape, I lay more branches in between and parallel to the outer structure. Think of these as the slats for the bed frame. Then I put down lots of soft bushy materials for my mattress, enough for about two-feet thick since much of it will mat down as I sleep on it and none of the slats I laid will be exactly flat and smooth.

I then fashion a roof in the same manner. Use the higher branches to lay slats and cover, if available, and if not, you can make a pyramid roof by angling long loose branches starting from the four corners of your platform and connecting at the center point above. Leave the open side away from the wind direction as best you can, and stack as much foliage as possible on the roof as the more there is, the less chance of wind and rain getting in.

The main concepts for the tree shelter are that it's off the ground, you have a strong platform, and there's a decent overhead cover. A lot of times it will end up looking just like a bird's nest, but these things are easy to build, require nothing but the trees around you, and they'll protect you and help you sleep well. Keep in mind that these take time to build.

These are very hard for kids in general, and are mainly for parents to build for their kids to make sure they are as safe as possible. But having this serve as a guideline will help you plan the best way to get through the night safely.

## Swamp Bed

A swamp bed is like the tree shelter, except instead of using standing trees as the "legs" that hold your platform, you create the legs by hammering three or four logs into the ground and then creating a platform frame on those. These are hard to make and often you won't have the wood or tools, but if you are stranded in a swamp, try to make a way to get your kids off the ground. You may have to pull guard duty all night as well, since there are often snakes and gators in the swamps at night.

## Ground Based Shelter

Let's say you don't have trees nearby, or that they won't work for shelter purposes. No problem! The ground is where most mammals live, and so can you. Just get comfortable with the idea and apply common sense to your situation.

If you plan to sleep on the ground, you'll want to get as separated as you can from the ground. If we have to find logs, rocks, piles of vegetation, even a stack of flat cacti can be used (make sure you tamp down the spikes if your boots are solid and the spikes aren't too long and hard!). After you've laid down your sticks, logs, or rocks, soften the base by covering it with sand or topsoil or more vegetation.

There are no limits to what you might find and use; the key is to look at everything around you as a resource and see it not for what it is, but for what you need and how it can be made to serve your purpose.

Survival situations are all about imagination and creative problem solving. This is why I find it one of the best ways to teach leadership and family counseling as it forces you to search for new and different ways to solve common problems.

*When you're building a shelter always be on the lookout for natural terrain features that you can exploit. Amber and Gabe made their shelter by taking advantage of a fallen tree. The wall on the left side is made entirely of the tree's root ball and then pine boughs were leaned up against it. (Photo credit Ruth England Hawke)*

So, be sure to keep harping on this point when the kids start to moan and groan; it's a great way to figure out how to solve problems for life and as such, these skills are always useful.

Once you've got the platform laid out, fashion walls and a roof—if you have the time, energy, and materials available. (You can just sleep right on the ground platform if necessary.) Again, many survival sources instruct you to build a classic "A-frame" structure, which is all well and good.

The A-frame is simple to make. Start by angling two long branches from the ground up (about three to five feet apart), meeting at a center point a few feet off the ground, and lash them together, creating a structure that resembles the letter "A." This will be the front end of the frame.

Then make another "A" for the back of the shelter. Then lash one end of a long thick stick to the top of one A, and the other end to the top of the other A. Now you've got the basic structure. Then lay many sticks on an angle from this top beam down to the ground on either side, or cover with as much foliage as you can find.

Remember that you can also use existing trees, rocks, ledges, and anything else to help create walls and a roof above your platform—just make sure you scout the area and make best use of all resources available.

Once you've got the platform, walls, and roof set, if you're in a cool climate, fill your structure to overflow with leaves and burrow into them to make a bit of a blanket. If you're in a really hot spot, try to give yourself more space in your hooch for air flow, like a higher roof or wider walls or edges, so the breeze can get in and you don't trap your own heat.

### When It Comes to Ground Sleeps, It's Better to Be On, Not In

On the ground is typically better than in the ground for numerous reasons. First, if it rains, you likely won't be flooded out. Second, insects naturally seem to find holes in the ground, and you don't want to wake up with bug bites or worse.

Next, the ground is colder and more wet if you dig into it, which is not usually a plus for the survivor. And perhaps most importantly, it takes hard work and energy to dig into the ground! So, unless you have the tools, time, strength, and necessity, it is better to go on the ground. Of course, there are exceptions to every rule.

Remember, the mantra is "in, not on." If it is excruciatingly hot or cold, try to get into the ground. Usually in such environments the ground tends to be very hard, so look for the soft spots.

If you are in a desert area that is all sand dunes, you're in a bad place. Be exceedingly frugal with all energy and make conservative decisions.

*Spanish moss makes excellent bedding, but only if you gather it from trees. If it's on the ground or dangling down to the ground, don't touch it unless you want an itchy bed full of chiggers. I can't express how important good bedding is both for comfort and insulation, particularly if your shelter is on the ground. Whatever you gather—leaves, moss, reeds, grass—your mattress should be at least a foot deep for a comfortable sleep. It squashes down to nothing very quickly. (Photo credit Ruth England Hawke)*

The key is to save water, so dig into the sand to get to a little cooler spot and then use something to shade you from the sun. If you have to, use the clothes on your back as the layer that separates you from the sun.

Next, make a small hole, lay your cloths across it, and put more sand on the edges to hold them in place. Then, get into the hole, rest by day, and work or move by night. In a non-sand-dune desert environment with similar weather, dig in where it's sandy or soft. Fortunately, most deserts have a rich variety of terrain.

Always try to use a tool if you can to prevent scratches and small injuries that could lead to infection easily and quickly.

In cold environs, like mountains or forest, look to dig a cave for areas covered in snow. Do so right away—as heat will surely cook you, cold will quickly freeze you. Get out of it.

Digging and burrowing into the snow will be warmer than the outside air. Also try to put a layer between you and the snow. As your body warms it, you'll get moist if not in waterproof clothes.

If there isn't enough snow to burrow into, but there is some, then try to fashion it into some form of shelter. I've found igloos are hard to make without a snow shovel to cut nice blocks. But you can make large snowballs, place them as you would bricks, and then fill in the holes and gaps with snow and pack it in. I find a pyramid shape works best because, as you stack your walls, each one a little closer in, the last row of snowballs will comprise your roof.

But again, in survival, building takes time and, without gloves, can be very difficult. So, weigh out the time and energy expenditure with the value added you expect. If you plan to hold tight for a while in the cold, it might be worth cold hands to make shelter the first day while your strength is good.

Again, the key point is if you don't have a shelter or something to make a shelter with, and it's really cold, don't stay on the ground—get into the ground. It will give warmth as it reduces your exposure to wind and precipitation. In the worst-case scenario, just scrape a burrow into the snow, lay in it, and cover up. This will buy you some time to rest and regroup.

After a rest, even if it's just a nap, it helps to decide if you need to build up the shelter more or if you need to move out and keep going.

## Time to Act and Act in Time

When you're really surviving, it's important to remember that everything is out to kill you. Always take a moment to think and question before you take an action. What could go wrong? Can I do this in a better way? Do I really need to do this at all, or are there other options? Make sure the kids are constantly reminded that every hour without food or water, without sleep, or exposed to extreme temperatures, is another hour closer to potential disaster if you don't keep busy trying to be found. Do not sit around and mope.

However, also teach your kids that when they do have time that they should take time and not rush, so they don't end up hurt or missing an important edible.

Often in urgent circumstances, where time is not an option, some decision is better than no decision at all. In other words, inaction will cause more harm or loss than a poor action.

For example, you might spill a lot of water by trying to catch a falling bucket, but you will lose all the water if you don't try to reach for it.

A good way to remember key points of shelter is using the acronym SITTING.

S is for shelter. Always find, build, and use one based on your environment. I is for improvise. Use wreckage if available, and improvise all other materials from what's around you. T is for trees. Always look to trees for shelter, whether as a quick sleep spot, as a frame with two or three trunks, or in a cluster.

N is for nature. Use everything nature provides, including caves, holes, logs, fallen trees, ditches boulders, foliage, dirt, rocks, and so on.

"G" is for ground. Make a platform on the ground as a last resort, and go underground in extremes.

Now let's look at types of survival shelters needed in specific environments.

## Making Shelter in Different Environments

### Jungle

Again, the best types of shelters are the store-bought kinds that are a combination of a hammock, rain fly roof, and mosquito net. There are great lightweight ones available.

Of course, if you're in an unplanned survival situation, you won't have the luxury of an already constructed shelter. But if you're traveling into, over, or through a jungle region, it's good to pack one of these in case.

Tents simply are not a good idea in jungle as it's hard to find a clear, level, dry place to put one down. Any rain or creatures are hazardous to tent shelters as well. Best to think hammock and get off the ground. We have had leaf cutter

*A face only a mother could love! Gabe demonstrating what happens to flesh exposed to a mesh hammock. Even with padding you can end up with pins and needles in bits of your face and other parts of your body. A hammock made from a sheet of fabric is more comfortable. (Photo credit Ruth England Hawke)*

ants actually eat a hole right into our tent because we were rushing and didn't pay attention before we chose the site.

When it comes to jungle survival, I find old-fashioned shelter is best. I recommend the jungle trio "HPN" (Hammock, Poncho, Net)—and I prefer these to be separate units. For hammocks, I prefer the US Army jungle hammock for their multipurpose utility. I can make them into a rucksack for carrying things, a litter for a wounded person, a trap for animals, or a net for larger fish. Hammocks are a good generic tool, but are not best for kids. The recommendations at the top of this chapter are the best for most families.

A good general rule in survival planning is to get the most use for the least weight and space. Most expensive specialty items that are designed for a specific use offer less practicality when surviving, as the basic day-to-day needs of a human require many implements to fulfill. So choose the best things for your needs, kids, funds, and uses.

## Jungle Shelter without Gear

If you or your kids don't have any gear, take to the trees. The swamp bed is smart to get off the ground but find the easiest way that works. In these situations, don't bother with the classic method of making a swamp bed.

*In environments like this mangrove swamp a hammock is the only way to go. Be sure to string it above the high tide mark and you'll remain dry (and out of the mouths of alligators). This silk style fabric hammock encloses you like a pod and is very comfortable. (Photo credit Ruth England Hawke)*

If you have to get your kids off the ground, think about a basic four-post bed, but make the posts with mini-tripods. Just take three smaller sticks/logs about one-foot long each, hold them in a bundle, and tie them with cordage (shoe string, ripped cuffs off your pants, natural material, whatever is available) and make one lash and a granny knot.

When securely fastened, open the sticks like a tripod and place them on the ground. Make four tripods and you got a swamp bed stand that you can take with you. These will set on the ground sturdily, no force needed, and they're easy to adjust as well. Once the four tripods are down, lay two long "poles" (branch, limb, thin log,) lengthwise onto the tops of the tripods, and two shorter poles as your width. Then lay slats and foliage. For the lashings needed to tie this all together, if you have no man-made cordage available, find some flexible vines, or pliant young sapling branches, or tough longer roots of small trees or plants, and wrap them into bundles; these should hold as a temporary lashing.

If you have nothing, it's dark, or you're zapped of energy, you can always grab a few large-leafed plants and make a sort of blanket over yourself while leaning

*A single tripod can be used as the frame for a teepee type shelter, or three or four smaller tripods can be used together as supports for an above ground bed shelter or swamp bed. It's important that the lashing is tight or you risk your shelter collapsing. The best way to do that is to stand your branches in a vertical bundle, tie your knot, and then splay the base out. (Photo credit Ruth England Hawke)*

against the dry side of a tree. Try to find a tree that rises on a bit of an angle, and always look above for loose branches that may fall. Be sure and lay a lot of foliage underneath you for that ever-important elevation, and you'll make it through the night.

If you're in the jungle, try to play with making shelters out of bamboo. Cut several fatter branches about six to twelve inches long with your machete. Split in half and lay down one layer on a lean-to frame with the inside half facing up. Then lay another layer of the split bamboo on top with the outside facing up. Place them so that the edges of the top ones lay in the middle of the bottom halves so that rain will roll off the top, into the bottom, and drain out on the ground. This is a super easy, highly effective emergency shelter.

Bottom line in the jungle: you need to get off the floor, mind the bugs, and do all you can to stay dry. Think of these things when it comes to shelter building.

## Desert

The desert is a very formidable environment. It can be scorching hot or downright freezing. So you must teach your kids to respect nature and understand the gravity

*Myke teaches the principles of a desert shelter. When there's no natural shade sometimes you have to dig down and then use your clothes or whatever you can find as a cover. Ideally you should place a second cover a few inches above the first to act as sun shield. Deserts can be scorching during the day and very cold at night so it's best to walk by moonlight if you have to travel. (Photo credit Ruth England Hawke)*

of the environments and the situation that they are facing. The desert can kill you if you're sloppy or disrespectful.

As always, teach your kids to start by looking at what is available. There will likely be some sort of physical terrain that will give you shade for a period of the day—find it and use it.

In the middle of the day when the sun is blazing, if you can't find any natural cover, then sit down, take off your clothes, and use them to create shade for yourself. If you can find or make a hole or depression to get into then all the better.

The key is to not leave your flesh exposed. Sunburn is fast, painful, and potentially deadly in the desert, and the resulting blisters only serve to suck even more water out of your circulatory system. So teach your kids to carry and use sunscreen, hats, sunglasses, lip balm, and long sleeves. These are all important in desert environments.

If you do have a tarp of some form, use it as a shelter during daytime. Place it a few feet above you to allow more heat to radiate off of it. Try to get to cover higher up so the heat is not radiating off it and cooking you below. Higher up means more breeze passing through too.

At night in the desert, expect the temperature to drop dramatically. If your overall plan includes trying to walk toward safety wherever it may be, then you may consider doing your traveling at night to avoid the crippling heat of the day.

If you need to sleep at night, then be sure to scout a good location long before dark, and to gather the materials that will keep you warm. Small caves, the underside of rock ledges, thick brush, and other natural formations can serve as cover or shelter. In the desert, if you have nothing else, a rock ledge with a small fire can provide enough warmth and safety to get you through the night.

## Cold Environments

When you're in any cold climate, the first order of business is to get out of the cold as soon as possible. As far as priorities go, water, fire, food, and all but immediate life-saving first aid, all come second to seeking shelter and getting out of the cold. Every moment you spend exposed reduces your physical and mental capacities, which leads to poor decisions and, ultimately, quick and final breakdown.

If you can find a field or cluster of rocks, seek shelter there. There will likely be good pockets of space between the snow and rocks, and they'll block the wind better than trees can. If there are no such rock resources, get into the trees.

Often there is space under snow-covered tree boughs that make for a nice, ready-made snow den. If the snow isn't deep enough, then use the tree as temporary shelter for breaks from the wind as you build up a snow or debris wall.

*Doug, his neice Oona, and two daughters made a snow shelter by piling snow up on top of a little drift that had formed by this fallen tree. They let it set for a while and then dug into it to make a cave big enough for all four of them, as shown by that little hole is the entrance. When they were inside, Doug lit a candle and checked a thermometer that he had with him. The girls were amazed by the temperature difference: outside it was 25 degrees and windy, inside the temperature rose to 45 degrees just through the warmth of their bodies and one candle! That made it much warmer and safer, and it's easy for a child to do. (Photo credit Doug McCallie)*

Debris includes anything and everything around you that you can simply grab, drag, pull up, break off, and gather around yourself to fashion a rudimentary shelter. It isn't neat or symmetrical, and they're not ideal shelters as they don't completely protect you from the elements.

But the very notion of having even a rudimentary shelter is extremely comforting, and psychologically, that mental security blanket can go a long way in reinforcing your will to live. But even debris shelters take a lot of time and energy to make, so plan accordingly.

The simplest and quickest technique of getting out of the cold in a snow-covered area is simply to dig into the snow and cover up. This will buy you time while you think about your next moves. Also, it is remarkably warmer inside a snow cave—even a small one that you quickly dig out.

It's not good for being found, but it's certainly a good stopgap measure for survival. Teach your kids to make lots of signals too. Laying dark branches in white snow, in groups of three, and making arrows pointing to your little snow cave is a great way to be found.

Ultimately, anytime you are stuck in a sub-zero environment, staying and waiting might not be your best option unless you have materials to sustain yourself for a long wait or you are fairly confident that a search party will be looking for you.

Without resources, merely waiting alone can do you in just like the desert. The environment is simply too harsh for us to survive for long without gear so getting out of it is usually the best plan. But where to go is a part of that plan. The bottom line is that without resources or imminent rescue, quick shelters and quick movements are the keys to survival.

## Seashore and/or Island

Unless you're stuck on a tiny islet with zero growth, you can usually fashion a decent shelter on or near a beach. There is always debris floating up on the shore

*Doug's niece and daughters—Oona, Thea, and Harper—in their snow shelter after they'd kicked the wall down. Doug says the girls couldn't believe that they were warmer surrounded by ice. They had a blast making the cave and also learned about molecules bonding together like concrete; the strength of an arch in construction; the insulating properties of snow and ice; and most importantly, how to survive in the snow should they need to. (Photo courtesy of Doug McCallie)*

*This shelter's bones are made from driftwood with large rocks to hold them in place. Dry sand is comfy to sleep on as you can dig a little nook for yourself in it. Beaches are good places for sleeping directly on the ground as there is less insect life to bother you, just make sure you're above the wrack line so you don't get swept away in the night.*
*(Photo credit Ruth England Hawke)*

that can be used to make an elevated shelter. The combination of a small burrow and your clothing as a cover will keep you out of the elements of sun

The seashore is a relatively easy environment for survival. You can pretty much get all you need in most cases on the seashore. Whether you choose to build a swamp bed or an A-frame shelter or something else, always first look above your chosen location to ensure that nothing is above you that might fall on you.

Coconuts are especially dangerous, although they are ironically also lifesavers since they provide water and food. I've seen them just drop at any time, and people die every year from coconuts falling on their head.

Also study the ground near your potential shelter location. Look for grooves in the ground that could have been made by flash streams of water. Also search for signs of animal life in the immediate area, such as tracks, holes, nests, or droppings, and if there are many such signs, find a different place to put down.

Another consideration in selecting a location is tidal movement—check the shoreline for signs of recent tidal activity, and notice whether the tide is moving in or out, and determine if it will soon cover the area you are considering for a shelter.

One good thing about seashore survival is that the leaves and branches often found near beaches are great for making a shelter. The best leaves for making a shelter are the ones that require the least amount of work to use. I prefer "elephant ears," which look exactly like their namesake. If they are not around, I'll reach for palm fronds or any other large-leafed plants. Round palm fronds work well just as they are; other elongated fronds work better if split down the middle.

All require a stick structure with slats, such as a lean-to, teepee, A-frame, etc., to build upon. If you have time, weave the leaves into the slats for additional sturdiness and weather protection. When there is no time to do so, simply lay enough slats to hold the leaves without falling through, and then lay a few more slats over all the leaves to give them security in bad weather.

Simply, find the right location, make a frame, lay the fattest leaves, anchor them, and rest. If you're going to be in such an environment for weeks or longer, you will have plenty of time and materials to construct a very fine shelter.

## Woodland

The type of shelter you can create in woodlands is relatively sturdier as the environment produces stronger resources. In most woodland, there are many branches on the ground that still retain a lot of their original sturdiness and, unlike equally-sized branches in the tropics, they have not been corroded by the fast-decaying tropical climate.

Also, the vegetation in woodlands is easier to deal with than jungles, as it doesn't grow as thick. Another helpful aspect of woodland survival is that there

*Short of burying themselves in leaves, a lean-to is the easiest shelter for a child to make. As the name implies this type of shelter is made by leaning branches or debris up against something solid. A lean-to can be quite a sophisticated construction where you build a frame containing a horizontal beam to lean your branches and foliage against, or you can simply find a rock face, boulder or tree to place them against. This one has been built by a child for fun, as there is not enough foliage on the walls to keep out the elements. (Photo credit Ruth England Hawke)*

isn't a real need to get off the ground; therefore the logistics are quite simple. Just lean some sticks together in an A-frame or teepee structure, construct a basic lean-to or use a tree as a lean-to, and start stacking pine boughs, various leaves, soil, and/or other resources, and you're sorted.

If it's still daylight after you've made your shelter, perform a quick "sun-spot check." Just lay inside your shelter and look up, and if you can see any sunlight, that's an area that will be susceptible for rain to come in—so quickly fill those spots in with more debris.

You can also do a similar leak-check by building a small, safe fire and looking for smoke leaks coming out. With the smoke-check technique you'll have the added benefit of repelling bugs.

## Mountains

Mountain-area shelters are similar to woodlands, except you might incorporate boulders as walls against which you can fashion your lean-to. You may also find clusters of boulders to serve as walls, meaning you'll just need to make a roof and fill in any gaps with brush and branches.

If there are no boulders to work with, there will likely be plenty of stones or rocks you can stack to make a good wall. Another technique is to make a shape of stones—square, circular, or triangular—simply piled one or two high. Then use them as a form against which you can wedge your sticks and make a nice little shelter.

Often a fallen tree or log can be found in the mountains, and these make a nice starter structure for a shelter, or even a good self-contained temporary shelter if you're wounded or too ill or depleted to make a shelter in time. Just pull up some soil or debris for coverage and get as comfortable as possible.

In fact, whenever you're building a shelter, make use of all your effort. What I mean is, when you dig up dirt or break apart sticks or rip up leaves, there will be debris from that activity. Use that debris! Put it to use by forming it into a small wall around your shelter, or as an insulator to keep out bugs, or as a stopgap to prevent leaks of water and wind, or as a small rain ditch around any ground shelter. The basic idea is to use all resources available in your situation, and to maximize all your efforts.

A good trick to teach kids for handling rain is to tie a piece of string where it is entering and angle it so the water will be diverted away from you. Or, for the edges of a roof or the top joint of an A-frame, have your foliage overlap a good six inches or more so that the rain is dispersed long before it gets to the joint and then flows

*A slip knot is the best way to tie a hammock, since it holds fast and is easy to release. This one has been tied above a knot in the tree trunk to ensure that the hammock won't slip downwards in the night. In an emergency you can carve a notch in the back side of the trunk for the same purpose, but this can be harmful to the tree. (Photo Ruth England Hawke)*

down the side walls instead of dripping into the middle. Teach them a few knots so they can build with cordage or vines.

If despite all that, it still rains into your shelter, dig a little channel and direct it out the door and sleep on the opposite side.

## Swamp

If you get stranded here, be prepared for a mental battle because it can be very intimidating when you're frequently submerged, which reduces your body temperature and softens the skin, which in turn increases exposure to damage and infection.

Also, swamps are often filled with gators and snakes. However, like the jungle, mountains, or island settings, one can survive there a long time.

But the chances of being found in a swamp are extremely slim unless a plane wreck left a good imprint in the ground. Even then, the marsh usually just swallows these up and the traces of a wreck are very hard to find. So, staying in the swamp is not a good plan, and you don't want to spend a lot of time making a shelter here. Therefore, swamp shelters should be the minimum needed to get through the night, and then you should continue moving by day unless you're ill or injured.

The ultimate rule of swamp shelters is to seek high ground. Often you'll find small patches of drier, harder ground to make a shelter on. It's still good to get off the ground even if it is harder, as it will often moisten very quickly while you work around your site and turn into quite a muddy mess. If you can get off the ground, take extra care and time to stack a very high pile of grass and padding to keep you dry at the top.

Try to take off your shoes to let your feet dry and try to make hooks for your gear to dry too. Just chop or break some strong branches, lay them into the forks formed by branches of a closely grouped set of standing tree branches, and build a platform to get you up out of the water. Then hang everything off the trees around you to dry while you rest, and do all you can to keep yourself dry as well.

Once you have a platform constructed to hold you up and get you out of the water, try to fashion a roof over your structure in case it rains. But if you don't think it necessary, don't spend the time on a roof.

The platform alone will take longer than you think. Again, the key is that you won't be staying long and therefore, it's more like a roadside motel instead of a nice vacation resort. Just get dry, get rest, and then get moving.

Regardless of your environment and your shelter, the basics of a good campsite still apply. Have a toilet plan, a trash plan, a fire plan for location and fuel supplies to last the night. Hygiene, hydration, some food and security are always part of a sleep plan. Here are some other things to consider for helping your kids make ready for shelter building.

*Bedroom camping in a giant orange frog, complete with stuffed alligator and lion for protection and two flashlights—one for fun; one for emergencies. For small children, camping in their own bedroom is an important first step toward coping with the unexpected. They're learning to be accepting of an environment that feels different to what they're used to. (Photo credit Ruth England Hawke)*

## Shelter Indoors

Children love building dens. Whether it's a full-on tree fort in the woods or just draping glittery fabric round their bed, I've yet to meet a child who doesn't find it exciting. This is good as it generally means there isn't any psychological hurdle to cross when it comes to training them to build survival shelters—it's interesting and fun from the get-go.

However, in most instances with a survival shelter you're going to need to sleep in it and that may take a bit of work with some kids, particularly the little ones. Children find routine reassuring so sleeping somewhere other than in a bed can be quite daunting. For the more confident or older child a few words of reassurance, a flashlight, and a favorite stuffed animal might do the trick, but for others the training needs to be more gradual.

Survival training for a child is often about exposing them little by little to new ideas and experiences so when they have to deal with the unexpected and the unfamiliar they have to the mental tools to cope, rather than melting down in fear and frustration. Achievements, however small, build confidence. This works for everyday life too.

## Bedroom Camping

Sleeping in a bed but somewhere that they're not used to can be a good start. Family vacations are a good way normalize sleeping in a strange place or staying at Gran and Grandpa's house or a sleepover at a good friend's house. Everything is different but it's safe and hopefully fun.

If you don't have these options, start with bed swapping. Have your kids sleep in a sibling's bed or in the spare room instead of their regular bed. The next leap is sleeping out of bed. This is where indoor camping comes into play. There are loads of options here: play tents; sheets and blankets; adapt a closet; use large cardboard boxes; and plenty more. Most modern outdoor tents stand up well by themselves without being pegged to the ground, so if you have a small one you could use that.

Make sure that they have suitable padding underneath them. Children don't need as much as adults when it comes to comfort, but you are insulating them from the cold floor. Unless you're lucky enough to have underfloor heating, even in summer the carpeted floor of your house can seem chilly. This is a good lesson to teach them as it becomes vital for health and survival when they graduate to sleeping outdoors. Also there is a chance that you might have to join them in their shelter at the last minute in order to get them to spend the night there.

Provide them with a bottle of water and a flashlight for the night. This is to get them used to keeping important things close while they sleep. Two flashlights are best, one for emergencies and one for fun. During these early days of shelter training the fun flashlight is important; kids should use it to burrow into their new environment and familiarize themselves with all the new corners and nooks and crannies once the lights go out. Strange shadows can be particularly alarming because the unknown is frightening. Playing a game of shadow puppets against the wall of your child's indoor shelter is a good way to illustrate that everyday items can look quite different in shadow form. When it's time for sleep, make a special flashlight storage place that's within easy reach, particularly for the emergency flashlight, so your child can easily grab it in the middle of the night. This is not only comforting for your little one but good training for survival situation.

I always recommend that the first night of indoor camping takes place in your child's own bedroom, that way if they're uncomfortable or scared they can crawl into bed.

Sleeping on the bedroom floor may seem like a far cry from surviving in Alaskan bush or up a banyan tree in the jungle, but believe it or not you're giving your child essential building blocks to be a true survivor. They're being exposed to something different, which will help them cope with the new and unexpected.

The next step might be camping in the living room or in the backyard or a friend's back yard, you'll have to judge when your child is ready for each new step.

*Shelter building in Fort Living Room. This is good practice for emergency situations where you can't leave your home. Robin and Luca have used an Army poncho liner for the roof of their shelter so they've been able to use its ties to secure it to the dining chairs. If you use weights to hold blankets in place, make sure you use items that won't cause injury if they roll off in the night or during play. (Photo credit Romy Melville-Evans)*

The key, as always, is to make sure that the overall process is enjoyable. That's not to say that every aspect of everything has to be fun, that's not realistic and seeing what works and what doesn't is all part of learning.

## Fort Living Room

Camping in the living room—or in Fort Living Room as it's known in the Hawke household—is actually a good dry run for any real life survival situation that necessitates that you should stay at home. Think natural disasters like winter storms or hurricanes where your home might offer you physical protection from the elements and also events that could trap you at home by cutting off routes of egress, like floods and landslides. Or maybe something more sinister like a contagion sweeping the nation or a terrorist's dirty bomb.

In these types of situations it's often better to gather the family together in one room, particularly if you have a large house. This is for practical as well as emotional reasons, so your dry run should involve parents too.

*Painting toenails as the sun sets in the jungles of Borneo. One of the things I learned out in Borneo is that it's helpful to have some activities up your sleeve that work when there is no electricity to help with the evening's entertainment. This is particularly true for families during power outages. (Photo credit Tasha Isaacson)*

In most crisis events, the power goes down. In the darkness or in dingy visibility you really want to know where your children are and what they're up to. Even normal activities like walking or going up and down stairs become problematic because you can easily trip over the everyday detritus of family living. That's not to say that you and the kids can't slowly and carefully move around the house, but it's best to minimize unnecessary wandering around. A sprained foot or broken bone is painful and inconvenient when life is normal, but it can make a monumental difference to the outcome of a survival situation and not in a good way.

Basing in one room also reduces flashlight use and saves valuable batteries. In a real life survival situation you should only use your flashlights when you absolutely have to, so during your Fort Living Room camping session, you should practice sitting in the dark and seeing what you can do to entertain the family without light. During a fun dry run scenario it probably won't actually get completely dark, as light from the neighbor's house, road, or distant town will invariably bleed in through the drapes. Nevertheless, it will still be a worthwhile exercise for children used to the convenience of constant electricity.

These days most of us have had access to constant power for our whole lives, and therefore we take it for granted. In a survival situation, you'll have to rely on yourselves for entertainment.

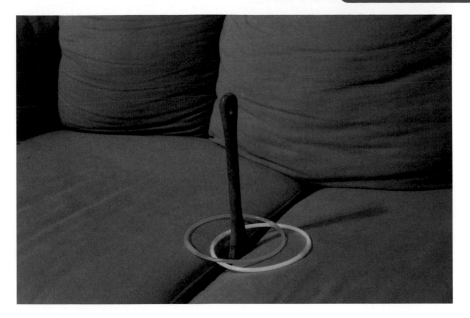

*Camping in your living room is good training for those survival situations that necessitate that you must stay in your house, and doing it without the lights on makes it more realistic. Games like homemade glow-in-the-dark ring-toss help keep little ones entertained. Life is easier if you plan entertainment for these eventualities beforehand.*
*(Photo credit Ruth England Hawke)*

Obviously in a lowlight situation with adults who speak the same language you can just chat, but with children to keep amused you need more than one trick up your sleeve. Here's a few ideas.

You can create a "power-out pack" in advance. This is different than a "bug-out bag," as it is designed for when you're stuck at home and is purely about entertainment. Fill a backpack or a box with toys, art supplies, and treats that your family normally does not have access to. Make sure it contains some things to help facilitate play in low light such as glow sticks, novelty flash lights, glow-in-the-dark paints, and as many different fluorescent toys that you can stomach buying.

Teaching your children some traditional songs is also a good way to keep them entertained—folks songs have stood the test of time because they're memorable and easy to master. A good singing game, which doesn't require anyone to know the entire song, is to select words or themes and come up with songs that include them. You can just say the song title or to make it more challenging, have every one sing a requisite number of lines. Try making music with improvised instruments. Making shadow puppets is also fun in the dark. You can draw and cut out silhouettes and put on a play by flashlight or just play hand shadow puppets. Telling spooky stories is another perfect nighttime activity for your Fort Living Room Camp Out. During an actual blackout it's probably better to keep the mood light. There are many games that you can play and most are really simple. Just make sure you have some planned out before the power goes out.

### Candle Use

Candles cause lots of house fires. According to the National Fire Protection Association, an average of twenty-four candle home fires are reported every day and we tend to burn our houses down with them most at Christmas and New Year. The NFPA goes on to recommend that during power outages we should use battery powered light sources and never use candles. In the 2017 guide on how to practice safe candle use during hurricane season, the National Candle Association and the National Association of State Fire Marshals state that approximately 26 percent of fatal candle fires occur during power loss.

During prolonged power outages, however, you may be left with little choice other than to use candles, so here are a few tips. Most are fairly obvious but important nonetheless, and all are good to pass on to your kids too:

- Keep pets away from candles.
- Supervise children at all times. Children, like moths, are drawn to the flames. Gabriel always likes to poke his fingers into candles (while they're still burning) and carve channels for the molten wax to flow through.
- Place the candle on a non-flammable surface like a ceramic plate or a baking sheet.
- Where you can, try and use a thick chunky candle rather than a traditional tapered candle. They're more stable and less likely to fall over. A candle in a container or jar is even better.
- Never leave a candle unattended.
- When extinguishing a candle, try and use a snuffer rather than blowing it out. If you don't own one, lick your thumb and index finger and give the wick a quick squeeze to cut off the oxygen supply—it's hot but it won't burn.
- Keep your candle at least twelve inches away from anything combustible, like curtains, furniture, bedding books, or clothing. According to the American Red Cross, more than 50 percent of candle home fires are started because flammable items were just too close. Additionally, never go hunting for things in a closet or a drawer or other similar confined space using a candle.
- Last but not least, make sure your smoke alarms have fresh batteries. In a crisis situation the emergency services may not be available or able to get to you but the alarm should give you and your family notice to extinguish the fire or escape the building if necessary.

Ideally, in addition to regular battery-operated lights, candles, kerosene lamps, and the like, you should also have hand-cranked lamps and flashlights and also solar-powered light. There are some amazingly bright ones available these days. Solar-powered garden lamps don't produce a great deal of illumination, but if that's all that you have, they are great to stick on the stairs or in the bathroom.

### Other Factors to Practice Beforehand

When surviving at home without power, it makes sense to choose a room that has the most insulation from the outside world as you'll need all the help you can get to maintain a comfortable temperature. In most instances that means a room that is surrounded by other rooms that act as a buffer. During a winter storm, you'll be trying to keep your family warm, and in a post-hurricane environment you'll be trying to keep everyone cool. In a two-story house, the upstairs area acts as a layer of insulation. The living room is a good choice because in most homes it's next to the kitchen, so you'll have easy access to food and water, if it's still flowing. Additionally, living rooms often have fireplaces, giving you warmth, as well as a means to cook and purify water by boiling.

*Breakfast time in Garner State Park, Texas for Pack 12, Den 2. Scout Camp not only teaches children outdoor skills, they get to play and socialize old-school style, without electronics and video games. Hunter, Kaiser, Gabe, Joey, Eddie, and Adrian look to be having a blast, and there's not a smartphone in sight! (Photo credit Ruth England Hawke)*

*Taking your children camping is a really good start to their wilderness survival training.
If you're a camping newbie and want to know how it all works, having your child join the
Scouts is a great way to get your family under canvas with support from others.
(Photo credit Ruth England Hawke)*

In terms of what to eat when you have no power, make sure to practice well beforehand. Camping in Fort Living Room weekend is an ideal time to introduce your children to your dry, stored survival food and concepts such as eating cold beans directly from a can. If they get used to eating camping food then it makes it a lot easier for them to eat survival cooking. A fun and useful survival technique to teach kids is how to cook using an empty can and a tea light for heat. First wash an empty can and punch some holes in the sides of it for air flow, some at the open base end and some at the top near the intact part of the can where you'll place the butter and pancake mixture. Once your can is ready have your children light the tea lights and carefully place the can over the top, then you're ready to cook.

It's also a good opportunity for you to problem solve how you can conjure up some family favorites using only one pan and no oven. This is when a fireplace is handy or a backyard grill. Don't be tempted to bring a gas grill inside as the carbon monoxide fumes can be lethal.

Another reason to keep your family close by when disaster strikes is to protect them from those people that would do harm to them in order to help themselves. It's a sad reality of life that when a catastrophe happens and the power goes down for an extended period of time the fabric of society starts to disintegrate and in the absence of a fully functioning police force to hold them accountable, some people start to behave very badly indeed.

This is not the time to have your children venturing into the backyard alone or scattered in the far reaches of your house where someone might break in without you realizing it. Keep them close to you. And do the same on practice night. Be sure to make a safety and security plan and teach it to your kids. In short, brief and rehearse these IADs, or Immediate Action Drills.

For you and your family's security, immediate plans are your IAD, or reaction drills to say, rain, a critter, etc. But also, when you can, consider teaching your kids to put up early warning systems to help wake them in the night if a creature comes, for example.

Finally, whenever you are at a campsite, consider writing and leaving messages. Write on wrappers, put notes in any cans, jars or bottles, or make messages on trees with a knife or leaves with a twig. And always make signals of where you are going so anyone who picks up your trail can go in the right direction to find you!

# CHAPTER SEVEN

# NAVIGATION

A walk in the woods can be an easy thing—if you know where you are, where you're going, how you're going to get there, and how long it should take you. But in a survival situation, you might not know any of these things. And you might be in mountains or desert instead of woods. So, the very first question you must teach your kids to ask themselves if they ever get lost or separated is, "Should you stay or should you go?"

In this chapter we will tell you what you need to know to find your way out of the woods and back to the comfort of home and what to teach your kids as far as staying put or trying to travel.

But before you learn how to travel in a survival situation, you'll need to decide whether to travel at all. You might be better off where you are. Should you stay put, signal for help, and wait for help to arrive? Or should you set out for civilization on your own? This is perhaps the most important decision you'll make in a true survival situation.

If you stay, you might never be found, or you might not be found in time. Choosing to move raises other questions. Do you know which way to go? How far it is? Do you have the resources, internal and external, to overcome the terrain, weather, and distance?

Note: Rescue teams fly, sail, or drive to the survivor's last known location, whether it be the entrance to a national park or the source of a "mayday" signal. Prepare to depart if:

- You are completely lost and far from anything man-made.
- You are alone and no one has any idea where you are.
- You are almost certain no one will be looking for you, they won't begin looking for a long time, they won't be looking in the right place, or you've waited

as long as you can at the boat, car, plane, or house. You are running out of supplies. A member of your party requires emergency medical care.

If you are with a group, you may have to make a decision about whether to strike out on your own, leaving the others behind. If a member of your group is in a bad way medically and can't make the journey, and neither you nor others in your party can transport the sick or injured person, you may have to go it alone. If your party includes elderly persons, infants, and/or children who would not be able to make the journey, you may have to leave them behind.

If you must break up the group, give the travelers their best chance at success by giving them the critical supplies. Write down their names and next of kin, with contact information, in case they are lost. Write down or commit to memory their intended route. Estimate a travel time and return date. If the group is divided over whether to stay or go, try to divide survival assets equally to avoid fighting, but favor the mobile group—their road is harder. Ninety percent of the time, you will be better off making camp and waiting.

Let's say your group was with a plane. Chances are the pilot called for help and gave coordinates when it was going down, and a search team will be sent. Even if the plane went down suddenly and unexpectedly, planes are fitted with beacon transponders that turn themselves on at impact, recording and reporting your location. That means a distress signal will have been sent when the plane crashed, and that means the authorities have been alerted and a rescue mission is being mounted. They'll be looking for the plane. Staying with the plane improves the chances that rescuers will find you with it. The same holds true for boats, cars, and structures, all of which are easier to spot than an individual person.

But, if the plane, boat, car, or structure poses some sort of danger, move to the nearest safe place. Try to find an area where you can safely camp for a few days, one that will be easily spotted by rescue teams. Assess whether you can safely salvage anything useful from the disabled vehicle or structure. Depending on what it contains—food, a two-way radio, flares, etc.—it could save your life.

While staying put and waiting for help to find you is often your best option, certain circumstances are going to force you to find your own way out. Stay where you are if:

• You are with a plane, boat, or other vehicle.
• You are at a shelter.
• You are with a group.

** (Unless any of the above is in danger of sinking, exploding, burning down, or falling off a cliff.)

Parents, these are only guidelines, and only you can make the final decision. Consider your options, think through the consequences, and teach your kids these principles so they can make good assessments too. However, kids will almost always be near the area they got lost and it's almost always better for them to stay.

Parents, your briefings are essential for your kids. When in the outdoors, have a daily morning and evening brief for where to meet up if kids get lost, something happens in the night, and there is a break in contact.

An even better way to do this is to do like the Special Forces: every time you cross a unique terrain feature, like a creek or a fallen tree, designate that as a rally point.

If you want to be like a high speed elite team of operators, you can designate a floating rally point, which means that anytime you get lost or split up, go back a certain set distance, say one hundred paces, which then provides comfort, confidence, and a point of reference for everyone involved.

Once you've made up your mind to stay, settle in for the long haul and build a shelter. If you decide to move, the following section is for you. By reading this chapter, you should have enough information to chart a course and follow it to safety with confidence.

# The Basics

## Situational Awareness

It's best to teach kids simple things first. If they have an awareness of where they are situated that is always a great start.

For example, you are at a camp site with your kids. You make a point of letting them know that up the mountain, on the right, is a ranger station. Down into the valley, on the left, is a river. About thirty minutes behind the camp site is the road the leads to the closest town, and in front of the camp site is a trail that leads to the entrance of the park.

Directions like the above provide a sense of where you are on the small local scale. You have to expand it to a larger scale for worst-case scenarios.

Start by making sure everyone in your family knows that the sun rises in the east and sets in the west. Everything that follows in this chapter details how to navigate as a parent and what items are essential for teaching your kids. So much of this will depend on the skill of the parents and the abilities of the kids.

I am a fan of using technology, but you should plan on it failing, breaking, or running out of power. Teach your kids the skills to navigate without the use of technology.

## Dead Reckoning

The concept of dead reckoning is one of the most important things start teaching your kids. Once they know the sun rises in the east, but moves all day, they can use the dead reckoning to pick their morning target and then start walking.

Dead reckoning is a good place to start, as it's the simplest and most effective style of survival navigation. It works in all types of terrain. The method is easy, but it takes some work to do. Simply look in the direction you want to travel. Pick the farthest "target" or landmark object that you can see and begin walking toward it. Be sure to estimate the distance before you begin, and be sure to take a pace count as you go.

Estimating distances is an art, so practice this concept with your kids in various terrains and situations. Shortly after you set off toward your objective, turn around and look at your starting point for a moment to consider what it will look like from the perspective of your destination, or what it will look like from behind. That way, when you get to your target, you can look back and see where you came from, confirming that you're on track. Then pick your next target and repeat, making sure to keep yourself in a general line by making sure the last place you left, and the next point you're going, are on the same line where you are now, in the middle.

If you can, try to line up three destinations in your sights. If all three landmarks are in line, then you are on track. In the thick bush, the distance from landmark to landmark might be only fifty meters, but that's when it's especially important to use dead reckoning to keep you on a straight line, especially if you have no compass. In open terrain, dead reckoning might not be possible, as there may not be a target on the horizon.

## Orienteering

For the purposes of survival, we'll define orienteering as navigating with a compass but without a map. You may not have a map for reference, but you can use your compass to maintain your bearings and direct your movements. Teach your kids to find north with their compass and how to find their azimuth, line, or direction to walk.

## Terrain Association

The art of navigating with a map, but without a compass, is called terrain association. It is a bit trickier than orienteering, but also has its advantages. With a map, you have a good sense of the overall picture, and a much better sense of where you want to go, but it's not always so easy to know exactly where you are. And always be sure to put where north is located on the map.

When teaching this, be sure to instruct kids to try to match what they see on the ground to the features on the map. It doesn't work the other way around. Read the terrain, then find it on the map. Don't pick a spot on the map and then try to make it fit the terrain, as that is a sure way to get lost. To do this, you must constantly be aware of your surroundings. Look for anything distinct and specific. For example, a river is good, but a bend in the river is better.

When you find yourself surrounded by distinctive terrain, don't leave the area until you can place it on your map. This, of course, only works with a good topographic map, not a sketch for a kid. If you have a good relief map, it's much easier to stay on track once you have confirmed your location by matching terrain to the map.

# Maps: How to Read, Use, and Make Them

*Making a pirate's treasure map is a fun way to introduce younger children to the concept of navigation. First (as shown in the photo on the opposite page), brown the paper using coffee grounds and scrunch it up a bit before setting it out to dry. A hair dryer or the oven on a low level can help here if it's not a sunny day. When ours was dry we burned the edges with a candle but you can just tear it up a bit to make it look worn. Then get drawing: make sure your little one draws a path that goes through one or two different terrain features and leads to an X, this way it's definitely a map and not just an imaginative bit of artwork.*
*(Photo credit Ruth England Hawke)*

In-depth training for reading maps is beyond the scope of this book. But, if you have a map, use it. If not, consider making one. This is especially good for when you think you and your family are lost, or it's just a great way to have your kids get familiar with the area.

Making your own map forces you and the kids to visualize your surroundings from a bird's-eye view. It's a good exercise and can help you develop a better sense of awareness of the surroundings.

Making a map from scratch can also help you understand the terrain and its potential impact on you. Even if you are staying put, your homemade map might help you decide on a better place to make camp. And if you're planning a move, it's excellent help in planning a route.

Another great way to help kids visualize their area is by constructing a sand table. This is just making a model of the surrounding terrain in sand or dirt, using sticks as small trees and pebbles as rocks, or whatever else is available as a visual aid.

To make one, simply orient whatever you intend to write on toward the north and then build the map with your camp at the center. Add key terrain features and significant landmarks as you scout the area and discover new elements of your environment.

This is a really good exercise when you go camping and plan to stay put for a while. Once kids see the terrain like that, they just "get it" and know where they are.

Another resource is software programs and other digital media like Google Earth®. You can show the kids on their own tablets or iPads exactly where there are and what is around them. You can widen out to show kids the rivers, hills, roads, and such around them while pointing those locales out in the real world.

Another great tool are apps like the SPOT Satellite Messenger and Rhino. SPOT has a lower cost version that just tells you where you are on another device or a higher end version that has a map you can see, too. The Rhino is a similar device that is a radio as well as a map. There are many brands, types, and prices and they change often, so we won't go into them too much here. Ultimately, research what's right for your budget and level of expertise as well as needs and get those tools that are most right for your family.

If you're in cell phone range, you can turn on the locators on your kids' phones as a low cost option. If you're traveling somewhere very remote, you might consider devices that use satellite and GPS as trackers so you can always know where your kids are. Alternatively, strap a GPS locator on your kids and 90 percent of your issues will be solved.

Another way to introduce your kids to the concept of maps and GPS is to get involved finding geocaches. These are little treasures people hide for others to find. It can be quite an exciting game and you can do it safely in your own yard,

*Geocaching is the best way to get kids to learn how to use a GPS because it's basically a modern day treasure hunt. There are several apps that you can download that contain coordinates and terrain features that will lead you to a waterproof box full of goodies. The idea is that you take the items and leave some gifts in exchange, ready for the next Geocacher to find. (Photo credit Mykel Hawke)*

neighborhood, or local park. Visit https://www.geocaching.com/play for more information.

## Some Terms and Concepts

### Longitude and Latitude

Longitude and latitude are very complex and difficult to teach and are beyond the scope of this book. However, if you're into sailing or flying, then it may be a good subject to teach your kids.

### Scale

A map's scale tells you the size of the area it represents. More specifically, it tells you the size of the area represented by each of the map's squares. The scale can be found in the legend at the bottom or side of the map.

Many civilian maps are made by the U.S. Geological Survey at a scale of 1:24,000, where one inch on the map is equivalent to 24,000 inches on land. One square on this map is one square inch, and one inch represents 2,000 feet. These maps cover an area of 7.5 minutes of longitude by 7.5 minutes of latitude.

Most military maps use the metric system, which is more internationally applicable, and are drawn to a scale of 1:50,000. On these maps, the squares are one kilometer to a side. The distance from one corner of this square diagonally to another corner would be 1.5 kilometers, or "clicks."

Note: The larger the scale, the smaller the area covered, and the more detailed the map will be. The smaller the scale, the larger the area covered, but in less detail.

For example, on a pilot's map with a scale of 1:250,000, the area represented by each square contains a lot of ground, but not a lot of detail. Such a map might cover the entire continental United States. A smaller-scaled map, like 1:1,000, will contain lots of detail, but will cover only a very small area, like maybe a local campground.

### Grid Coordinates

Grids are formed by the vertical and horizontal lines drawn on the map, much as the lines of longitude and latitude divide the globe into square sections.

### Legend

A map's legend is like a book's table of contents and index rolled into one. The legend will tell you the map's scale, where and when it was made, and all the visual keys you'll need to understand the map's symbols.

Some things are considered standard on a map:

- Green = Vegetation (white areas contain few or no plants).
- Blue = Water (rivers, lakes, intermittent streams, marshes, etc.).
- Brown = Contour lines (which indicate elevation).
- Red = Roads (or place names or major destinations like airports, etc.).
- Black = Man-made structures (buildings, cemeteries, roads, etc.).

### Symbols

If you have a map while surviving, look for signs of civilization like cities or roads. If you cannot find any, look for other man-made structures like oil pipelines or railroad tracks. Any of these will eventually lead you to a populated area. If you are lost at sea and have an aerial map, look for black dotted or dashed lines that indicate commercial shipping routes, and try to get yourself near those to increase your likelihood of being spotted.

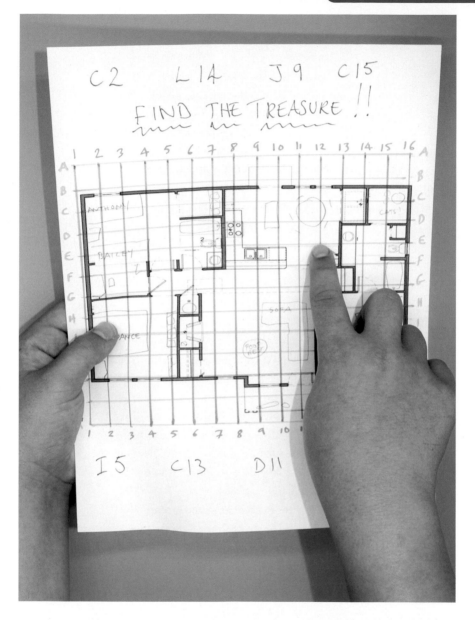

*After your children have grasped the basic concept of maps, it's time to teach them about grid references. This can be quite a dry lesson but you can make it dynamic and interesting by turning it into a treasure hunt. Print off the floor plan to your house, add in some landmarks like beds, sofas, the washing machine, and pet bowls, then create a numbered and lettered grid as in the picture above. Once you've done that, go and hide some treasure where a few of the lines intersect each other on the map and write the grid coordinates down for your treasure seekers. (Photo credit Ruth England Hawke)*

Black dashes usually mean some sort of trail. Blue dashes mean intermittent stream. It might be dry, but it's a good place to dig for water.

### Coordinates

Coordinates are the numbers used to pinpoint a location.

If a map starts at 25 at the bottom left corner and goes to 75 at the bottom right, then one of the fifty squares in between includes your east-west position. If the map's vertical coordinates start in the bottom left-hand corner at 10 and go up to 60, your north-south position would fall somewhere in one of those fifty squares.

To name your position, read right until you find the grid coordinate that corresponds to your east-west position, then read up until you reach the coordinate that corresponds to your north-south position.

When giving or receiving coordinates on a map, remember, "Right & Up." This is simply a standardized way of reading or describing a location in a way that someone else can find it. Right gives the east-west coordinate, which comes first. Up gives the north-south coordinate.

Say your position is 50 and 30. On a military-style map of 1:50,000 scale, this would place you in the map's middle square. But that square represents one square kilometer. That's a lot of terrain in the middle of the jungle.

To mark the location more precisely, divide the square into ten equal divisions. Since our square is 1,000 meters by 1,000 meters, dividing it into tenths narrows our square areas to one hundred square meters. So the new way to describe the more detailed coordinate would be as follows: Right 50 then, say, 5, then up 30, then, say, 5 again. It would look like this: 505305. This coordinate will bring you within 100 meters of your desired location.

At this distance you could make contact by screaming. This is called a six-digit grid, and it's about the best you can do without a protractor. With some practice, you can get good at guesstimating an eight-digit coordinate, which will bring you to within ten meters of your target. At this distance, you should be able to see your objective.

### Contour Lines

Each contour line, often a wavy brown line on the map, represents a consistent elevation, which will be indicated on the line. The contour interval is the distance between contour lines, and tells you how steep or how flat the terrain is. This will come into play when you plan your route.

If the lines are close together, the elevation changes a lot in a very short distance, which means the terrain is steep. If the lines are farther apart, that means elevation change in the area is gradual.

Look for areas that have lots of lines in increasingly smaller concentric circles. This indicates a hilltop or mountain peak. The ultimate elevation is usually printed near the mountaintop.

You'll mainly use contour lines for the following:

* To avoid peaks (or to find them if you need the vantage point for scouting).
* To avoid steep valleys (or to find them if you're looking for water).
* To avoid steep ridges, cliffs, or mountainsides.
* To seek flat ground for ease of travel.

## Compasses

When it comes to map reading while using a compass, there are three different norths to be aware of but the only two that matter are the North on the map and the North on the compass.

### Grid North

Grid North corresponds to the actual lines on any flat map you might be using to navigate. Flat maps are imperfect representations of the spherical earth, and so Grid North is not True North.

### Magnetic North

Magnetic North is the direction the compass points. Magnetic North is not True North. The earth's magnetic wave lines meet slightly off-center of True North, in part because the earth's rotational axis changes ever so slightly, and so the earth's rotation isn't perfectly consistent.

What this means is that near the poles, Magnetic North can be as much as three hundred miles from the actual physical location of True North. Again, 99 percent of the time this will not affect you, but it can be helpful to understand the differences as you navigate, especially over long distances or from locations near the poles.

### True North

True North is the actual point on the earth where all the longitudinal lines meet. It is a physical point whose location means very little to the survivor except as an aid in understanding the other forms of north.

## Map Tools

### Protractors

A protractor is usually a thin, clear piece of plastic with a lot of numbers on it and a few square and triangular holes cut into it for use in measuring distances and plotting routes. Its use is beyond the scope of this book, but it is a great tool to use if you're going to get your kids into advanced navigation, especially if they find themselves getting in to the fun of geocaching.

Tip: You can also use the protractor's straight edge to measure straight-line distances and get azimuths for your path to navigate.

### GPS, or Global Positioning System

GPS is one of the greatest things since sliced bread in our opinion. But it is not within the scope of this book to explain how to use it. Since there are many different devices with many different options, we highly recommend you research the latest technologies and get what's right for your budget and needs. You can use GPS in place of a compass, but if it breaks, you still need to know how to use a compass.

# Compasses

A compass relies on the laws of physics to tell you which direction you're going, and a decent amount of math is required to use one with precision. But in its simplest form, anyone can use a compass effectively, or even create one.

The earth spins. Just as the spinning of a windmill or waterwheel generates energy, the earth's spin generates electromagnetic waves. It is these waves that magnetize the earth, and it is the earth's magnetic pull that makes the compass needle point north. The compass needle is actually a magnet, and the pole's magnetic pull is very faint, so the needle must be as frictionless, or free-floating, as possible to allow for greatest accuracy.

If you have a map and compass, orient them both toward north, then turn your body so you are facing north as well. This will be your point of view and reference for the rest of your route planning. Whatever direction you must travel, keep your compass and map oriented north, and then face your direction of travel and the map will show you what terrain lies ahead.

### Parts of a Compass

### Bezel Ring

Your compass has a ring around the outside that turns called a bezel ring. The bezel ring is used for precise navigation. When you turn the bezel ring, it makes

*Compasses are tricky. The concepts of True North, Magnetic North, and Grid North are a bit complex for younger children to understand, so it is best to stick with the basics to start with. First make sure that they have grasped the nuts and bolts of geographic direction, north, south, east, and west—except on a compass of course, the order is north, east, south, and west or N, E, S, W. A little rhyme is the best way remember the order: Never Eat Sloppy Wheat. Here, Genesis and Gabe are lining up north on the compass and getting ready to walk east. (Photo credit Ruth England Hawke)*

a little click, and each one of those clicks represents 3 degrees. Turning the bezel ring five clicks to the left or right means an adjustment of 15 degrees to the east or 15 degrees to the west.

### See-Through Back

Many modern camping compasses have a see-through plastic back so you can lay the compass on your map and then line the map up with the compass, so that the top of the map, which is always north, is pointing the same way as the north arrow on the compass. This is called orienting your map.

## How to Use a Compass

Hold the compass level to the ground so the needle can spin freely. Some compasses have a bubble to help you keep the compass level. Keep the bubble in the center to ensure an accurate reading. Also, be sure to keep the compass away from metal objects. Let the arrow spin until it settles in one direction. This is north. Turn your body so that you are facing north. You are now oriented to your environment. The arrow, the lines on the bezel, and your nose should all be pointing in the same direction.

The compass face is divided with marks into degrees, which are usually marked in red.

The azimuth is the angle, in degrees, measured clockwise, between north and the direction you want to travel. North is an azimuth of 0 degrees. East is an azimuth of 90 degrees. South is an azimuth of 180 degrees. West is an azimuth of 270 degrees.

When you're facing north, your outstretched right hand points to 90 degrees, or due east. Your back is facing south and your left side faces west. Here's an easy way to remember:

Nose = North
Right = East ("right-ist" or "right-ish")
Sit = South (your butt is south of your head)
Left = West (both words have an "E" so it's easy to remember)

The easiest way to teach your kids how to get a sense of direction is to point out where the sun rose that morning. The sun always rises in the east, so point your right shoulder toward where the sun came up and your nose will be facing north, your backside facing south, and your left to the west.

For example, let's say you are facing north, where your compass arrow is pointing. You know that the nearest town is to your west, or your left-hand side, about five miles or so away. This means you want to travel on an azimuth of 270 degrees.

If you know which direction you want to travel, and want to find that azimuth, simply point your compass north, then turn clockwise until you're facing the direction you want to go. Look into the distance and find the farthest object you can see. Keeping your compass level, look down at the dial. Imagine a line from the far object to the center of your compass. Where that line crosses the degree marks on your compass dial marks your azimuth.

Setting the azimuth on your compass is also quite easy. Turn the compass body toward your target and line up the azimuth with the aiming points of your compass. Keep the north-pointing arrow lined up between the bezel brackets (these are the two lines on the bezel that bracket the north-pointing arrow when the bezel is set at zero). Then face the direction of your pointers and walk your azimuth.

By keeping the north arrow between the bezel brackets, you will ensure that your compass is always oriented toward north, and by following the direction of the aiming points on the compass, you will ensure that you are headed in the correct direction, always walking in line with your azimuth. As you walk, check the azimuth every fifteen minutes or so to keep yourself on track. After breaks, simply stand up, hold the compass flat, let the north arrow stabilize within the bezel brackets, and resume walking in the direction of your pointers.

*Spencer is using an improvised compass made from a magnetized needle floating on a leaf in half a coconut shell filled with water. The needle is pointing North-South. A magnetized needle floating in any other body of water would work, too. The best way to magnetize the needle is to put it next to a magnet; stroking it repeatedly with an object that contains iron also works. (Photo credit Ruth England Hawke)*

## How to Improvise a Compass

A compass is an important tool if you have to move. But what if you don't have a compass? As a last resort you can make one. To do so, you'll need a needle and, ideally, a magnet. A sewing needle is perfect, but many metals can take a charge to become a magnetized pointer. Try a paperclip, safety pin, staple, or bit of stiff wire.

First, you'll need to polarize the needle. If you have a magnet, leave the needle lying on the magnet for a while.

If you have a battery and some wire, wrap a piece of paper or a leaf around the wire to insulate it. Then wrap the wire around the needle and tie one end to the positive terminal and one to the negative terminal. It's best to use a C-cell or D-cell battery, but nine-volt batteries work well, too. Leave it connected for about thirty seconds, or until the wire becomes hot. Repeat this at least ten times to charge the needle.

Mark one end of the needle as the north-pointing end.

The needle will have to float free to point north. You can place the needle in anything that will hold water, like a plastic cup, the cut-off bottom of plastic bottle, or even a Styrofoam plate, as long as the container is not made of metal.

Place the needle on something that will float, like piece of cork or Styrofoam. Push the needle through the cork or Styrofoam so it's stable, but will spin freely. If you have nothing that floats, try a leaf.

If that doesn't work, try rubbing your finger on your nose and coating the needle with oil from your skin. That may float the needle on the surface of the water, but this method will require occasionally re-oiling the needle.

If no water is available, you can tie a thin piece of string around the middle of the needle and let the needle hang so that it spins freely. But mind the breeze, as wind can make this sort of compass difficult to use; however, it's better than nothing.

Note: Always keep your compass, manufactured or homemade, away from metal.

## How to Read the Sun, Moon, and Stars

If you don't have a map or compass but have an idea where you are and where you want to go, then learning some basics about reading the celestial skies can help you keep your bearing.

Remember, the sun rises in the east and sets in the west. Once you have that locked in, you can always find north by orienting your right shoulder toward the east, which points your nose north. It's that simple.

## What Time is It by Day?

Most kids know how to tell time, but a lot don't know how to estimate time. Luckily, it's easy to do and it's a fun thing to teach.

You can make a good guess at the time of day by where the sun is in the sky. When the sun is highest in the sky, it's noon. When it first rises, it's approximately 6 a.m. And when it sets, that is approximately 6 p.m.

To tell the other approximate times of the day, divide the sky into sections. The eastern horizon is 6 a.m., the western horizon is 6 p.m., and the middle of the sky, directly overhead, is high noon. To see what time it is, just look to see where the sun is and guesstimate.

If the sun looks like it's halfway between 6 a.m. and noon, it's about 9 a.m. If it's halfway between noon and 6 p.m., it's close to 3 p.m. It's pretty simple.

If you test this a few times, you'll usually be within fifteen minutes of the actual time.

A great trick to teach along with time estimation that is extremely useful for practical survival too, is how to tell how much daylight or nighttime remains.

Usually, when the sun is setting you can put up your four fingers in front of you in line with the horizon. Depending on a few factors like finger size, each finger represents approximately five minutes. So, three fingers until the sun hits the horizon at sunset means you have about fifteen minutes of light left.

This skill becomes really important when you're trying to assess how much time you have left to finish a shelter or set up a fire.

The opposite works for sunrise, too. Not that you can measure darkness in fingers, but you can tell by that very first hint of glow in the early morning, about how much longer you have until the sun does come up.

## What Time Is It by Night?

You can use the skies to tell the time at night as well (provided you have a clear sky), but I find using the stars to tell time very complicated and not practical for most.

I recommend sleeping at night anyway, in which case knowing the time isn't critical. But maybe you want a general idea of what time of night it is, want to know how long you've been resting, or how much longer before the sun rises. In these cases, you can estimate time by using the moon.

A full moon can be used just like the sun—it rises in the east and sets in the west. And you can use the same basic principle, top of the sky is midnight, low in the sky early evening is 6 p.m., bottom of the sky near the horizon in early morning is 6 a.m. These are rough approximations for teaching kids broad strokes of reading night skies.

Telling time by the moon when it's not a full moon is a two part process. First, look at how much of the moon is lit up. If half of the moon is lit, then the moon will be up half the night, or six hours. If one quarter is lit, it will be up only three of the night's twelve hours. If the moon is three-quarters lit, the moon will be up for nine hours.

For the second part of the equation you have to know when the moon came up and where it is in the sky. You can guesstimate from there.

For example, if the moon is half full, you know it will be up for six of the night's twelve hours. If it came up at dusk, and is half way to the "high noon" position, then it's 9 p.m. If the moon didn't show up until midnight (you'll know this because it first appears in the high noon position) and the moon is only half lit, and it's halfway toward the horizon, or 6 a.m. position, then you know it is 3 a.m.

Knowing the time can help you plan your movements based on available light. There is another part to using the moon as a quick fix cheat for navigating, so we'll look at that next.

## How to Travel at Night

Generally speaking, you shouldn't be traveling at night. But if you're stranded in the middle of the desert in the middle of summer, when movement by day will surely kill you, here are some tips for how to move at night without a compass.

### Navigating by the Moon

The moon orbits our planet every 29.5 days. This means we get about two weeks of a moon with one side lit up and about two weeks with the other side lit up.

We really get only one night per month of proper "full" moon, but for survival purposes, there are roughly three days before and three days after the true full moon that we get a full moon's worth of nighttime lighting.

The same holds for the new moon phase—there is really only one night of pitch blackness, but the little sliver of moon that is lit a few days before and after that mean we get about a week of effective darkness.

This is significant to the survivor planning to move at night. If you know you're facing nearly a week of fumbling in the dark, you must weigh very carefully the decision to move or not. Likewise, the full moon has a strong effect on tides and if your movement involves crossing water, this factor must be considered as well. At least you know you'll be walking in a lot of light, almost as bright as a dark cloudy day.

Now let's look at how the moon can be used for navigating. If you look up at the sky in the early evening, you will notice one of two things. Either the sun will go down and there will be no moon until about midnight, or the sun will be setting and you will see the moon is already up. Here's what either case means to you:

If the moon doesn't come up until around midnight, then the side that is lit is pointing east. Since the sun is already down, you have only one celestial body to point the way. The phrase "one at least, to show the east" may help you remember.

If the moon is up at the same time as the sun, then the bright side of the moon is pointing to the west. Remember the phrase "two is best to show the west."

### Orienting to a Full Moon

When the moon is full, provided the sky is clear, you can use the shadow tip method to orient yourself. Since the moon also rises in the east and sets in the west, all the same techniques apply.

### Orienting to a Crescent Moon

Regardless of which side of a crescent moon is lit, either will show you south. Just imagine a line from tip to tip of the crescent, and then continue that line down to the horizon, and that will point you generally due south every time.

## Navigating by the Stars

### The Big Dipper

The Big Dipper is a gift for navigators as it stays in the position of true north throughout the year. Depending on where you are and the time of year, it might be near the horizon or even obscured by mountains in the distance, but it will always show north, and it can always be found in relation to other supporting constellations.

The Big Dipper is known by other names, like The Plough in Europe, or seen as part of a larger constellation called Ursa Major. But in the US it's called a "dipper" because it looks like a soup ladle, and it's called "big" to distinguish it from a smaller dipper in the same section of sky. It's one of the easiest-to-recognize constellations.

### The Pole Star

The Pole Star is the North Star. Find it first by locating the Big Dipper, and trace from the handle down to the ladle, around the bottom of the ladle, and up the front of the ladle to its upper lip. If you extend an imaginary line along the front of the ladle and out beyond its upper lip, that line will point the direction to the North, or Pole, Star.

The North Star is actually the last star at the end of the handle of the Little Dipper. It's easy to confuse the North Star with the planets Venus or Mars, which are very bright in the night sky and can be mistaken for stars by novice stargazers. One sure way to differentiate between them is that Mars is red and Venus is blue, and while both will be bright, neither will twinkle.

Once you have the North Star located, you will know for sure where north is, and you can determine the other directions from there. If you're headed east, keep the North Star off your left shoulder, and you'll be facing and walking due east.

I still find a quick glance at the moon will tell me both time and direction, as long as I was paying attention at sunset.

If I see the moon and the sun up together, "two is best to show the west." (The lit side of the moon is my crescent pointing to west.)

If at sunset, I don't see the moon anywhere in the sky, when it finally does rise, I will know the lit side of my crescent will point towards the east. ("One at least to show the east.")

## Getting Your Bearing During a Full Moon

### The Shadow Tip Method

As the sun rises in the east, it will cast a shadow pointing west. As the sun passes the high-noon position, toward the western horizon, the shadow will move to the opposite side, or toward the east.

Find an open area, place about a one-foot stick in the ground, and look to see where the shadow falls. Mark the tip of the shadow with a rock, a small stick, or a line in the dirt. Wait about five minutes while the tip of the shadow moves. Now, mark the new position of the shadow. Mark a line connecting the two positions. This is an accurate east-west line. Extend the line in the dirt about a foot to each side so it's long enough to stand on.

Put your left foot on the end nearest the first mark and your right foot on the end nearest the second mark. You are now facing north. Your left shoulder is pointing west, your right shoulder is pointing east, and south is behind you.

# Weather

It helps to have a basic understanding of how weather works. In the simplest terms, the earth rotates, facilitating night and day. The earth also orbits the sun, accounting for the four seasons. During each season, general patterns prevail, such as heat in summer and cold in winter.

Start by explaining the obvious to kids: The sun heats the earth by day, and its absence cools the earth by night. Wind patterns are caused by changes in temperature, and the sun evaporates water from the oceans into the atmosphere, where it rains down onto the land below. All these processes work together to give us what we experience as weather. Understanding that helps us figure out what we need to do, or not do, in survival situations.

Weather doesn't do much for us in terms of determining direction, but it does mean a great deal in terms of travel, movement, and shelter. In these instances, you are at the mercy of Mother Nature and you must respect that.

Where you are on the planet and what time of year it is will determine what types of weather you can expect to be exposed to. If the skies look like rain, you'll want to make sure to pitch camp on high ground. If the wind is whipping, you'll want to avoid exposed ridges.

These are factors to be considered as you decide whether to hole up or set out to find help. My purpose in this section is to give some general weather-prediction tips so you can do a decent job of reading basic weather patterns. Plan your moves accordingly.

There are a few pithy sayings that go a long way toward reading the weather:

- Red sky at night, sailor's delight. (This means the sky is dry and it's not likely to rain for a while.)
- Red sky in morn, best to warn. (If the light of the sunrise is redder than yellow, expect stormy weather.)
- Gray-breaking day, all is ok. (This is the normal morning sky before the sun comes up, and means a normal day.)
- Gray at night, wet all right. (This means the clouds are so thick they cover up the setting sun's light. Expect rain.)

## What Kids Should Be on the Lookout For

Sometimes you can smell moisture in the air, or things sound different. Or you can see the smoke from your fire dancing about instead of just trickling upwards. Or you can feel the drop in atmospheric pressure, or change in temperature, or just feel the wind either stop suddenly or pick up rapidly. Other signs of weather to look for include:

### People

Some folks get aches and pains in anticipation of wet weather, or their hair curls up with moisture, indicating that rain could be approaching.

### Animals

Excessive activity in the middle of the day may be an early warning of bad weather. When animals go all quiet, a storm is imminent.

### Skies

A rainbow usually means the storm is past. If there's enough moisture in the air, you can sometimes see a ring around the sun or moon. If the ring is large or loose, then the moisture is thin and the weather will be ok. If the circle around the sun or moon is tight and small, it means denser moisture in the air, and an increased chance of precipitation.

### Clouds

Aside from hard and increasing winds, one of the best ways to predict oncoming weather is to look at the clouds. There are many different types, in many varied combinations, and all indicate different things when you're stuck outdoors. It's important to remember that when they're dark, they're full of water. When they're close to the ground, they're ready to dump on you. That said, here's your class on clouds:

> **The Good:** Bright, white, puffy, cotton ball–looking clouds; rippled, sand dune–type clouds; high-flying, light, wispy, thin-looking clouds; ground fog in the morning usually means a sunny day is ahead.
>
> **The Bad:** Clouds that look like someone stretched out a big cotton ball over the sky, leaving small pockets and slight gaps where the cloud is thinner; clouds that look like a solid grey blanket has been unrolled across the sky. These usually mean precipitation is coming. The time of year will determine whether it's rain or snow, and the speed and strength of the wind will determine how long before it gets to you.
>
> **The Ugly:** These are those very serious tropical storm-type clouds that move in rapidly, and the sky goes black before it pitches down on you. Also, when you see any of the above cloud formations with one large, tall, fat, pillar-looking cloud, usually with a flat head at the top, it's pushing a bad rain. When you see driving rains moving like a shower wall, these are from a mean storm.

If you're in the mountains, a storm can overtake you in minutes. In the desert, you might want to make tracks toward ominous-looking rain clouds in hopes of finding life-giving rainwater.

### Lightning

If you can see lightning in the distance, prepare to seek shelter before it gets to you. If you can hear it, take shelter right away. Shelter is way back in a cave or at the base of a tree in a large cluster of trees at the lowest point you can find. Stay away from high ground and single trees. In open terrain, lay down flat on the ground or in any small gulley or ravine.

To calculate lightning's distance from you, start counting seconds from the moment you see the flash until you hear the thunder. Then divide that number of seconds by five. For example, if you count ten seconds between the flash and the boom, the lightning is two miles away.

### Choosing the Route to Get There

When choosing your route, choose the path of least resistance. You will probably be weak, tired, and hungry, or maybe even ill or injured. At that point it's time to put theory to practice in the real world. Mind how you go. Route selection is everything.

Try to stay on the high ground. Don't drop down unless you have to, since climbing down and back up will wear you out fast. Walk the ridge lines as much as possible. That way you can see both sides of the mountain, and double your chances of spotting water or civilization.

If you have to drop down to lower elevations, try to read the ridges and stay on a path that keeps you as high as possible. Beware of dead ends that force you to backtrack and waste energy. Don't walk in valley bottoms unless you are shielding yourself from the wind or looking for water. In low-lying areas you are more likely to encounter thick brush that can make movement difficult. In these cases, drop low to the ground and try to find a trail to follow out. Then stay out.

Try to give yourself "handrails" by using terrain features such as rivers and ridge lines to keep you on track in case you get disoriented in thick cover or dark. Additionally, try to avoid traversing swamps and mountain ranges. Better to take more time and go around them, unless you're running out of time and forced to take the risk of not making it at all.

Be aware that on sloping terrain you will inevitably drift downward. Try to offset your elevation loss by walking back up a few meters every click or so. If you find yourself fighting too hard, consider altering your route to an easier path.

Don't dogmatically push to reach a planned destination, and kids especially can't be pushed too hard. Most kids don't have the same self-awareness as adults. Go gentle with kids is the rule and incorporate food and water stops and rest and sleep areas into your route.

## Estimating Distances

If you have a map, use a straight edge to estimate the distance to where you want to go before you set out. The straight edge can be the compass, a protractor, a ruler, a piece of paper, a piece of string, or any flat object that can be held against the scale in the map's legend and transferred to your azimuth.

Try to estimate the distance to your destination before you set out. After a day of traveling, you should try to estimate how far you've come, and compare that to how far you expected to get. The difference can help you adjust your planning to better match your actual performance.

A piece of paper is handy for estimating distance on a route with many legs or curves. Simply place one corner of the paper at the start point, then move the paper, keeping the edge on your line of travel at all times and making little pencil marks at each change of direction for a new leg or at each bend of a twisting route.

In this manner, you can "walk" your paper edge along the entire route, making marks along the way, so that when you are done you can look at the distance along the straight line of the paper's edge. Place this against the map's scale legend to see how far your journey will be on the ground.

Remember that elevation can be deceptive. For example, a 45-degree incline will add about fifty meters for every one thousand meters, or "click," travelled. A ten-click journey on a steep gradient could add an extra kilometer to your overall distance. This can add up over the course of many miles in mountainous terrain.

A good rule of thumb is to allow one extra hour travel time for every one thousand feet of elevation gain. An eight-mile journey that might take only two hours on flat ground will take three hours if the path climbs a thousand-foot hill.

## Estimating Distances with a Map

The easiest way is the way you know. Use whatever point of reference you're familiar with. Most folks know that a football field is one hundred yards, and a basketball court is about twenty-five meters long. Use these known quantities to estimate unknown distance or whatever is a good point of reference that your kids might know.

## Keeping Track of Distances without a Map

### Pace Count

Pace count is a technique used by the military to determine distance travelled. It is important for helping you know where you are at all times. It is also essential in planning how far you can expect to go in any given terrain and amount of time, especially when traveling with children. Hopefully, with some experience, you can modify your pace count for variables such as terrain, load weight, weather, and other factors including food, fatigue, and morale.

In its simplest form, pace count is just a matter of counting your steps. For this to have meaning, you need to know how far your step carries you. Take a look at the example below.

On a flat surface, I walk one hundred meters at a comfortable speed in sixty-three paces. Ruth will walk it in seventy-two paces. If the terrain is uneven, but still fairly flat, like out in the woods, it may take a few more paces to make one hundred meters.

Try to do this with your kids. Have them walk one hundred meters counting each time their left foot hits the ground. Have them do this three times, then take the average, which will be their pace count. This makes the kids feel empowered with knowledge and instills some self confidence as they have some idea how far they have traveled and feel like they are part of the team by keeping the pace count.

The more difficult the terrain, like thick jungle, or the steeper, the more steps I take, so my pace count increases. If I'm carrying a full rucksack, moving at night, or sick, tired, and hungry, I will take smaller steps, and so again my pace count will increase.

**Basic Measurements to Know**

- One meter is approximately three feet.
- One hundred meters is the distance you'll be measuring with your pace count (approximately sixty-five paces).
- One thousand meters is a kilometer (KM), or one "click." This is one hundred meters times ten, or 650 paces.
- 1.6 kilometers is one mile. (This is good to know if your map scale is in miles.)

These measurements are just one of the reasons I recommend having a conversion app on your phone, but of course, it's always better to have these things memorized.

**Pace Cord**

A pace cord is the most common and easiest-to-use strategy for measuring distance traveled. It only requires a few minutes to make, it's super fun for kids, and it really does help them to keep focused on the mission.

First, take a piece of cord or string. Double it up a few times if it's very thin. Make it about one foot long. Tie a knot at the top and a knot at the bottom, and one more about two-thirds of the way up. Then take nine smaller pieces of string and tie them into knots around the longer segment of the cord. Now tie four smaller pieces in knots around the shorter segment. Make the knots tight enough to stay put, but loose enough to slide up and down the cord. Now you have a pace cord.

Tie it to your shirt or belt loop. Slide all the knots to the top on each segment. Begin walking and counting your pace. When you get to your one-hundred-meter pace count, slide the bottom knot on the nine-knot segment down to mark one, one-hundred-meter segment walked.

After your second one-hundred-meter pace count, slide down another knot. Keep repeating this. Let's say you get to your destination, a watering hole down the hill from your base camp, and there are six knots at the bottom of your pace cord. That means you have travelled six hundred meters.

After nine knots, you'll mark your tenth one-hundred-meter walk by sliding down the bottom knot of the four-knot segment. Each of these four knots indicates one thousand meters, or one kilometer, or one click. Rest your nine knots to the top of the cord's longer segment and begin again.

With this technique, all you need to do is count your hundred-meter pace mark of sixty-five steps or so, and let the cord keep track of the rest.

Some alternatives to the pace cord are to pick up a pebble or break off a piece of twig and put it in your pocket every one hundred meters. Once you have ten of them, just move them from one pocket to another until you've travelled a click. Move them back to the first pocket for the next click, and so on.

If you want more accuracy over shorter distances, you can chop your pace count in half to the fifty-meter mark, or in quarters to the twenty-five-meter mark. After a while, you will find many uses for your pace count, including using it to move around your camp safely in the dark.

### Tracking Distance with Time

Sometimes, you may have too much on your mind, or other matters to deal with, to effectively calculate a pace count. If you have a watch, another—though much less accurate—way to measure distance is to let time doing the counting for you.

It takes a person in decent shape and average health, on average, about fifteen minutes to walk one mile at a normal pace on a flat road. This means the average person walks about 4 mph. Folks who are older, ill, or not in shape may walk at only 3 mph, meaning they cover a mile in twenty minutes.

If 1.6 kilometer = 1,600 meters = 1 mile = 20 minutes, then: 400 meters = 5 min, and: 100 meters = 1 minute, 15 seconds

Generally speaking, and depending on your rate of speed and specific circumstance, you'll travel about one hundred meters every minute or so.

Now, take this info and factor in your terrain and circumstances. Are you carrying a litter? Is someone on crutches? That might mean only one mile per hour. If you are in extremely thick terrain like a swamp or a jungle, you might only move one mile in an entire day.

Keep in mind that if you're one hundred miles from anywhere, that could mean three months of walking.

When using this method, remember to factor in a wider margin of error with these less accurate methods.

**Give Your Journey Legs**

You will rarely walk in a straight line. You have to take the actual terrain into account and break it into manageable portions. Give your journey some legs.

For example, say you need to walk ten kilometers. There's one mountain and two rivers between the start and end points.

So look at how far it is to the first of these obstacles, and call that the first leg of the journey. It might be two clicks to the first river. Then you have to walk another four clicks to the mountain. Call that the second leg. From the mountain, it's three clicks to the second river, and then one more click to the destination—each of these segments becomes a leg.

Take a look at the terrain contained within each leg. For example, you might be going due south and gradually downhill on the first leg toward the river. After you cross the river, you might travel southeast on a steep uphill slope toward the mountain. From the mountain, you might turn due east and follow a gentle downhill slope toward the second river.

In this way, you can chop up a long journey into smaller sections called legs. Within each leg, look at the distance, the direction, and the terrain you must traverse, and approximate the time we think it will take us to get there. By envisioning the terrain in your mind's eye, you familiarize yourself with what to expect, and when and where to expect it. And you can brief your kids on what to look out for and keep their minds engaged.

Also, if you lose your way, get hurt, or someone becomes separated from any members of the family, it might be easier to get back on track having already been told the route and what to be looking for.

## Travel Tips for Safer Movement with Family

### The High Road

When moving uphill toward high ground, go slow, and try not to get kids' pulses and respirations so high that they get sloppy and slip and fall.

### The Low Road

Moving downward toward lower ground can be deceptively difficult. Not only can it cause injury through the pounding of your heels as you go down, but there's also a tendency to want to move quickly, which could lead to a sprained ankle, an open fracture, or a fatal tumble. Best to go slow and safe.

## Open Ground

This type of terrain can also be deceptive. Try not to go too fast. Speed can lead to injuries and cause you to miss a lot of subtle signs like tracks and trails.

## Thick Vegetation

This presents certain challenges in that you often can't see very far ahead of you, and so can get disoriented. Try to look as far ahead as you can and pick a target to walk toward, like a dead tree or a hill, etc. Watch your step as you go, looking for holes, and try to look over logs before you step over them.

## Wet Ground

Wet ground can be extremely challenging. Try to stay as dry as you can. Look for little islands of dryness as you go, but try to plot them on a line so that you keep to your general direction of travel.

Swamps can be some of the most difficult terrain to travel because it's hard to lift your feet out of deep, sucking mud, over and over again, and also because the tendency to "island-hop" can take the traveler well off the path. If you have no choice, get in the water and walk as straight as you can, taking breaks to dry out along the way. It comes down to which is the greater risk: parasites and predators, or jungle rot and being lost?

## Boot Check

For any survivor, the most important concern for movement is your feet and your footgear. A good rule of thumb when traveling in standing water or rain is to stop for ten to fifteen minutes every hour and take your shoes and socks off. Let your feet air-dry for five minutes or at least enough to keep the skin from disintegrating for the next forty-five minutes. Put your feet in the sun if you can to dry them out. Wring out your socks and swing them around while you're waiting to help them dry as well.

You might even consider having your kids not wear socks at all if you all are traveling in swamp or very wet jungle. Surprisingly, most decent shoes or boots won't tear up your feet without socks. In fact, when they get wet they stretch a bit, and actually become more form-fitting as a result.

## Cliffs, Ridge Lines, and Rivers

You will most likely come upon natural obstacles during your travels. Most can be surmounted or skirted. Here are a few ground rules:

- Never jump off a cliff into unknown water. There is almost always a better way down, and it might even be better to try climbing and fall halfway than to jump and risk death from not clearing the cliff or landing on rocks in the water below.
- Never try to climb up anything if you can help it. Try to walk out, always looking for the easiest path out first. Climbing is a last resort, and you should never need it unless you're trapped, since civilization and water and rescue are almost always in valleys.
- Stay out of freezing cold rivers. You will become hypothermic within forty-five minutes and could very well die. Best to either build a raft or just keep walking beside the river.

There's a multitude of scenarios one might encounter in the process of navigating your way toward safety. Hopefully we've covered techniques and strategies to allow you to adapt or improvise your own unique techniques.

Whatever environment you live in, be sure to give your kids the skills they need to have to survive in it.

# CHAPTER EIGHT

# FIRST AID

One of the first things we want to cover about medicine is that everyone gets ill and injured in life. Keep this in mind when you decide how much time, money, energy, and effort you are going to allocate for yourself and your family's medical portion of survival training.

That means that you will get sick. So, if you start from the point of view that you will be the ill or injured person, then you can ask yourself a hard question: "What would my kids do, and what could they do?" Unfortunately the answer very likely is not much.

So, it helps to focus on what you need to do to make your family better prepared. The entire focus of survival is about staying healthy and alive. That said, we can't recommend highly enough, that you make first aid training one of your biggest priorities of family readiness. It is an investment that will never go to waste and will always come to good use.

I don't want to belabor the point, but I feel it is worthwhile to mention again here that I was a Special Forces medic, trained in dental, veterinary, laboratory, obstetrics, surgery, anesthesia and every other type of medicine with specialties in tropical medicine and definitive care trauma. On top of that I was a Medical Service Officer and a National Paramedic. So, while my perspectives can be somewhat extreme, that view comes from military guidelines for wilderness medicine.

Most medical professionals agree on the concept of the golden hour, which means if someone suffers a traumatic injury, the care they get, or don't get, in the first hour will have a significant impact on their chances of survival. Put bluntly, if you get severely hurt out in the wild and don't get some kind of serious care to counter it, the chances are you might not make it.

To help save lives, the medical community has recognized that any one out in the woods may be more than an hour from professional medical care, so they established guidelines that anyone with some training can do some level of intervention to try and save a life and still be protected by law if the care was reasonable and not willful negligence. This was done with the intent to make folks less afraid to help someone in extreme need due to litigation and to encourage more people to get first-aid training for medical emergencies.

# Ground Rules

Much of this section is proper medicine, recognized as such by authorities as acceptable practices, but some of what you'll learn will be suggestions for extreme medicine. So, please take this medical information on board as one loving parent to another. And that is also why I cannot recommend strongly enough that you get every bit of proper medical training from authoritative sources whenever and where ever you can. Now, let's do a quick review of law, medicine, survival, history and reality.

There's a connection between medicine and law that doesn't always fit a survival situation. Medicine has been around since the beginning of time. No one knows it all, and no one owns it. You have a fundamental right to learn as much as you can to be able to do as much as you can when your life or the life of someone you love is at stake. As such, no law restricts what you can do to save yourself. The laws governing medicine were created to protect patients and regulate practitioners. When survival is on the line, the law cannot hold someone responsible for what they do to save themselves or their family.

Further, laws do provide you some protection under what is called the "Good Samaritan Act." If you try to help someone using reasonable measures, you are protected from punitive legal action. The protection varies from state to state, but the spirit of it allows you to help without fear of being prosecuted later if something goes wrong. In fact, some places require you to help. Whatever you decide, once you intervene, do not abandon your patient unless you have no choice or are turning that person over to someone trained to continue rendering care.

Finally, the first rule of medicine is known as the Hippocratic Oath: "First, do no harm." And as a guideline, that is true. But sometimes you have to be downright brutal to save a life and ultimately do the patient more good.

For example, if a man has a dislocated arm, you are going to yank that thing back into place to help him. Or if a woman fractures her femur, you are going to have to pull the bone hard to splint it. Or if a kid slices open his arm and it won't stop bleeding, you will reach into the wound and pinch that artery closed. Get it into your head now that the practice of medicine is a labor of tough love.

*Children learn best if they're enjoying themselves and participating rather than just passively sitting back. When you're teaching them important and complex stuff like first aid, get them involved and try and get a laugh out of them from time to time; that way you know that their attention isn't wandering. Myke is teaching these Scouts the sequence for hemorrhage control and by using a bit of gallows humor about squirting blood, he keeps them focused and smiling. (Photo credit Ruth England Hawke)*

## Anatomy & Physiology

My purpose here is not necessarily to teach a full-blown Wilderness First Aid course. Those courses exist and I highly encourage any families that are going camping in remote areas or folks with older kids who are going on extreme hikes, climbs, and adventures to take one of these courses.

That said, I will cover a lot of ground to give a sort of "one over the world" view of extreme first aid to get you a baseline familiarization. Hopefully, I will motivate someone in the family to be the primary designated medic. However, everyone else in the family should be trained in basic first aid and everyone should carry their own immediate first aid kit.

Now, for a quick review, the human body can be seen much like a car, with a series of systems that cooperate to make the machine work. A fault in one system may show up as an improper response in another system, but usually, an electrical issue shows up as an electrical issue and an engine issue as an engine issue. So let's learn the systems of concern for survival and how they might get fouled up.

## Basic Systems Review

- Integumentary (skin): Watch for rashes and infections.
- Musculoskeletal (muscle and bone): If they don't work, you don't work.
- Respiratory (breathing): If this stops, it's game over.
- Circulatory (blood): Got a leak? Plug it fast!
- Digestive (food): Sometimes things get blocked up, or won't stop flowing.
- Genitourinary (water and sex): Dehydration is the main problem.
- Nervons (brain and pain): Headaches and injuries.
- EENT (eye, ear, nose, and throat): Something going awry with the senses.
- Endocrine (hormones): Outside the scope of survival medicine.

## Basic Symptoms Review

### Fever

This is the human body's "engine" light, if you will. When something is wrong, the body tries to fix it. And, whether ill or injured, white blood cells get mass produced and go to work. As they do, their increased presence in the blood stream increases body temperature. This is a simple explanation so don't get too hung up on it.

The key thing is a fever is a symptom, not a cause. Still, it needs to be controlled because it reduces the body's overall function. A fever above 106 degrees can damage brain cells or cause death. Be on the alert for black urine, which is a sure sign that the brain is cooking and your patient needs to be cooled down!

As we review indicators of problems, just remember there are two things to help us assess our patient's problems: their signs and their symptoms. The best way to remember what these are is simple: signs are what we see and symptoms are what they say.

Pain is a symptom because you can't see it. You can only go by what they say. And pain is also, very subjective, based on the person's background and perceptions. So, consider that, as well when you ask them how much it hurts. A child may feel a cut a lot more than a soldier, for example. However, there are some aspects of pain we can see and as such, these are used as primary assessment tools.

## Four Main Pain Levels

You'll need to gauge pain levels in addition to temperature, pulse, respiration, blood pressure, and pulse oximetry, if you want to understand your patient's pain. The basic classifications are as follows:

### Alert

If you can hear a person yelling and screaming, they're okay for the moment. The noise means they are conscious, breathing, awake, and talking. In short, it's a good sign that his body is stable enough that all systems are still functioning. So, you can see they are in pain, and assess it's not enough to knock them out. That's good news for you as the health care provider.

### Verbal

When someone clearly traumatized stops yelling but still responds when spoken to, even if it's only a groan, things have actually gotten a bit worse. Still, a reply shows they are still hearing and processing what's going on.

### Pain

When a patient is no longer chatting, you will have to resort to more extreme measures to get their attention and figure out how much pain they're suffering. One way to do this is a sternal rub, rubbing your knuckles hard on the sternum (the hard flat bone in the middle of your chest) to elicit a response. (It hurts like heck. Try it on yourself.) The patient should shudder or groan in response, even if unconscious. If the sternal rub doesn't work, try plucking them in the eye with your finger to see if they twitch or blink. Any response means your patient is still functioning at some level. If there is no response at all, that isn't good.

### Unconscious

Unconsciousness means your patient shows some kind of vital signs of life but they aren't responsive at all, not even to pain. And we can see they don't respond to pain, so, it is used as an assessment tool for us. Now, for these cases, we need to look a bit further to assess how damaged they are so check the following:

#### *Eyes*

Remember PERRLA, which will tell you to look at your patient's eyes to see if the Pupils are Equal, Round, Reactive to Light, and Accommodating (meaning they focus when they should). If so, chances are that brain function is still okay. If they don't dilate or constrict at all, that's not a good thing.

#### *Ears*

If blood is coming from the ears, that isn't good but it is better than clear liquid leaking out. The clear stuff is cerebro-spinal fluid (CSF). If you see this (and, if you do, it will be mixed with blood), it indicates that your patient has suffered a head wound that caused a leak from the brain cavity to the outside of the skull. Subsequent blackening around the eyes, also called "raccoon" eyes, will confirm this diagnosis. There isn't anything you can do about it except understand your patient has a serious injury and factor that into how you triage.

Understand that pain is very subjective. It's relative to a person's perspective and experience. I have seen grown men crying from small wounds, and women and children hacked with machetes merely whimpering as they patiently awaited treatment. The best way to get an idea of how bad someone hurts is to ask him or her, on a scale of one to ten—ten being the worst pain of your life—how do you rate this pain?

Next—and remember this—the operator feels no pain. Pain is the patient's problem because pain is not a cause; it is only a symptom. Trauma assessment sometimes demands measures that will cause the patient to feel some pain on the way to healing. Pain is a healthy sign that the body is working and only indicates that something isn't working right. You are there to fix it.

## The Four Characters of Pains

### Throbbing

Throbbing usually means some sort of circulatory problem and the throb is the result of the heart beating and pumping blood to/through the area in pain.

### Stabbing

Stabbing pain is usually associated with muscle tissue and is the normal kind experienced with trauma to an area, however, it can be associated with an acute issue with an organ as well and as such is considered a more urgent pain to address.

### Shocking

Shocking or shooting pain usually indicates some sort of issue with nerves.

### Dull

Dull aches and pains usually indicate an issue with organs or bones.

## Vital Signs

Vital signs are a measure.

In general, most folks have the same vital signs. Below are the normal ranges. More fit people tend to have them just a bit lower, and less fit folks a bit higher.

The main vital signs are temperature, pulse, respiration, blood pressure, and pulse. Temperature means they are usually hot (but can be cold) and the range assesses status. Pulse is the rate of heart beating, often, really fast is shock, or slowing towards death. Respirations, similar to pulse, fast breathing means responding to shock and slowing down usually means getting closer to death.

Blood pressure just helps you get an idea how much fluid is in the circulatory system, very important with heavy blood loss, but it also tells if heart is malfunctioning.

Pulse Oximeter tells how much oxygen is actually getting into their body. A simple, tiny, inexpensive finger clip can tell this and more and is worth being put in every family's first aid kit for these reasons.

### Temperature

Ninety-eight point six degrees Fahrenheit (37 degrees Celsius) is typical, but normal temperature may vary one degree Fahrenheit in either direction. Without a thermometer, body temperature is very hard to estimate so all you can do is try. Begin by factoring in the ambient temperature and feeling your own head as a baseline then, if the patient is conscious, ask them if they feel fevered. If you are sick, and alone, try to record what you observe when you are with it enough to write.

The three basic ranges of temperature are low, medium, and high.

- 98 to100 degrees F (37 to 38 degrees C) is a low-grade fever. Usually, the body will handle it fine.
- 101 to 103 degrees F (38 to 39 degrees C) is a mid-grade fever. Control the temperature with acetaminophen and consider employing antibiotics if they are available.
- 104 to 106 degrees F (40 to 41 degrees C) is a high-grade fever. Keep cool at all costs. Try submerging in cold water or placing cold, wet cloths under armpits, on neck, on groin and behind knees. Strip naked.

In a worst-case scenario, do what you can and hope to pull through, eating food and drinking water if possible. Keep patients from becoming delirious and hurting themselves. Many people have recovered from days of fever, and supportive care is all you can do if nothing else is handy.

### Pulse

The pressure we feel on arteries close to the surface of the skin tells us how fast the heart is beating. This is important to measure and anyone can measure it by feeling the neck, the wrist, the ankle, or anywhere arteries are close to the surface. The average pulse is sixty to one hundred beats per minute (bpm). Fit people might have a pulse up to ten bpm lower than typical and unfit folks could have one as much as twenty bpm higher than normal. Pulse may also be affected by exercise or stress.

Take a pulse by placing two fingers on an artery and using your watch to time the beat. Do not use your thumb as it has an artery and you'll only measure your own pulse. You only need to count the beats or "pulses" you feel for fifteen seconds. Multiply what you count by four to get one-minute pulse. For example, if you count twenty pulses in fifteen seconds, the person has a pulse of eighty, which is normal.

Note: In trauma or illness, there is usually an increase in pulse and breathing during the early stages. In the late stages, both of these can slow down below normal.

### Respiration

The amount of times a person takes a breath in one minute is their respiration rate. On average, this is sixteen to twenty breaths per minute, which translates into four to five breaths in a fifteen-second period. Trauma and pain, working, and running will cause an increased breathing rate.

### Blood Pressure

Another important vital sign is blood pressure. It is difficult to measure without the right tools, however it is an important assessment tool, especially when there is traumatic blood loss.

Blood pressure is measured in two ranges. The top range (systolic) is the higher pressure caused when the heart contracts and pushes blood through the system. The bottom range (diastolic) is the pressure that stays in the system, even when the heart is relaxed or dilated.

Measuring blood pressure requires a stethoscope, blood-pressure cuff, and some practice to get the skill. However, there are new electronic devices that do this easily, quickly, and much more efficiently, especially in a noisy environment like when a patient is screaming in pain. I recommend families get one of these for their first aid kit.

- Systolic blood pressure ranges from 100 to 140, averaging about 120.
- Diastolic blood pressure ranges from 60 to 100, averaging about 80.
- Pulse oximetry should normally read between 95 to 100 percent.

The PulseOx measures the amount of oxygen that is saturating the arteries. It is usually written as $SpO_2$. The actual medical term is long but if it helps you can think of it as saturation perfusion of oxygen or $O_2$. The main thing is that most folks aren't at 100 percent so no worries there, and the time for concern is if it gets below 90 percent.

These ranges are important because they allow you to understand what's typical versus when there is significant blood loss. Gauging this will tell you a lot about how bad off a patient is and what survival measures you need to consider.

Say that your helicopter crashes and you find a fellow survivor in the wreckage who has lost an arm. He managed to get a tourniquet on himself using his belt but then passed out. Check to make sure the scene is safe, determine if you need to move or not, and then assess the patient.

The patient's blood pressure can be estimated by looking, in order, for a pulse at the following locations:

- Behind the ankle bone = blood pressure about 90 systolic; still low but far enough from the heart to be good news
- Femoral pulse (groin area) = blood pressure about 80 systolic
- Wrist = blood pressure about 70 systolic
- Neck (side of windpipe) = blood pressure at least 60 systolic; worst-case scenario

If the first pulse you can find is on a patient's neck, you know he's alive and has a chance if you prevent further blood loss and get fluids into him.

If you don't have an IV, water enemas may be the best bet for a while since the patient will be unconscious and unable to drink water.

That may seem like a rough scenario, but survival medicine is harsh. The good news is that the patient has a pulse and a chance at survival, and that you always have a way to approximate blood pressure in the field without tools.

## Triage

Triage should occur when you have a "mass casualty" scenario. That means more patients than the system can properly provide for. In survival, two people injured at the same time constitutes mass casualty and may force you to have to make a "triage" decision.

In a major accident, chances are some people with you will have died and more will die soon. No matter who you are, where you are, or who is with you, not everyone can be saved all the time.

When a mass trauma event occurs, you will be faced with enough casualties to overwhelm the system. If you are the only first responder, you must decide who gets what care, and in which order.

These are four categories for triage, which you can remember with the acronym D-E-A-D (although the technical terms are in parentheses):

## Dead or Dying (Expectant)

These patients will die no matter what. Also, patients in this category could be people who would require so much effort to save that others who could recover might otherwise die. Do not attempt to save the hopeless. Leave them be and attend to others.

## "E" mmediate (Immediate)

These are patients who will die without help but absolutely can be helped. For example, a quick tourniquet can save the life of someone with a leg amputated at the thigh. Without it, he'll be dead in one minute. Deal with immediate cases on discovery.

## ASAP (Urgent)

These patients have serious wounds and require treatment soon but could survive for up to sixty minutes without treatment. A typical instance of this triage level includes a gut wound with no massive bleeding. Another example would be someone with some fingers chopped off. Get to it as soon as you can.

## Delayed (Minimal)

These injuries range from a broken forearm to an eye hanging out or a deep cut. The patients can make it up to six hours without attention and still be okay. Address these cases at your first chance but understand that they can wait.

After doing the best you can on the people with a chance, go and look at who you assessed as expectant. If they're still kicking, do what you can.

Once you've made it through the first round of triage, begin reassessing your patients and the treatments you rendered. Some may still be bleeding; others will have loosened their dressings. On the bright side, you'll have a bit more time the second time through.

Unfortunately, your patients' vital signs will have become more complicated as the true effects of their trauma take hold and shock wears off or worsens. Below are a few additional assessment tools to use while remembering that triage is a continual process.

## More on Pain

The sensation of pain as experienced by your patients will help you understand which systems are damaged. There are a number of ways to categorize pain and a few different theories used in the field of medicine. What's important is that pain can tell you about what you can't see or measure any other way:

- Throbbing pain usually indicates that something is restricting blood flow, maybe swelling from a bite or a fracture. Move the fracture just a little to allow the blood to flow better and stop the throbbing. Try to reduce the swelling by elevating the limb, loosening a dressing that might be too tightly applied, or applying cold or hot compresses on the affected area.
- Electric Impulses and tingling usually indicates an issue with a nerve. A slipped disk in the spine or a pinched nerve in a fracture is the usual suspect. Do what you can, but treatment is very limited without pain control medications. This type of pain sometimes feels like fire and is sensitive to hot and cold.
- Dull, constant pain is usually found with musculoskeletal injuries like sprains, fractures, and strains of bones, tendons, ligaments, and joints.
- Sharp pain usually indicates actual damage to something and is the type of pain felt in most traumatic events where lacerations occur.
- Colicky or spasmodic pain is usually felt when something is wrong with an organ or large muscle mass. The cause could be a lack of oxygen due to decreased blood flow, which in turn could be caused by either swelling from a hard impact or loss of blood from hemorrhaging. Not much can be done in the field for organ damage other than to make the patient comfortable by treating signs and symptoms while offering rest, food, water, and time to recover.

## First Focus: Trauma, then Medicine

Now that you have a good handle on the basics of what is normal in terms of vital signs and traumatic events, actions to take and outcomes to expect, let's get into the real matter of medical issues and actions for survival: how you approach patients or treat yourself in order of assessment and treatment priorities.

### First and Foremost is Safety and Security

If you get hurt entering the situation, then there will be two patients that need treatment. And if you two are the only two, you both might not make it.

So check the scene for safety, and if it's not safe for the other person, your first challenge is how to either make them safe or make the scene safe.

### C-Spine

The cervical spine has to be on your mind before everything else. Controlling the c-spine is taught religiously in modern para-medicine, with one thing beat into every paramedic's head: control the c-spine. Fortunately, there's a way for you to remember anyway.

*Mia and Abbie are practicing bandaging basics during a wilderness first aid class. Your family should have at least one first aid kit and your children should be familiar with the contents and know how to use them as soon as they're old enough. (Photo credit Jeffrey Coit)*

Since the airway is first point in methodical checking, and the airway opens to the mouth and nose, you can take control of the c-spine while checking the airway. To do so, place your hand on the patient's forehead and, from that point onward, make sure not to move the neck. Free your hand up by stabilizing the neck as soon as possible with either a brace or by placing something near the sides of the head to keep the head from turning like the patient's shoes or some logs or rocks. Movement risks damage to the c-spine and can cause paralysis or even death.

Reality check: Nearly all the time, the c-spine is not important. If there are no impact injuries, there is likely no damage to the neck and, as such, c- spine is not an issue.

## ABC vs CAB

For decades, first responders were trained that airway, breathing, circulation as the priority of treating trauma, but it's now generally agreed that the priority of work in trauma is CAB; that is stop that bleeding first, then fix any airway and/or breathing issues, and then circle back to check circulation. Nonetheless, the ABC system is a good way to teach beginners.

### A is for Airway

Traditionally, clearing the airway is considered the starting point for medical care. However, if there is trauma, circulation is the number-one priority. Stop the bleeding first and foremost because massive bleeding can kill a patient in one minute. If someone is not breathing, they can last a couple of minutes without oxygen—and you can supply air to your patient but not blood.

When you come upon a survivor and have assessed the scene as you approached, begin calling to him to assess his level of consciousness. A response means he's conscious to some degree and that his airway is open because he can speak.

If the patient doesn't respond, check the following:

- If he's unconscious, make sure he's breathing and turn his head to the side to keep him from choking on his own tongue.
- If he's unconscious and not breathing, check his pulse because he might be dead already. If there's no pulse, he's dead. Consider CPR if no one else needs help.
- If there is a pulse but no breathing, your patient might need CPR. Before beginning CPR, open his mouth and make sure nothing is blocking the airway. If the airway is blocked, stick your finger in and try and sweep it out. Be careful not to get bit by his gag reflex or push any obstruction deeper.
- If there is a pulse but no breathing and no obstructions, give two quick breaths. Do this by pinching the nose, making a good seal around the mouth with yours and giving a good deep breath. You should see your patient's chest rise. Then, let go of your patient's nose and break the seal with your mouth to let the air come out. If your patient was just winded and needed a kick start, this should do it.

That procedure will cover checking the airway and responding the vast majority of the time. Very rarely, though, the airway will be obstructed because of trauma.

If your patient's face is torn off, don't panic. They can still recover, and plastic surgery can do a lot of great things. For now, treat the damage as a wound and stop the bleeding, making sure any blood, flesh or cartilage is cleared out of the throat area. The key is to not freak out, so the patient doesn't freak out.

Notice that I keep using the word patient as I find that helps me to be more clinical and calm so I can focus on treatment.

### B is for Breathing

Checking the airway means just making sure the passage way is open; breathing is making sure the patient is actually sucking air in and out. But what if the patient is breathing with difficulty? Here's what to look for and what to do about it.

Look very quickly at what other injuries he has. Is it just panic causing rapid breathing or is trauma causing it? Checking for a sucking chest wound will tell you.

### Pneumothorax or Collapsed Lung

When you have a hole in your chest, it's easier for the air to come in through the hole than through the throat. So, every time the chest rises mechanically when you try to breathe, air rushes into the chest cavity through the hole rather than through the windpipe. That air then gets trapped inside the chest instead of blowing back out because the tissue around the wound seals in expiring air and keeps the air inside the chest.

As this happens, the lungs start to get smaller. The more air in the chest, the smaller the lungs get until they can't hold enough air to oxygenate the blood. If you see the neck veins protruding like they're under a lot of pressure or see the trachea or throat moving opposite to the hole, your patient is in a bad state. You must get the air out of his chest.

The treatment is fairly easy. Cover the wound with your hand—or with your patient's hand if they are conscious. Find something waterproof like plastic and cover the wound with that. Put a dressing on it and secure it. Turn the person onto their uninjured side with the hole pointed to the sky if possible. (Think about an air bubble in a water balloon where the air rises to the highest point. Wherever the hole is, lay your patient so the air gets nearer the hole.)

It might be necessary to "burp" this wound every once in a while, anywhere from every five to sixty minutes depending on its severity. If the patient is conscious, he can do it when he feels pressure building up by sticking a finger into the hole, letting the air out to relieve the pressure and then covering the wound back up. The ribs have a lot of nerves, and burping will hurt, but it will save your patient. Ultimately, surgical intervention will be necessary.

If there is only a small puncture into the chest but the same symptoms are present, you won't be able to burp it with your finger. If you have a medical needle with a hole in the center, stick it into the wound to drain the air. You can also try forcing your finger in or, in the worst-case scenario, cut with a small knife to make the hole big enough to drain air. Only incise enough to widen the hole and drain the air. There will be small amounts of blood but failure to drain the air will result in death.

### Hemothorax

If there is an injury to the chest and no is air sucking in and out but breathing is getting increasingly difficult, then chances are your patient is suffering from a hemothorax, or blood in the chest. The effects are the same as a pneumothorax, as blood fills the cavity around the lungs. Do not drain this blood. The blood will only fill up so much space and will then cause enough pressure to stop itself from bleeding. In this case, you cover the wound and do not "burp" it. You lay the person on their injured side so that some pressure on the bleeding can help to stop it. If your patient does not lose too much blood into the chest, he will be okay, but this too, will require surgery.

Pneumothorax (air-lung) = injury up, air rises.
Hemothorax (blood-lung) = injury down, blood sinks

Tell the difference if you're not sure by *auscultating*. You can do this with a stethoscope if you have one. If you don't have a stethoscope, you can still do this by tapping on the chest to hear what sounds it makes. Practice on yourself, and you'll hear the difference. Take your two main fingers from one hand and place them flat on the patient's chest, then take the two main fingers from the other hand and tap on your fingers. You will hear a thud.

Tap your right side on the top half of your chest and then your right side on the bottom half. This is the side without the heart, so it is all lung and will sound hollow. Then tap on the left side of your chest, first the bottom, then the top half where your heart is. You will hear a distinct difference between the hollow areas of lung tissue and the solid area filled by the heart. This is the difference you'll hear when you auscultate a patient with a chest injury.

If their chest is filling with air it will sound "hyper-hollow" and if it is filling with blood, it will sound "hyper-dull."

### C is for Circulation

Circulation means blood, so basically it means stop the bleeding.

### *Different Types of Bleeding*

- Desanguination is loss of major amount of blood.
- Arterial blood is the bright-red spurting kind that squirts out with every heartbeat.
- Venous blood is the dark, oozing kind; while it might be copious, it's rarely fatal.
- Minor bleeding is what you might see from a small cut or laceration.

The type of bleeding must be taken into account with the location of the bleeding to have a better picture of the situation and what kind of treatment is warranted.

### Examples of Bleeding

Minor bleeding inside the brain can cause major neurological signs and symptoms very quickly whereas a minor bleed on the arm will clot and heal even without treatment in most cases.

Major arterial bleeding from an amputated leg can be controlled with a tourniquet in seconds, but major bleeding from a ruptured spleen or torn aorta will cause enough internal bleeding in a minute to cause death without one drop of blood being shed.

Most venous bleeding will hurt but will clot fairly soon on its own. A venous bleed on the scalp could cause a person to lose enough blood that they go into shock and die because the scalp is so vascular that it just keeps bleeding.

So, the type of bleeding and the location are the two major factors for considering what the final outcome might be, but the treatment is always the same: Stop the bleeding!

It's easy to do. Put your hand directly on the wound and push down. If your patient is conscious and coherent, make them do it while you find or improvise a dressing. In case of an amputation, go straight to the tourniquet. If blood is spurting, reach in and pinch it off. Get aggressive, go after the source of that bleed, and stop it as soon as possible. If you have to stick your finger into an open gut wound and pinch a piece of intestine to stop it bleeding, do so.

For parents, it's easy to be aggressive and stop multiple bleeds so long as you remember, pain is the patient's problem and tough love will save the day.

This is not the time to be worried about infecting the wound. You are already dirty so the wound is already infected. If they lose too much blood, they won't get any infections because they'll be dead! If they live because you saved their lives by stopping massive bleeding with dirty hands, you can give them antibiotics later.

## Hemorrhage Control and Action Sequence

### Direct Pressure

The first thing to do is put your hands on the wound or a dressing covering the wound.

### More Pressure

Add a dressing if there is none or add a second dressing and pack it into the wound more by tying the dressing down with the knot on top of the wound to create more pressure in an attempt to stop the bleeding.

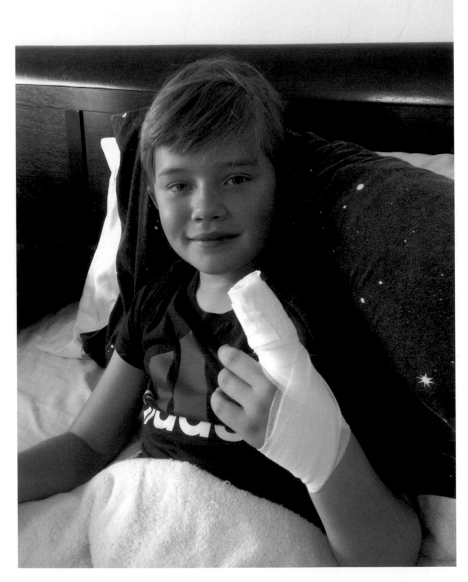

*Live by the sword, die by the sword. Or in the Hawke household that translates as: if you use knives a lot, you will eventually get sliced. The point here is, however carefully supervised your child is, if they use a knife often they will most likely have an accident at some time or another. Both you and they need to know what to do in that eventuality. First up, don't panic. Fear is contagious and you need your child to remain calm. Apply direct pressure to the wound, ideally with a dressing and raise the wound above the level of their heart. If in doubt seek medical attention. (Photo credit Ruth England Hawke)*

### Elevation

Raise the wound above the level of the heart to decrease the blood flow by reducing the amount of pressure on the hole in the circulatory system. This is particularly useful for a bleeding arm or leg if the person is sitting. If you can't get the limb above the heart, get the heart below the limb by laying the person down then raising his arm or leg.

### Pressure Points

On some locations on the human body, blood vessels are closer to the surface and, as such, pressing down at these points will reduce the blood flow through the vessels to the wound. For instance, if pressure and elevation weren't stopping the blood flow in a hand wound, you could squeeze the area on the wrist where you would normally take a pulse which will reduce the blood flow to the hand. Pressure points coincide with the places where you can take pulses and this method is particularly useful to a survivor if you are treating yourself or need to hold off the bleeding until someone can produce a suitable dressing.

### Tourniquets

Tourniquets are considered a last resort in modern medicine; however, combat medicine holds that a good tourniquet, quickly and correctly applied, is often the first choice for any significant bleeding. A tourniquet will staunch blood loss and provide the caregiver more time to get the right dressings ready to apply. After the dressing is applied, the tourniquet can be eased up gently, striking a balance during the transition. Also, you can re-tighten a tourniquet while adjusting a dressing. Finally, once the dressing is in place and the bleeding is under control, the tourniquet can be removed completely.

Rules for Tourniquet Usage:

- Tourniquets should be two inches wide or wider but not narrower unless nothing wider is available.
- Tourniquets should be placed two inches above the wound or amputation. Placing lower could damage the wound.
- Placing higher could mean that, if the tissue below the tourniquet dies from lack of blood, the patient will lose more tissue than necessary.
- Tourniquets should be tightened only enough to stop the major bleeding; some oozing is okay.
- Tourniquets should not be loosened until you have a proper dressing in place and ready.

- Tourniquets should be kept ready to be tightened or re-applied if the bleeding begins again.
- Tourniquets should be placed below joints when possible. If the patient loses a limb later due to amputation, the joint is important to having a better prosthetic.

## Dealing with Disconnected Body Parts

Amputations are obviously treated initially by the application of a tourniquet, but what do you do with the body part? Most likely, you will simply bury it later if the survival situation gets extended. But for the short term, try to salvage the limb, provided circumstances allow taking these extra measures. No body parts should be re-attached in the field unless done so by a trained person. Re-attaching is an invite to infection, gangrene, septicemia, and possibly death.

When it's gone, it's likely going to stay gone. However, you should wrap the part in some clean plastic or other waterproof material and put it on ice or snow if you happen to have some. If not, a cold lake or river water is near and can be used to keep the body part cold.

Try not to let the water get to the body part, however, as the part will absorb the water, rupture the cells, and destroy the appendage. Also, do not let the part freeze as this too will rupture the cells and destroy the tissue. Depending on how well the temperature is regulated, the part might last up to three days.

Eyeballs pop out. It happens. If they do, try to place them back inside. It will only get worse when left out, and without the chance of immediate first aid, most of the time, it's best to put the eyeball back in. If the orb is destroyed, the eye is lost. It cannot be repaired or replaced. In this case, do not place it back in but treat it like any wound and cover it with a clean dressing. If the orb is intact, some muscles that move the eye are probably torn but the vision should still be okay since the optic nerve is like a tough piece of stretchy plastic. Try to place the eyeball back in gently after cleaning it the best you can. Finally, cover the eye and dress it like a wound. If the eyeball can't be placed back in the socket but the orb is intact, put it in something like a plastic bag, keep it moist, cover it gently, and secure the whole contraption to the patient's head. Cover both eyes in most cases because wherever one eye looks, the other will turn. This twitching will cause more pain and discomfort to the patient.

## DEFs of Tracking Patient Progress

### D is for Disability

This is mostly addressed when you determine the patient's level of consciousness (alert, verbal, pain, unconsciousness) but becomes particularly important when you notice a significant change, one way or the other. If your patient is starting to come around after your treatments, this is great. But if you notice that they are deteriorating, you need to reassess what you are doing and what you have done.

### E is for Exposure

In a survival situation exposure is not usually warranted or desired. However, if there was a major crash, or a person tumbles down a cliff, or you found someone unconscious and there are no obvious causes, you might need to remove their clothing in order to find problems and treat them. In the cold, this might not be ideal, but it will help you look beyond the obvious. For instance, someone might have fallen and broken a leg, which gets your attention right away. Meanwhile, no one notices that they also suffered a puncture wound to the chest cavity. Exposure and inspection will find this.

### F is for Full (of vital signs)

In a survival situation, you are very limited without tools. But you can get a basic amount of info by measuring vital signs, knowing what they mean, and then reassessing to see if they're getting better or worse. Remember, breathing and pulse increase initially in response to trauma and shock, and then slowly decrease. Keep this in mind when you first begin treatment so that you're not lured into a false sense of security because the vitals look good early on. Reassess regularly, and when you're not sure what to do next, reassess again with systems checks, body part checks by function, and reexamination of all your dressings and treatments.

## Carry Techniques

Sometimes you will need to move patients from the scene of an injury, either right away to get them out of harm's way or after you stabilized them. Here are a few tips I find useful and practical enough even for kids.

### Moving an Unconscious Adult

Always get your patient's help if he can assist in any way. Always use as many people as you can to move someone. Always try to squat while lifting, letting your legs do the work.

### If You Have to Carry a Patient Alone

Stand behind your patient and hold him under his arms, your fingers interlocked across his chest. Drag—don't lift—using your legs instead of your back to walk backwards.

If your patient is a child, carry him in your arms.

If your patient is heavy and the distance is great, an over-the-shoulder carry is best. Begin by putting a knee on the ground and pulling your patient's arms over your head. Slide your shoulder lower while wrestling your patient onto your shoulder. Slowly stand up while holding onto something. Then get comfy and get moving.

If you can, use a rope or something similar to make a loop under your patient's arms. Then tie the loop across your shoulders and you can carry your patient like a backpack.

Finally, if time permits, make a pole stretcher. Place your patient in it and drag the poles. This works well, but the sticks will wear down and need to be replaced so make them long. In some situations, for short distances in emergencies, you may just lay them on a blanket and drag them, or tie a rope to them and drag them.

## If Two People Are Carrying Your Patient

The stronger carrier holds the patient under the arms with fingers interlocked as above. The weaker one holds under the thighs while standing between the patient's knees and lets the ankles lock under their armpits; the carrier locks their fingers together. This works much better than trying to hold a tight grip over any period of time or distance. The two carriers lock arms like a cradle and let the patient sit in your arms like he was in a chair. Again, time permitting, make a pole stretcher or litter to drag.

## Leaving an Unconscious Patient

Sometimes, a person is not conscious, but you can't move him and need to leave. If at all possible, once the person is treated and stabilized, turn him on his side, the uninjured side if possible. Raise the top leg so the knee is bent and place his top arm with the elbow bent so his hand supports his head. This should keep him from choking on his tongue or vomit. Try to leave a message in case the patient comes to and make sure you note where you left him.

The hard part here is abandoning someone with no idea where you're going, if you'll make it, and whether you'll ever be able to find your patient again. Chances are that your patient will perish if he is ill or injured and you cannot take him with you for whatever reasons. Also, trying to carry him might actually kill you. It is not an easy decision, but it is one that might need to be made. But do your best to mark the location, and make a lot of signs on the trail as you move so you or others can find their way back.

Now that we have looked at trauma or injuries, let's take a look at diseases or illnesses.

# SAMPLE: A Different Diagnostic Tool

It starts when the patient says something is wrong, they don't feel right, or they may simply be presenting by acting odd or out of sorts. Parents are pretty good at reading their kids, but sometimes, the parents may be the ones getting sick and they could be so focused on surviving and caring for the kids, that they don't even realize they are acting out of character.

Once someone says they're not feeling well, the first thing to do is check the obvious by looking at them and making sure they don't have any injuries that haven't been noticed. Once you survey that it's not an external physical injury, make an assessment of what might being going on internally that is making them feel unwell.

We do this by asking a set of questions that helps us narrow down the problem. We do this primarily by asking them for a "SAMPLE."

SAMPLE is another medical acronym used to help get a handle on what might be going on. While not so relevant in trauma scenarios, it is good for illnesses.

SAMPLE stands for:

- Signs and symptoms: Remember, what you see is a sign—a bruise for example. What they say is a symptom, such as "no feeling in the hand."
- Allergies: Always ask people if they have allergies.
- Medicine: Ask a patient if they are taking any medication.
- Past medical history: Ask patients if they've had something similar in the past and what was done to make it better. This single most important question could give you everything you need to know to help them.
- Last meal: This is especially important in case of a rapid onset sickness when surviving because people might be trying to eat new things around you.
- Events: Ask what's happened recently and why and how you might be able to make it better. With injuries, ask about the mechanism of injury, or how they got hurt. Have them demonstrate or explain so you can visualize how something might have been hurt and what else might have been injured but is being overshadowed by the pain of the main injury.

Armed with this basic assessment methodology, you are ready to do the best you can to help yourself and those around you. You can even ask yourself these questions so that you can best understand how to help yourself when something unknown is making you sick or causing you pain.

# Prevention

Prevention is the most important thing anyone can do for first aid and health. This is especially true for the survivor since there is limited or no access to health care and medicines in survival situations. So, everything you do in a survival situation must err on the side of caution.

Survival situations are no time to take chances and unnecessary risks. If you need to climb a tree, descend a cliff, cross a river, or even just use a knife, go slow. Take some time and think about what you want to do, why you need to do it and how you can do it in the easiest and safest way possible. Simply slicing your finger from being too hasty can change everything.

Prevention is pretty much common sense. If you're thirsty, drink. If you're cold, get warm and stay dry. If you're tired, get rest and sleep. This is the number one key to a good prevention plan. Rested people think better and better decision making decreases the chances of unnecessary injuries and illness.

The first question for prevention should be, how can this go wrong? From there, you can plan around potential problems. If you have no choice, then take whatever chances as cautiously as you can.

## Hygiene as Health and Medical Care

Try to maintain your personal hygiene and general cleanliness as a top preventive strategy. This will also help with your sense of general well-being and positive mental outlook. It also decreases diseases by reducing the bacteria that grow naturally on the human skin and multiply quickly in dirty conditions. These become opportunistic infections waiting to happen if you get a cut or scrape while your skin has this excess build-up of bacteria. So, keep clean. You can do this under almost any circumstances.

**Hygiene Tips**
- The sun kills bacteria. If you have no water, try to take off your clothes and expose your skin to the sun for a while, being mindful not to get sunburned.
- The air itself can still help kill some bacteria if there is no sun. Just airing out your body for a little while each day can reduce the amount of bacteria on your body.
- Sand can be used when there is no water, especially in the armpits and groin. Be careful to get it all out of the butt cheeks to prevent chafing and a rash.
- Ash from fire can be used to clean hands.
- Hand gel can be used as one of the best all-around cleaners without water.
- Fire can be used to clean metal utensils.

*Bath time in Borneo with little Iban girl, Jessica. Bathing in rivers can be a lot of fun, especially when you have a wriggly little lovely on your hip! We were actually washing here, not just playing (note the soap on the dock). Iban women bathe in sarongs for modesty so I followed suit. It's very important to stay clean in order to avoid fungus and skin sores, which can become infected. You're at particular risk from this in damp tropical places. If you're somewhere where there is no water to wash in, strip your family down from time to time and let the sun and breeze get to their skin. (Photo credit Tasha Isaacson)*

- Rain can be used to wash body, clothes, and utensils.
- Water of any type can be used for all hygiene needs.
- Shower in the rain if you get the chance or use some snow if practical.
- Teeth are vitally important in life and become even more so in a survival situation as dental problems can cause misery and grief unlike any other. So, keep your teeth as clean as possible. You only need a stick or some cloth to do so. Many folks use a twig of sassafras or pine to scrape all their teeth. You can also take a piece of cloth and wrap it around your finger and then rub your finger over your teeth, very firmly. The key is to take your time, and go over every area of every tooth. Do this at least twice a day.
- Feet are the most important thing for any soldier, and this rule applies to the survivor as well. Take care of them! Massage them every day before you start your day and every night before you end it. Keep them dry at all cost. If you can't keep them dry, stop frequently and air them out. No matter how cold it is, air them out. No matter how wet it is, take them out of your boots, even in a downpour of rain, and air them out. Try to rotate socks and keep them clean.

- Rashes can happen to anyone at any time. The general rule is if it's wet dry it out, use air, sun, sand, ash. If it's dry, moisten it with water, oil, lotion, lip balm, Vaseline, fat, vehicle grease, or anything else you can think of to use.
- Poison oak and ivy can be a miserable experience for anyone. Bleach is the very best treatment if you have it. If not, soap and water, early and often is the best way to get the oils off your skin and stop the irritation. A key point here is that if the oils got in the clothes, it's best to throw them away or reinfection will happen. If disposal is not an option, wash them very well and hope that sorts it.

That takes care of your body. Clothes are the next most important thing to keep clean. They will keep you warmer in the cold and will last longer in the heat if they're clean.

### Clothing Tips

- Sun will kill germs on clothes just like on a person. Lay or hang your clothes in the sun whenever you can.
- Air will also work on clothes to reduce bacteria loads. Air out your clothes when you can. If you're wet, get naked and let the clothes air dry.
- Boil your clothes if you have the luxury of fire and a pot as this will kill all the bacteria. Or just rinse your clothes in any water or sand you can come by.
- Post-defecation contamination is the number one way that many campers and survivors get sick. Do your best not to contaminate your hands during defecation. Use some nice, safe-looking broad leaves for tissue. I prefer to use the dry leaves on the top of the leaves on the ground because it reduces the risk of sap causing irritation if the leaves are already dead and dried.

Most important is to always wash your hands, all the time, after everything, before everything.

## Nutrition

This is another key element of the prevention strategy. Most likely, as a survivor, your food intake will be very limited. However, if you understand nutritional basics, then you have a chance of balancing your diet. In long-term survival situations, this alone could mean the difference between life and death because weakness that results from these deficiencies leads to higher degrees of incapacitation from which death could result. If left to scavenge in a survival situation, see if non-survivors had any vitamins or supplements in their personal effects.

## Food Basics: The Four Food Groups

There are essentially four food groups, even though nutritionists will get technical and divide these into further sub-categories. For a survivor, it's very simple.

- **Meat:** This includes nuts, beans, eggs and fish.
- **Milk:** You won't find butter or cheese, but you might just get some goat milk.
- **Fruits and vegetable:** These are obvious and we don't care if a tomato is not a vegetable.
- **Breads and cereals:** You're not going to find any bread out there, and cereals actually take a lot of work to make, but you can find some good substitutes like roots and plant stalks that provide starches and carbohydrates.

But the bottom line is that you will not eat a balanced diet. You will eat what you can get. That's why for the survivor, it's more important to understand what you need and what can give it to you out in the wild.

When you are surviving, basically, you need to think "caveman diet," as that's pretty much what you're going to be on. This is mainly meat and some fruits and veggies if you're lucky.

- Protein is the number-one thing that is going to give you strength and you are going to need it. The best source of protein is meat, which means hunting, traps, snares, and fishing now come into play. If you're lucky, you'll find some nut-bearing trees or some occasional eggs or legumes. But mostly, you'll need meat.
- Fats are one of the best sources for energy there is. They aren't great for you when you work in an office, but when you're out in the bush, using all your muscles in ways you never have, fat tastes delicious and keeps you going. The bottom line is to never waste fat and throw it away. Eat as much as you can. Use it for storing other foods, or making soap or candles if you have to, but try to eat it all first!
- Carbohydrates that we normally get from breads and pastas aren't naturally occurring entities. But many roots will provide carbohydrates, as will many plants like cattails. Carbs are important for energy so eat them when you can.
- Vitamins and minerals kind of fall into the same category for the survivor. You're not likely to get all you need, and surprisingly to most health nuts, you don't really need that many, but the lack of them will cause you major problems over a long period of time. For now, it's important to know that you need them and they are harder to get so this is why you need to try to find some fruits and veggies around you, as these contain the trace minerals and

occasional vitamins humans need. Mentally prepare yourself to try some as you do need them to survive. The following section explains why.

## Vitamin Deficiency Diseases to Be on the Lookout For

I won't cover all the deficiency diseases here, but I do want to make parents aware of a few that can manifest in kids in any extended survival situation. In the absence of trauma or an illness that you can fairly easily identify, nutrition deficiencies are not common in our society so most people won't recognize them. So, let's just touch on these and if it's a keen interest, definitely research more about it. This is especially important for parents who have sensitive children or kids who have unique dietary requirements.

- Vitamin A deficiency causes blindness.
- Vitamin B1 deficiency causes beri beri and lack of energy.
- Vitamin C deficiency causes scurvy, gum bleeds, and slow healing.
- Vitamin D deficiency causes rickets and weak bones.
- Lack of calcium causes weak bones and teeth.
- Lack of iodine causes goiters, swollen neck and glands.

These are just some classic examples of issues a survivor can possibly experience in a long-term survival situation.

## Sample Medical Questionnaire

Minerals are in the same category for the survivor as vitamins. You'll get what you get from whatever you eat and you'll eat whatever you can get. It's important to point out here that bugs are a complete nutrition source. You'll get more vitamins, minerals, fats, and proteins from bugs than any other food source.

Further, almost everything you need nutritionally to survive is provided by meat, and the same is not true for surviving by plants alone. It's just a harsh reality. So, for parents who are taking a noble path of raising vegetarians, consider those practices to be temporarily suspended while in a survival situation.

The only two vitamins not provided by meat are Vitamin E, whose deficiency causes no known disease, and Vitamin C, which is one of the most widely occurring and easy to find vitamin sources. Seaweed at sea, cacti in the desert, lichen in the arctic, and many plants in the jungle, mountain, and forest can provide Vitamin C. With meat and one plant from each of the world's environments, you can survive with a healthy diet.

The human body has naturally-occurring enzymes to pull vitamins and minerals from the meat of animals, but we cannot pull the essential vitamins and minerals from the plants. We need animal meat to do this for us because animals have their own special enzymes that break down grasses and grains and absorb the nutrients we need. These are just some biological facts to consider.

Fiber, simply put, is purely a nicety. Yes, it's nice to keep regular, and that is important. Without it, you can become constipated and that can cause debilitating pain. But constipation is easily treated by drinking a lot of water and consuming some oil or a lot of fat. Either will lubricate feces causing the blockage and the resulting pain. Get fiber if you can, but plan to live without it. Enough fruits, veggies, fats and water will usually suffice for the survivor.

## Immunization

It is very important to keep your shots up-to-date and make sure your kids get all their immunizations too. I won't belabor the point too much here except to say, especially if you're going to travel, check with the CDC in the US or the NHS in the UK and see what they recommend. As a parent, you'll have to research what you think you'll need and then decide what to get for your kids.

Some folks will opt for a rabies vaccine, while others won't. Some get the flu shot each year, some don't. I usually don't recommend flu shots for healthy persons, but for kids and elderly, sometimes it's good. In short, immunizations are very important. Diseases are real and they do kill. Take the steps to prevent them. Check your shot records and get them up to date.

## Disease

Simply put, diseases are naturally-occurring organisms that cause a reaction which has a negative impact on the health of the human organism. Diseases come from many sources, can cause many symptoms, and not all have cures. Some go away on their own, some are easily treated, and some are fatal if untreated. Most diseases can be either treated or cured. Treatment means the disease can be controlled and managed to make it less harmful but not stopped or killed completely. Curing means the disease can be completely removed as a problem.

Since most diseases can be cured, or at least treated, the key will be lasting long enough to get treatment or a cure. To this end, it is helpful to know what diseases are out there and what causes them so you can try to prevent them when possible while recognizing signs and symptoms if you do get something.

This way, you can understand what is going on if you get sick, try to keep any sickness from getting worse, have some idea what to expect so you don't despair, and have a concept of the timeline you are up against to help make better decisions to effect a rescue or escape to civilization.

I will touch on some diseases that are more common and I will include some treatments just in case you happen to have medical supplies.

How to use medications will depend on more variables than I can cover here. Read the label, then use your common sense and best SWAG (scientific wild-ass guess!).

## Some Diseases to Watch for as a Survivor

- Bacterial infections: respiratory, intestinal, genito-urinary, skin, and eyes
- Viral infections: respiratory, intestinal, and eyes
- Fungal infections: skin, nails, and respiratory
- Protozoan infections: intestinal and bowel
- Internal parasites: lungs, heart, brain, eyes, and intestines
- External parasites: skin, hair, nose, and ears

There are far too many diseases to list each one, and the region, the signs and symptoms as well as the treatments, both FDA approved as well as holistic herbal remedies. It's best to make a study of the things in the area where you live and/or where you plan to go and then make a simple chart of the diseases, key signs and symptoms and the treatments for them. Memorize the list and laminate it and put it in your first aid kit for yourself and your family.

The key here is to make you aware of the different types of vectors that you can face as a threat to you and your family's health, any time, and especially in a survival situation. And once you know what you face and can identify whatever you think it is, then you'll have to make an assessment of what medications to use to cure or treat it. That requires a little more skill than just identifying signs and symptoms.

## Antibiotic Therapies

### Rules

There are a lot of rules, regulations, and laws out there regarding antibiotics and their use. These are mostly good things because, if antibiotics were readily available to everyone, many folks would take them for the wrong reasons.

### Reasons

What's the harm? Humans develop immunity to things the more we're exposed to them. Many diseases that can kill people are easily cured by antibiotics but these antibiotics took time to discover and develop. If people take a lot of antibiotics, then the chances are we will no longer have effective treatments for many diseases and might not find new cures in time. So, in the big picture, doctors are trying to save lives by controlling and restricting the misuse of antibiotics.

### Exceptions to the Rules

The survivor has but one mission, to stay alive. Illness can cause this mission to fail. So, antibiotics are to be considered fully acceptable for use in a survival situation. That said, you need to know some basics about bugs and drugs.

### Two Types

There are primarily two types of bacteria that have significance to the survivor, the kind that need oxygen and the kind that don't (called aerobic and anaerobic bacteria, respectively). They have different shapes and such, but that is only important in a lab with a microscope.

### Three Terms

There is some terminology that will help you: gram negative and gram positive. In a lab, a stain on the bacteria differentiates between the two and this information tells what type of antibiotic will work better against it. The other key term to know is broad spectrum antibiotic, meaning the drug works against both kinds. These are what you need.

### Two Ways

Antibiotics usually work in one of two ways. Bactericidals either get inside the cell and destroy the nucleus or attack the outside of the cell and destroy its membrane; either way, the bacteria dies. Bacteriostatic prevents the bacteria from dividing, stopping its proliferation throughout the body.

### Diagnosing

The types of bacterial infections you might get on a cut on the outside of your arm are usually aerobic and gram positive and less severe. The types you might get inside you, where there is no air, are usually anaerobic and gram negative and are usually more severe.

When you attempt to diagnose a bacterial infection in the field without the benefit of proper tools and lab techniques, this is called an empirical diagnosis, based purely on experience and observation. Use the info you gather to try and decide what kind of infection is being presented. That will drive the determination of which drug might be needed. In short, it is a best guess.

A good rule of thumb is that green is bacterial, yellow is viral. This is useful for determining if you actually need that antibiotic or not when there is a cough, runny nose, or phlegm.

It is important to grasp that not all antibiotics work for all bacterial infections. So if you are taking an antibiotic for something that it is not designed and intended for, it might not be doing you any good at all and you've squandered a valuable resource that could have been of benefit later if used for the bugs it was intended to work against.

What it all means to you is this: incorporate what you now know about the basics of antibiotics and bacteria and make the best guess for what will work based on what you have available to you. In most cases, a broad-spectrum antibiotic will work. If in doubt, take the antibiotics.

## Treatment

When it comes right down to it, it is best to have some broad-spectrum antibiotics. Try to get them, try to keep them in any first-aid/survival kit, and if you have them, chances are, they will help.

**Note:** Most medications will last much longer than their shelf life. Very rarely is an out-of-date medicine actually more harmful as a result of being expired. Consider the temperature and conditions of storage and time expired, but if the container looks good and the medication looks normal, give it a try.

### Systems Symptoms: Diarrhea

While the biggest full-body symptom that we see often manifests as a fever, the biggest sub-system symptom we see is the perennial plague on the survivor. It has many nicknames but will be experienced by almost all survivors and it is diarrhea.

There are simple general concepts and rules for dealing with diarrhea:

- Let diarrhea go for the first twenty-four hours to clear out any causative organisms.
- Unless you are moving or already ill, then you need to treat it right away.
- If you are moving or already dehydrated, try to stop it up.
- If diarrhea lasts more than a day, chances are it is a bug, not just bad food.
- Viral diarrhea will be very aggressive, hit hard and fast, and pass in one to three days.
- Bacterial diarrhea takes a while to build up and is slower to go away.
- When fever, vomiting, blood or pus are present, consider antibiotics.
- Antibiotics will not help with viral causes of diarrhea. In all cases, drink fluids, stay hydrated, treat symptoms, and reduce fever.

Now, for tackling what could be one of many different causes, here is a chart of some of the causes of diarrhea and how to help you determine what type you might have so you can best determine how to deal with it. It is important to know that the majority of diarrhea is from a bacterial cause.

## Causes of and Treatments for Diarrhea

There are many other causes of diarrhea but the most common ones are bacterial or viral. Usually, bacterial are less vicious and last longer. Often, the body can beat it with some nutrition and rest. Sometimes antibiotics are needed to end the suffering. The other main cause is viral. These usually hit hard, fast and have a fever but the good news is they usually pass quickly and the person recovers.

The key in survival is to try to let it pass for one to two days, while keeping hydrated, treating the symptoms, and when all else fails, trying some antibiotics. Use the anti-diarrheal medicines if you have some and, if not, some of the alternative remedies listed in this section. Also worth mentioning here is that many of these are internal, and therefore, without oxygen—as such, they are of the gram negative variety.

Also, the other primary sub-system symptom of illness the survivor will encounter is nausea and vomiting. Often it will coincide with diarrhea and taken together, give you a slightly different diagnosis of the causative organism than diarrhea alone. If you have vomiting by itself, it's almost always a direct result of ingesting something the body doesn't like and is rejecting. It's usually very short lived and once empty, with some water and rest, it resolves itself.

Vomiting can also be a side effect of something else such as motion sickness or worry, but in almost all cases, it passes quickly and as such, is not usually a cause for concern unless accompanied with other symptoms like fever and diarrhea. In all cases, the treatment is usually the same: anti-emetics, like Benadryl, and rehydration.

The last of the sub-system symptoms that most survivors will encounter is a headache. There are over thirty different types of headaches, and migraines are just one kind of them.

Migraines usually require specialized attention and if someone in the family suffers them regularly, they'll usually know what brings them on and how best to deal with them. For these special issues, like any other medical issues the family members might have, it's always good to have their specific medications on hand.

For most survivors, headaches will manifest and most of the time, they will be the result of dehydration with the primary treatment being water and rest.

# Real First Aid

We've covered a lot of ground for all the basics of trauma, disease, and illnesses. Now, let's look at the other types of medical and health problems a survivor might encounter. But first, let's clear the air about a commonly misunderstood practice: CPR.

## CPR: The Real Deal

The fact is that everyone is going to die. Sometimes, in very rare circumstances, this can be reversed by CPR. In some states, the out-of-hospital survival rate for CPR patients is as low as 3 percent. Most persons that survive as a result of CPR were already in a hospital, with professionals looking after them and all the follow-up care that goes with the cause for needing CPR in the first place. The rest of people who actually survive after CPR was administered survived because they were witnessed at the time they dropped.

This means two very important things to a survivor. First, if you didn't witness someone go down, and you come upon them, assess them, and find no breathing or pulse, chances are, they will not recover. Second, if you do recover them, consider what might be the cause of the problem in the first place. Most likely, you won't have heart monitors, drugs, IVs, and oxygen to sustain them if you do recover them.

Now, I'm not saying not to try CPR. If you're fit and strong, there are no other patients, you're not in danger from the environment and you think you can recover and sustain them, then give it a go.

There are two reasons for CPR in a survival situation. The first reason is trying to do something for yourself. If you don't want to accept your patient's death, then get down there and try if the situation permits. The second reason is to help the surviving loved ones who may be in too much shock themselves. CPR in a survival situation is mostly for you and the other survivors, not for the dead and dying. It is hard work and will drain you and this must be considered, especially early on in any traumatic crash type scenario.

### Exceptions: Lightning and Drowning

Now, for every rule, there are almost always exceptions and this is true for Survivor CPR, too. If you see a fellow survivor get struck by lightning, or have a bad fall, or drown, and you rescue them, in these cases, CPR is very effective and can very much stand a chance of bringing someone back to life! Therefore, we'll cover some CPR basics since this is not a certifying class. Still, you'll have the concept in case you need to apply it.

The first thing is always to assess. If you try to do CPR on a conscious person they're either going to hit you or hug you! If they are unconscious but breathing, they might puke on you and now you've created a choking situation. If they have a pulse and you start pushing on their chest, you might actually throw the heart out of synch and kill them, so assess first. No breathing, but pulse, give two breaths. No pulse or breaths, then do CPR.

**Precordial Thump**

CPR has already been covered in the early assessment phase. But before you do CPR there is a great little trick to know about called a precordial thump.

This is old school, and some CPR classes no longer teach it, but for the survivor, it is the closest thing to a defibrillator you're going to get in the field.

The heart is amazing and works by automaticity, meaning that it generates its own electrical impulses. It has built-in backups as well. Nodes at the top fire quickly and regulate most things; when they fail, nodes in the middle pick up the slack, but at a slower rate; when they fail, the emergency nodes at the bottom kick in, usually too slow to be healthy, but enough to sustain life. When someone falls, gets struck by lightning, or has drowned and the heart has shut down so it no longer creates a pulse you can detect, often, the little electrical nodes are still firing away but either very weakly or out-of-synch so that the heart is just quivering. In a short period of time, without blood flow pushing oxygen, major organs start shutting down and dying from the lack of oxygen. Your job is to get the oxygen there by returning the blood flow and getting the heart pumping again.

Because the heart is like a little electrical battery, sometimes a jumpstart is all you need to get it back to work. And that is what the precordial thump does. Execute it with one good blow, striking with the bottom (palm aspect) of your fist, right on top of the center of the heart. Use a firm blow but pull back so as to not break ribs.

Very often, if you witness a case of cardiac arrest, a precordial thump will kick start the heart back into operation. It can save a life and save you a lot of work. It shouldn't really be done more than once, or two to three times tops.

**Golden Sixty, Sixty, Six**

This is a guideline to help you understand the bigger picture and what things might mean to you in terms of realistically planning and managing expectations for yourself and other survivors.

### Golden Minute

The first sixty seconds will often dictate a lot about the chances for a patient's survival. If they have a leg chopped off and are bleeding out, chances are, if you don't intervene within that first minute, they will bleed out and die.

If someone has their face smashed and can't breathe for over a minute, chances are they will suffocate and die. If you see this, or it happens to you, stick your fingers right into their neck and hold open a hole for them to breathe out of. The chances of someone surviving without the two critical requirements of blood and air, after more than a minute, are very slim indeed. If there are other pressing matters, you might opt to not attempt rescue. This point is usually where first aid rendered by first responders makes all the difference.

### Golden Hour

The upside to the human response to trauma is a shock response that makes a patient hyperventilate to get more air while blood vessels constrict. This passes quickly, however, and the blood flows and the breathing shallows. During this time your treatments will most impact a patient's chance of survival. If you can get good dressings on the wounds to stop bleeding, and make sure the airway and chest injuries are treated so your patient can breathe effectively, chances are good that he can survive—if he can get further medical treatment. This is the level where, back home, a good paramedic saves lives a lot.

### Golden Six Hours

After first responder aid and stabilization care is given, your patient will need medical or surgical intervention, depending on the damage done. For the survivor, these first six hours will likely come and go without rescue or aid. Most trauma victims with significant organ and tissue damage will begin to expire without surgical intervention.

You must understand this concept. If you are the caregiver in a mass casualty situation in some remote area, chances are that a lot of your work and effort to save some folks might come to naught if no real medical care can be rendered so you must weigh heavily some considerations.

- To whom do you give limited time, energy, and medical supplies?
- Who do you move or not?
- Do you let the person know they are likely not going to make it?
- Do you tell their loved ones what the realistic expectations are?

The golden six hours isn't necessarily when your patient will die. It just means that, by then, major damage will have taken its toll and death is likely not stoppable in the field. Without lots of antibiotics, infection sets in. Major organs start to fail as a result of diminished function and systems begin collapsing. Understanding the long-term importance of the first six hours should help you mentally prepare so that you can better manage the remainder of your survival strategy.

Note: I have found that most of the time, people prefer the truth, so be honest in your assessments to both the dying and the living. Only in a few cases have I seen that people actually know they're going to die but can't or don't want to face it.

## Other Possible Medical Issues

### Dehydration

This a real problem for most people in a survival situation. You can survive for a very long time on small amounts of water if you're not losing too much to the environment or exertion. Survivors, however, will often get diarrhea or other illnesses that cause vomiting. Both of these can significantly contribute to dehydration.

### Kidney Stones

Kidney stones occur a lot in the field for people who are dehydrated over long periods of time. They result from low fluid levels that allow naturally-occurring crystals like calcium to build up into deposits that become like small rocks or pebbles in the ureters, or tubes that drain the waste fluid from the kidney to the bladder.

When these occur, there is sudden and very severe pain in the flanks often accompanied by fever. Usually, they will pass. Have the person rest, often on the opposite side, to allow gravity to help move the stone along the ureter into the bladder. Give pain medication and water if available.

Sometimes, kidney stones build up and cause an obstruction in the urethra near the bladder. This is a medical emergency as the person cannot urinate, and urinary retention has the bladder full and hyper-extended to the point of extreme pain from loin to groin. In these cases have your patient lie upside down, with their back against a tree and their feet up in the air, and massage the bladder area so gravity can help dislodge the stone.

### Jaundice

Jaundice causes yellowing of the eyes and skin. It is nothing more than a byproduct of bilirubin backing up into the blood stream and turning the external tissues

*Ouch! Shells are sharp. Beach shoes are a good idea when you're foraging for seafood. In a survival situation a cut on the foot like this could become infected and dangerous. Best avoided. (Photo credit Ruth England Hawke)*

yellowish. It only backs up when the liver is inflamed, a condition called hepatitis. But this too is only a symptom because something must cause the liver to swell up, such as a virus, parasite, or physical obstruction.

## Diabetes

Diabetes affects a lot of people and as such, you might see it manifest in a survival situation. There are two main types: the kind where the patient needs insulin and the kind where they need sugar.

If your patient needs insulin, they'll have some, or will have told you or will have told you they're out. The bad news is, without more insulin, your patient will not make it. The good news is that only about 10 percent of diabetics are Type 1 diabetic, meaning the patient has too much sugar in his or her blood. Often, stressful situations like survival will worsen the condition, which takes time to set in, anywhere from hours to days.

If your patient's breath smells fruity and they are thirsty and urinating a lot, their skin is hot and dry, and they are breathing deeply and rapidly, they are worsening. The problem is exacerbated by starvation as this causes the liver to start generating more ketones and glycerol, which in turn worsens the condition. In a crash situation, search for insulin among the wreckage since finding some is your patient's only hope.

If your patient needs sugar, the problem has a much easier fix—a shot of sugar—but, without it, your patient could be in real trouble, too. If they are suddenly hungry, confused, angry, and clammy skinned, chances are they are going into insulin shock, meaning too much insulin in the blood. Check to see if your patient is wearing any diabetes tags. Be sure to get them to drink a sugary drink or eat something sweet. If you're having trouble telling which way your diabetic patient is going, the good news is that giving a candy bar to the other type of diabetic won't hurt them. If in doubt, whip it out.

## Poison

There are really only two courses of action available to the survivor for first-aid responses to poisons. If poison is ingested, vomit it out. If you can't do that, or it's been too long, try to neutralize the poison internally by consuming charcoal-based fluids. If the poison comes from contact, then suck out poisons from bites with something other than your mouth and clean the wound. Clean off the area and treat the symptoms.

## Shock

Most people have been exposed to and understand allergies. Allergies occur when something in the environment comes into contact with the patient and their body has a negative response to that stimulation. Sometimes, the reaction is mild like a runny nose and watery eyes; sometimes, it's worse like a rash or difficulty breathing; sometimes it's so extreme that without intervention, the body kills itself by over-responding.

This is true of anaphylactic shock. For example, when someone is stung by a bee, the body might have a strong response that ends up killing the person because a constricted airway prevents breathing and swelling constricts circulation. This is a life-threatening emergency if untreated. The good news is that only a few hundred people die a year from it, but many of those who lived had two things handy that you likely won't have during a survival situation. Epinephrine or adrenaline injections and diphenhydramine or Benadryl are the two drugs used universally to treat anaphylactic shock. These can be purchased from most pharmacies and should live in every first-aid kit.

The chances of surviving true anaphylaxis are slim without these. If you have them, get them into the person right away or they could die within minutes. If you do not have them, be prepared to put something down your patient's throat to keep that airway open. In time, chances are that the swelling will go down, but you must keep them alive long enough for the body to do that. In a worst-case scenario, consider cricothyroidotomy. Also, any antihistamine-type drug is better than none, so if anyone has motion sickness tablets or sleeping tablets, try them while your patient can still swallow.

The other types of shock are nice to know but not really relevant to the survivor.

- **Neurogenic:** When the brain is damaged and the nerves are not passing their signals correctly, major organ functions are impaired. In the survival situation, this is mostly fatal.

- **Hypovolemic:** Losing too much blood can cause shock. Without stopping the bleeding quickly and replacing the volume of fluids lost with IV fluids, chances are someone in this type of shock will die, and quickly. Stop the bleeding right away, at all costs. During hypovolemic shock, try elevating the patient's legs, even wrapping the limbs tightly to reduce—but not prevent—blood flow to the limbs. That way, the blood can stay concentrated in the chest and keep the vital organs functioning.

- **Cardiogenic:** This accompanies a heart attack. Chances of surviving in a survival situation are extremely low. If someone is having a heart attack, here are some field things that might help. Put the patient's face in a bowl of ice water, as doing this invokes a mammalian drive reflex that slows heart rate down and can stop a potential "V-fib" heart problem, when the ventricles fibrillate and can't pump. Rub the patient's neck where the jugular veins are located. This can also cause a slowing down of the heart rate and preclude a heart attack.

This is called a carotid baroreceptor response and can be used to calm people down when stressed as well.

- **Septicemic:** When your patient has a systemic infection, they'll be burning up with fever. Without antibiotics, they will not make it.
- **Psychogenic:** This is my favorite kind of shock. Sometimes, people just see things or hear things that cause them to faint. When this happens, momentarily, the brain lets go and the blood vessels all expand or vasodilate at the same time, which causes blood pressure to drop and the brain to temporarily lose oxygen. This will pass quickly and completely. Just make sure the patient doesn't hurt their head when they pass out, lay him down, and wait a minute. The same goes for when someone hyperventilates; they will over oxygenate, pass out, and stop breathing for a minute or two but as soon as the carbon dioxide builds back up in the lungs, it will trigger restarted breathing.

The best thing for any type of shock is to try and treat the cause. Keep the patient comfortable, care for the symptoms, and hope.

## Elements and Exposure

Braving the weather is mostly common sense. If it's hot, stay cool. If it's cold, stay warm. If it's wet, get dry. If it's dry, find some wet. But what about when you can't get out of the elements? Here's what to look for and what you can try to do about it. In severe cases, you might not be able to do anything except take it with the hopes of making it out or getting rescued: your only real chance of surviving.

### Sunburn

Sunburn is something most of us have experienced. Essentially, sunburn is like any other burn in that there are three degrees. Chances are that you'll never live long enough to see the third. The treatments are the same as well.

First-degree burns cause the top layer of skin to turn red. These hurt but aren't serious. Second-degree burns go deeper and cause blisters. Later infection is the real danger. Third-degree burns go past the skin and do not hurt but are the most dangerous.

The treatment is the same for all burns, as follows:

- Keep cool and dry.
- Use pain medication when needed and available.
- If the burn is deep, consider using topical antibiotics. Burn victims need a lot of fluid, as they will ooze white blood cells and dehydrate.

- Do not lance blisters. If you must, lance at the base, not at the top.
- If the burn is third degree, the skin will be grey and painless; the nerves are burnt. Victims will need antibiotics because the skin is open and the body exposed to infection.
- If a large surface area is burned, like an entire limb, consider escharotomy. This is done by slicing through the burned flesh with a scalpel or knife, not too deeply. If the entire limb is burnt, there will be swelling inside, but the skin will not give so make a slice along the entire outside and inside burned part of the limb. This will allow circulation and promote healing and prevent necrosis, or the dying of the tissue, which causes gangrene to set in. Gangrene of an extremity, without amputation, will lead to septicemia and death.

## Lightning Strikes

Lightning strikes can cause burns and are to be treated in the same way depending upon the severity. Unfortunately, serious internal damage might be done as well. Dark urine indicates that the prognosis for survival is poor. The good news is that while thousands get struck every year, less than 10 percent of strikes are fatal.

## Heat Exhaustion

Heat exhaustion is merely getting overdone in the sun. The key to avoiding it is to rest regularly, drink lots, stay cool, and don't work too hard in the heat. If your skin is cold and clammy, you're still okay; just take it easy as heat exhaustion can quickly lead to heat stroke.

## Heat Stroke

Heat stroke is a flat-out killer. It strikes when the body gets so hot and dehydrated that the cooling mechanism of sweating stops. If a person passes out and presents hot and dry skin, they are in a bad way. If you're working, and don't feel well and notice that you've stopped sweating, stop immediately. This is a life-threatening emergency. Cool down by any means. Get into shade, jump in cold water, strip naked, fan yourself, or put a wet cloth on your forehead and face, underarms, groin, side of the neck, behind the knees and in the arm joint. The same places you can take a pulse or use for pressure points can be used to cool the blood and reduce the core temperature. Dark urine is a bad sign and means the brain is already cooking. Without fluids and reduced temperature, someone in this state will expire.

## Sunstroke

Sunstroke is some people's way of saying sunburned and dehydrated. It is not to be confused with heat stroke, which is a life-threatening emergency.

## Prickly Heat

Prickly heat is an interesting phenomenon. In hot environments, when sweating a lot, especially on the oily parts of skin, the pores will become blocked. This stimulates the tiny nerves on the hair follicles and will be interpreted by the brain as a burning or electrifying sensation. The solution is simply to wash the area with soap and water.

## Jungle Rot or Immersion Foot

Jungle rot or immersion foot is simply another name for when the tissues of the feet begin to disintegrate as a result of being wet too long and then being torn off from too much friction, usually from the boot during walking. The treatment is easy: dry your feet. Take breaks and air them out. Failure to do so will invite infection and become debilitating. This can be fatal if it immobilizes you in a bad location or infection is systemic.

## Ingrown Toenails

Ingrown toenails happen a lot for soldiers and there are many techniques for dealing with them. As a long-term survivor, chances are that you will encounter this if you have to make a long-distance movement as most people do not own or wear shoes designed for such. There are two main schools of thought on this problem, as follows:

### Trimming

Shave the top of the nail so it is paper-thin. Then trim a deep "V" into the middle, and the toenail will come away from the side, easing the pain and pressure.

### Removal

I go for this. It's painful, but if it doesn't solve the problem permanently, it certainly solves the problem for a long time and right away. The trick is to simply slice the very edge of the toenail out. Take a small blade, with the cutting edge facing up, slide the point under the nail and try cutting the nail only, with as little damage to the quick below as you can. The secret is to cut down past the cuticle to the root. Once the blade slides easily without resistance, you're past the nail and can stop. Slide it out. Drain the pus, stop the bleeding, clean the wound, and put a good dressing on it. Contrary to popular opinion, a person who undergoes this can walk that day. Still, it's best to wait. Rest with the foot elevated, and the pain will subside in a day or two.

## Frostbite

Frostbite happens when the skin is damaged by cold, rupturing cells and causing blisters. You'll know when you have frostbite because it burns or stings at first. And like third-degree burns, once the body part stops hurting, you're in trouble as it's then frozen. Treat the symptoms just like a burn but remember some important differences about recovering from frostbite.

Do not thaw things out unless you can keep them thawed. Re-freezing of digits or limbs will worsen their condition and outcome. Use the body to get frostbitten parts warm again: feet against stomachs, hands in armpits. Do not use water or fire for re-warming; this must be a gentle process or tissue damage will result.

## Snow Blindness

Snow blindness happens very easily when your eyes experience direct, prolonged exposure to the strong UV rays from bright sunlight reflecting off snow or ice. Protect the eyes when you can with glasses or goggles. Two sticks worn like glasses so you see through the slits or a strip of cloth with a small slit you can see through will also work. In a worst-case scenario, put something dark like shoe polish or mud under your eyes to deflect some of the ultraviolet light.

# Commonplace Health Problems

Okay, now that we've covered some serious stuff, let's look at some of the more commonplace, and less life-threatening, health problems a survivor might face.

## Boils

Boils are an accumulation of pus and dead tissue—occur as hygiene deteriorates. They can become quite painful and unnecessarily infected but treatment is rather easy. Use a warm compress to try and raise the infection closer to the surface. Then lance the boil with a hot pin and drain the boil from the head. If the boil is very large, use a clean piece of cloth as a drain by stuffing it into the wound and leaving a piece hanging out so the remaining pus can ooze out as the wound closes and heals. Keep clean afterwards.

### Fungus

Fungus, athlete's foot, crotch rot, and ringworm are all fungi that can form anywhere on the body and are common complaints of survivors. The best treatment in a survival situation is sun, but this will only keep the fungus at bay and will not cure it. Only anti-fungal drugs will remove these once they take hold of human tissue. They are unpleasant and uncomfortable but will go away once treated.

### Hemorrhoids

Hemorrhoids cause a lot of people grief and this can be especially true for the survivor suffering from ailments that cause excess strain on bowel movements. Avoid hemorrhoids with the following tips:

- Maintain a balanced diet.
- Stay well hydrated.
- Don't push too hard during defecating.
- Lubricate bowel movements.
- If these don't keep you from getting hemorrhoids, try sitting in some water to let it reduce the swelling a bit.

Deal with persistent hemorrhoids by using a rubber band or piece of string. Tie off the offending protrusion and cut off all circulation, which will kill that piece of tissue and stop the pain. Eventually, it will drop right off. Sounds rough, but it will work.

### Ticks

Ticks are a common problem in the woods. Whatever you do, do not burn them off. This is just like squeezing them. You defeat the whole purpose of taking them off, which is to stop disease. Use tweezers or string tied around them or even a small toothpick-sized twig to slowly dislodge a tick. Don't squeeze to get them off or just rip them off. If you leave the head, this will get infected fast.

### Leeches

Leeches are the ticks of the jungle and swamp world. Don't rip them off since that'll cause open sores and infection. The best way is the same way as with the tick: slowly take them off by separating the sucker head (small end) from the flesh. If leeches get up into your nose or somewhere you can't use the gentle removal technique, do burn these boogers with a match or cigarette cherry, or use salt, ash, or tobacco spit.

## Bugs in the Ears

The best way to get rid of bugs in your ear canal is with oil. Digging can lead to rupturing the ear drum, which not only hurts (although it does heal with relatively little scarring or hearing loss) but could open you up to a bad infection since there will be a dead bug carcass rotting inside there. Try some oil, any type, as this will drown the critter quickly and then you can drain him out.

# Sprains and Strains

Sprains and strains are typical injuries for survivors, as they do many physical activities in an unstructured environment. The two types of injuries are often confused.

### Muscle Experience Strains

Muscle experience strains occur when you lift too much and the muscle tears or tendons stretch from hyperextension. You'll know it when it happens, as there will be a lot of pain in the muscle group.

### Ligament Strains

Ligaments connect bones to bones, holding the skeleton together. Sprains often happen to ankles when people are running and step on something that cause the weight of the body to force the ankle into an over-extended position. There are three types of sprain. Here's what they mean to you as a survivor:

- If you twist an ankle, but don't fall, it is a Type 1 sprain with a one-week recovery.
- If you twist and the pain makes you fall, it's a Type 2 sprain with a one-month recovery. If you twist and hear a pop, it's a Type 3 sprain with a one-year recovery.

All three sprains hurt and all three swell; the difference is the healing time required. You can move on a sprained ankle the same day as the injury if you need to, but rest time is required in order to prevent it from happening again and becoming a permanently weak point in your structure. Many athletes hurt their ankle and are too impatient to let it mend properly.

The good news for a survivor is that treatment of strains and sprains is the same regardless of severity. The bad news is that you won't likely have the main component: ice. When treating strains and sprains, remember RICE during the first forty-eight hours.

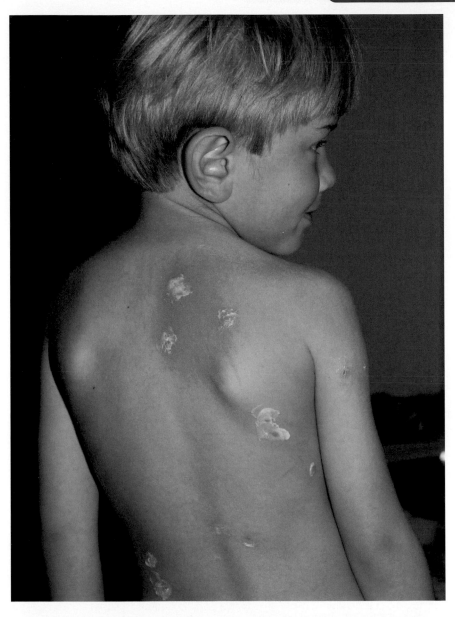

*Prevention is always better than the cure when it comes to bug bites, particularly in areas that harbor insect-borne disease. The best way to avoid mosquito bites is to wear long-sleeved shirts and long pants made from a thick tightly woven fabric, I've watched mosquitoes poke their nasty proboscas straight through light materials. For children it's better to use a natural citronella-based repellent on exposed flesh; these are very effective in most cases although in heavily-infested areas you may be forced to break out the DEET. If you don't have access to shop bought repellents, oils such cooking oil and baby oil are a good barrier. Mud also works though you have to keep applying it.*
*(Photo credit Ruth England Hawke)*

R: Rest, get off the injury, and give it a break if you can. If not, favor it, a lot.

I: Ice reduces swelling during the initial twenty-four to forty-eight hours following a sprain or strain.

C: Compress the injured area using an ACE bandage for support.

E: Elevate the injury to take your weight off it and reduce the inflammation.

After the first forty-eight hours, the equation changes and you should apply heat to the damaged area, which increases circulation to the area and speeds recovery. So you keep the RCE and swap the "I for ice" with "H for heat" and get CHER. Remember: when you sprain you ankle, eat your RICE for twenty-four hours before meeting CHER.

## Dislocation

Dislocation is a possible medical issue in the wild that is extremely painful but easily managed. It's also relatively easy to diagnose. If someone else experiences this injury, follow these steps to relocate the limb:

• Take a seat on the ground beside your patient.

• Wrap something like a towel around his wrist so you can grip it; it will likely be sweaty.

• Place your foot into your patient's armpit.

• Slowly pull backward until the arm is stretched out towards you.

• Let the arm slide back into place; the muscle will guide it there for you.

The arm will ache and not be right again for a long time but the immediate pain relief will be extreme and your patient will thank you for it. If you experience the injury, relocation is more challenging:

• Wrap something like a rope around your wrist, padding it if you can.

• Tie the other end of the rope to a tree.

• Place your feet against the base of the tree.

• Push yourself away at an angle so the rope extends your arm.

• Allow your arm to pop back in.

• Try not to pass out.

The same principles apply when a leg is dislocated to the front or back. Instead of placing the foot into the armpit, you'll use the groin and pull. Common sense will help you get the leg back into the groove; you'll know it when you've done it.

# Fractures

Fracture is a fancy name for a broken bone. There are many different kinds but it comes down to two major ones for the survivor.

## Closed Fractures

These break the bone but keep everything still inside the person.

## Open Fractures

These are the kind where the bone is not only broken, but it's decided to go and stick out of the person's body. These present the additional problem of deciding whether to try and put the bone back in or not.

## Fracture Checklist

The fracture checklist will move you through the few key considerations for treatment:

1.  Assess Bone
    These indicate the presence of a fracture. Check for an obvious deformity like a right angle where it shouldn't be. Check for crepitus, a crunchy sound of moving broken bones around. Be gentle and don't cause additional damage even though you must feel and manipulate a bit.

    If there is pain upon any manipulation or movement of the joints, consider the bone broken.
2.  Assess Flesh
    If the answer to any of these is "no," you've got repairs to do before splinting:
    ○  Pulsing: Is there a pulse below the fracture?
    ○  Temperature: Is the part of the fractured limb below the break as warm as the part above it?
    ○  Feeling: Does the patient have feeling in the part below the break?
    ○  Movement: Can they move anything below the break?

## Preparing to Splint a Closed Fracture

If there is no major deformity, you can splint the break mostly as it is. If there is some major bend in the road, you have to move it. Normally, you'd only move it enough to get a general sense of normalcy and to keep the pulse flowing so the limb doesn't lose circulation and die, *but*, for the survivor, the chances are that you will be there awhile so you must consider moving a highly-deformed broken bone so that it can heal properly. That means moving the deformity all the way back to a normal position. Follow these guidelines when doing so:

- Assess the patient's pulse before and after the manipulation. The pulse must be kept open. If the limb is cold, there isn't enough blood flow and you'll need to move it some more.
- Stroke the patient's skin with your fingernail to assess whether he has feeling. If so, great. If not, that's not great but it's okay. The same goes for whether your patient has function or not. If he can wiggle his fingers or toes, super. If not, it can wait.
- If your patient can wiggle an extremity, see how much strength he has by having him push a little against your hand in all the normal directions.
- The key is to keep the same amount of function after splinting as your patient had before you applied the splint.

Assessment is important because it allows you to make sure you are setting their splint the best you can without the benefit of x-rays.

### Preparing to Splint an Open Fracture

You will encounter additional challenges from an open fracture. All modern medical practice says not to put the bone back inside and this hold true for almost all environments. The exception is when infection could sneak in—then try to get the bone back inside. If you have a clean dressing to place on the bone, and can pad it so it doesn't get bumped or moved around, then this is the recommended course of action. Dress it and keep the dressing dry, so it doesn't invite more bacteria in. Pad and protect the break, splinting the limb the best you can, and keep the patient immobilized.

If you are sure help is nowhere near and dressings and antibiotics are in short supply or nonexistent, consider placing the bone back inside and letting the body be the dressing and the immune system be the antibiotics. Clean the bone the best you can before you place it back in the body.

If you make it back, your patient can always have surgery to repair and correct the break. Reapply the principles of assessment to determine if your job is done.

### Splinting a Fracture

The principles of splinting are simple:

- Splint broken bones in a functional position or as close to it as you can get.
- You can use boards or sticks or anything inflexible as a splint.

- Tie the splinting board in two places above the fracture and two places below it.
- Immobilize one joint above the fracture and one joint below it.
- Pad all the boney parts to avoid causing ulcers or sores.
- Reassess the pulse after you place each tie to avoid cutting off circulation.
- Use ice and heat to promote healing as with sprains and strains.
- If you have them, use anti-inflammatory drugs for fractures, strains, and sprains. If the wound was open, use antibiotics if you have them.
- If you have nothing, use an anatomical splint. Tie the broken limb to the body to immobilize it. Tie a broken leg to the other leg, tie a broken arm to the chest, etc. Broken fingers and toes are easily taped to the neighboring good digit.

## Animal Issues as Medical Problems

It's imperative to teach your kids about the animal threats in your environment and to train them how to react to an encounter. Animals are a food source for the survivor, but they can be a threat as well. After all, we're in their environment and must respect the rules of that situation.

Some animals like tigers, sharks, alligators and the like see humans as a food source. The secret to not becoming a meal is making yourself a hard target. But you can only do this by understanding your environment.

"Always make noise" should be the first rule for survivors. This contradicts everything I learned in Special Forces but you do not want to be stealthy if you are surviving, for two reasons. The first is that you hope someone hears you and comes to your rescue. The second is that you want to give all the animals out there every chance you can to get out of your area. Most animals will leave humans alone. The exception to being noisy is if you are hunting.

So, what do you do when you encounter animals that can hurt you? Let's take a look.

### Water-Based Creatures

We'll just cover a few things about sea creatures in this chapter. For now, be concerned with the dangers and treatments for these.

Poisonous sea creatures to keep an eye out for include surgeon fish, zebra fish, stone fish, cone shell, auger shell, blue-ringed octopus, weaver fish, toad fish, and sea snakes. If it's brightly colored, avoid it. If it bites, stings, or pokes, consider the bite, sting, or poke poisonous.

Poisonous creatures to avoid eating include trigger fish, porcupine fish, and puffer fish. If you're unsure, and it doesn't look like something you'd see in the supermarket, chuck it.

Poking, puncturing, or stinging sea creatures should be handled carefully. These include sting rays, which have the extra kicker of being a poisonous poke; sea urchins, with nasty puncture infections and venom too; box and Portuguese man-of-war jellyfish, which can kill; and even catfish and the like can poke you hard when you try to handle them. Be very careful when fishing and removing any fish from your line or net.

## Dangerous Sea Creatures

Piranhas can be dangerous if you're trapped in their environment, but mostly, you can get away. Just brush them away as you exit if they start on you upon entering the water.

### Crocodiles and Alligators

Crocodiles and alligators of any kind should be respected and steered clear of, but mostly they'll steer clear of you, or at least grant you passage. If in the water above the waist with them, be wary as you are technically on the menu. Those in salt water tend to be particularly ornery, and can move very fast over short distances. You can fight back when they're not too big and stand a chance, but in the water, once they get a good grip, your chances are slim. Avoid water at night and movement near water at night when they're most active hunting.

### Sharks

If they're bigger than you, and you're in the water, you're on their terms. You might get lucky and be left alone, or get some good whacks or pokes in their nose and eye, and deter them. Try and skip this step. Otherwise, try not to urinate in the water or make irregular panicked swimming motions. Be prepared to fight hard if attacked.

### Barracudas

Barracudas are rarely a concern for a survivor, but if caught on a line they can be fierce. Be careful when capturing, but they are mighty tasty.

### Moray Eels

Moray eels are usually not a concern for the survivor as they hunt at night, are generally shy, and will avoid people. If free diving for lobsters you might get bitten, but try to never stick your hand where you can't see. Moray eel bites aren't poisonous, but they can get infected. If bitten, stop the bleeding, clean the wound, and apply a dressing. Do the best you can to avoid these and if it happens, treat it the best you can in a survival situation.

With stinging and poisonous creatures, there are a couple other things to think about. Box jellyfish, Portuguese man-of-war, fire coral, and many other stinging sea creatures use similar mechanisms, called a nematocyst, to cause a sting. These cause a painful burning sensation. Factors like how much skin was contacted, where on the body the stings were situated, and the condition of the victim (whether elderly, ill, etc.) will determine your patient's systemic response. Sometimes people get sick, nauseous, vomit, have anaphylaxis, or even paralysis and death. Usually, they just get a bad sting that passes in an hour or two and then leaves blisters within twenty-four hours.

The first treatment is obviously removal of the cause. Get the stingers off the person. Don't use your bare hands. Even dead creatures can have some sting left in them. Use vinegar, ammonia, or alcohol to stop the nematocysts from firing. If you have nothing else, use sea water, not fresh water as this will trigger the stinging. Baking soda or shaving cream is helpful for removing the nematocysts. Treat the sting site like any burn, by relieving the pain and dressing the wound.

There is very little that you as a survivor can do for poisons from bites, stings, or ingestion. But a little knowledge, a lot of caution, and some common sense will serve you well for prevention.

## Land Animals

Knowing habitats is one of the best methods of preventing conflict with critters, many of which like to live in and under things. Carelessness and complacency will get you more times than not, so stay hyper-vigilant. Every time you lift up a stick for firewood or to build a shelter, look first. Stir the foliage with your stick and give anything that might be in there a chance to either leave or make its presence known to you so you can avoid it or eat it.

I don't recommend anyone try and take on any big game when surviving. The chances are that you will lose, or even if you win the battle, you might lose the war by incurring injuries or losing or damaging supplies. If confrontation is unavoidable, below are some species-specific recommendations to help you deal with it the best you can follow. That said, if you can't prevent an animal injury or bite, treat the wounds, bites, scratches, and fractures like any other.

### Bears

Bears should be avoided at all costs. They're great hunters, can smell a good distance, run fast and far, and climb. So, it's not like you can really escape. If it looks like they're headed your way, consider your options at that moment and see if gently walking away will get you out of there. Never turn your back and run; this will make a bear see you as prey. If you have food, toss it to them. If you think the bear wants to attack, look for a river or a tree. Be prepared to engage. Try the passive technique of balling up, letting it whack you a few times and then it might leave you alone. If fighting back, a sharp poke or stab in the eyes and face with a heavy, strong stick or spear just might discourage them.

## Cats

If you encounter a big cat in the wild, try and make your physical presentation bigger so you look less like something small for them to prey on. Raise your arms and your voice. Wave your weapon above you but not at them just yet. You want to discourage, not challenge. If the big cat tries to circle you, it is determined and you will have to fight. If it starts looking off to the sides, give it room to pass you by.

General principles of fighting and self-defense apply here. Wait for the cat to swing and draw inward with your spear during its swing, and as soon as the swipe with the paw passes by you, strike straight inward for the eyes. This will prevent the animal from trapping your spear within its grasp since your pole will be on the outside of its arm, allowing you to thrust into its face and neck with all your might and reducing the chances for it to spin around towards you. The cat will have to peel away from your spear and, psychologically, this breaks part of the animal's momentum as it must now square back up on you to refocus its attack.

## Dogs

Direct is the best way. Any wild dog-like creatures that have decided to directly confront you must be directly confronted. You can't hide from their amazing sense of smell and you can't outrun them. If confronted by a wolf or pack of wolves, keep eye contact. If you must look around, do so slowly and purposely so as to not convey a hint of fear, panic, or intention of flight.

The upside to fighting wolves—unlike big cats—is that wolves only have a mouth full of teeth to contend with. They are, however, team hunters and one or two will attack while the others flank you. So get your back up against a tree if you can, channel the attackers to your front, and then begin eye-poking, neck-gouging, and throat-jabbing with your weapon.

## Bulls, Rhinos, Hippos, and Elephants

These animals are simply too big for you to fight. Your best bet is to outmaneuver them. Find a strong tree and run circles around it. If they can't touch you, they can't hurt you. And if they can't pummel that tree over, chances are, you can turn circles around that tree over a shorter distance and faster than they can. With enough frustration, hopefully they will give up. If you don't see a tree or boulder, try waiting until they get close and then step or jump quickly to the side bullfighter-style. Do not get off your feet, or you might not get on them again.

## Toxic Land Aniamls

Many creatures in nature have the ability to defend themselves with some sort of bite or sting. They often inject venom with this bite or sting. Poisons come from contact or ingestion; anything else toxic is delivered by envenomation. There are many different types of venoms but they can be broken down into three main categories.

### Hemotoxins

Hemotoxins get into your blood stream and cause the rupturing of cells, preventing clotting or destroying organs by *lysis*, or breaking the cells. With these kinds of bites, the bleeding usually doesn't stop and there is a lot of pain and swelling and fever. These symptoms usually present with blood or blood-filled blisters at the bite site and a lot of pain.

### Neurotoxins

Neurotoxins paralyze the victim by attacking the nervous system and cause death through respiratory failure. The key indicators here are very little pain and bleeding at the site but rapid onset of heart palpitations and abdominal cramps.

### Cytoxins

Cytoxins actually destroy cells. This type is not so much of concern for the survivor except for the brown recluse spider.

### Snake Bites

Many snakes only bite humans out of fear from a surprise encounter, which means most snake bites are non-envenoming. Even then, there is still the chance for a nasty infection so the wound must be cleaned; also, the person should be treated as if there was envenomation until time and lack of symptoms prove otherwise. Snake toxins are usually quick-acting so if you don't see signs and symptoms within a few hours, chances are, you are okay.

The treatment for snake bites is very simple. Keep calm. The venom will act faster if you panic so move slowly, relax your breathing, lie down (away from the snake hopefully), and raise the bite above the heart if possible. Remove rings, watches, or any articles of clothing near the bite that might cause constriction once the person swells up. With hemotoxins, swelling can be quite severe.

Do not:

- Cut. This will only cause wounds while letting the venom contact more blood.
- Suck with your mouth. The venom will get absorbed into your blood stream.
- Use ice. It won't help, though it won't really hurt either.
- Use a tourniquet. The venom will get in anyway and this hurts the limb if there is no venom.

Do:

- Use suction devices if they are available at the time of the bite. These have been shown to reduce the amount of venom by some 30 percent if applied within the first three minutes. After that, what is done is done and there isn't any point, but hey, I'd try anyway.
- Use a constricting band two fingers or two inches above the bite—between the bite and the heart. This reduces the amount of venous blood flow, or blood flow through surface vessels carrying blood back to the heart. Test the difference between a constricting band and a tourniquet with two fingers, which you should be able to get under a constricting band but not a tourniquet.
- Treat the symptoms. If you suspect a hemotoxin, try not to give aspirin as that is a blood thinner and will only speed up hemorrhaging.
- Clean and dress the bite. Always apply the principles of wound management.

The truth is that bees kill more people every year than snakes do. Most snakes won't attack people and will flee the first chance they get but, if cornered, most snakes will fight back. This is when they are ready with venom waiting.

### Other Biters

Scorpions, wasps, and ants bite. They hurt but most either do not inject venom at all or rarely inject enough to be dangerous for healthy, full-grown adults. Children, elderly people, and, unfortunately, weak and famished survivors can succumb to these venoms. So, it is good to know that some scorpions are venomous and others aren't and the same is true of tarantulas and other spiders. But treat them all like they have venom, by trying to avoid them; if bitten, treat it. As a survivor, there isn't a lot more you can do.

For most bites of this nature, wilderness first-aid treatment calls for cryotherapy or ice. Chances are, however, that you won't have ice, so clean the wound, dress, it, keep your patient calm, and look for signs of hemo- or neurotoxin. Remove stingers gently, by scraping away from the point of entry so as to not push more venom into the injection site. Gently brush off brightly-colored critters like caterpillars as these things can sting and some have barbs. The rule of thumb is to go gentle with the little creatures.

Spiders come in many shapes and sizes and a bite is a bite, but if you get bit and see the spider, the basic rules of which ones have venom are: yellow, red, or white spots and dark black or brown bodies. Most spiders do not kill humans.

The brown recluse is an interesting case. It is a little brown spider with a big bite but often people don't know they've been bitten until they find a little swollen area with blister and a bulls-eye look. It might have a little pain that, after a few hours, turns itchy. The reason is that this spider injects a cytotoxin that kills cells. What's happening is that all the tissue is being killed: the nerves, the blood, the muscle. Usually, the toxin wears itself out as it spreads and stops killing cells. The skin usually stays on the top, looking dead and grey until the whole thing sloughs off and leaves a small crater.

Normally, cytotoxin wears itself out after only one to two inches but wounds have been known to be up to ten inches. This becomes significant when a person can't afford to lose six or seven inches of flesh at the bite location. As they're not aggressive, most brown recluse bites are on the butt or back from sleeping on these spiders. But if someone is bitten on the neck or face, you should not let the necrosis spread. A medical person would excise or cut it out to stop the necrosis. For most survivors, this is not a medically-viable option, but should be considered depending on confirmation of the necrotic bite in an area where a serious threat to health might result. A little digging into the bulls-eye will show that it is all dead tissue under the wound. It's up to you. Treat what's left like all wounds.

Bees deserve special mention. Not because they kill, although they do, but because the key here is avoidance. Bees normally make a hive ten to thirty feet off the ground. Avoid these; getting honey is too risky for any survivor to consider. Give way and move away. If you happen to stir them up and they come for you, try squatting and holding still. If they spot you, run through thick brush to keep them off you and head for water if you can. They'll give up pretty quickly, but do not hang around, and keep moving.

**Worms**

Now, for everybody's favorite—worms, also known as helminths or internal parasites. Most people have them and live with them just fine. As a survivor, there is a good chance you'll get them as you'll be subjected to uncontrolled food and water sources. Mostly, you'll be fine, but in some circumstances, they might immediately cause poor health. Over a period of time, they could become very medically significant to you.

The bottom line is to expect to contract worms, but know that you'll mostly be alright. Seek testing and treatment once you're rescued or recovered if any long-term abnormalities present after the experience. (Note: wear footgear at all times to prevent many worms!)

Consult the CDC or NHS to find out what parasitic worms are in your area, research how they manifest as signs and symptoms, and what medications treat them and then get some to have on hand in your med kit. The upside to worms, is that they are mostly all treatable and the drugs to cure them are usually not too expensive.

### Rabies

Rabies cannot be cured. Rabies is pretty rare, especially in people. To contract it, you have to be bitten by a rabid creature within the few days they can spread it.

Rabies is a virus that can affect all mammals. It gets into the nervous system and causes great pain to all the senses and makes it difficult to swallow or speak, causing excessive salivation and tearing of the eyes. It is extremely painful and death is always the result.

There are preventive vaccines that will help increase the chances of the post-exposure vaccines working. The post-exposure vaccines will work most of the time if given early enough. The incubation period is about two weeks to two months. Once rabies kicks in and the first signs appear, there is almost no hope of surviving, no matter what level of medical care is available. As a survivor, treat all aggressive animals as if they have rabies. Avoid being bitten. If attacked by an animal under circumstances that seem out of character, assume rabies exposure. Make all attempts to get to medical care ASAP. If you or another survivor starts to manifest rabies symptoms, consider quarantine measures for the protection of everyone else.

## Being Well in the Wild

There are no limits to the trials and tribulations that a family surviving might encounter. This chapter gave you a decent foundation in the basics of the body, health, medicine, trauma, and general first-aid care as it applies to someone with limited means of surgical treatment, physician counsel, and pharmaceutical support. There is no way to teach years of medicine, training, knowledge, experience, and science in the short space of any one book. Our purpose is to give hope to people in extreme situations by telling them what to realistically expect and supply emergency measures to consider during extreme circumstances. The best treatment is prevention, and the best prevention is preparation, avoidance, caution, and common sense. Remember to go slow and be safe, in all ways and in all things.

# CHAPTER NINE

# TOOLS

When it comes to survival weapons, we prefer to call them tools as they are primarily meant to help you survive. So, we encourage parents to use the word tool to enforce the concept that these things are only meant to help save lives.

The first thing your family needs do in a survival situation is to make an inventory of what you do have. Take anything in your vehicle that can be used as a tool or weapon. Everything else you need to survive—in terms of weapons and tools—you'll have to make with the materials you find around you in your environment.

*You should always have at least one survival kit packed and ready to go. As you might imagine, the Hawke household has many placed strategically in various spots. Always rotate any perishable items like batteries and food and make sure your children know where the kits are and also that they know how to use the contents. If they have their own kits that they are responsible for, even better. (Photo credit Ruth England Hawke)*

Of course, you will likely be in an environment in which you may cross paths with predators. So, as you begin looking for shelter and fire materials, and water, the first thing to do is to pick up a stick or rock to use as a protective weapon.

## Weapons First

There are two things that must be with any survivor at all times: a stick and a knife. It will be up to the parents to decide what kind of knife to get for their kids based on needs, skills, and maturity, but even a simple knife is important for them to have at least in their backpacks.

We recommend a small folding knife for most kids to just have in their pocket or back pack. We recommend all folding knives have locking blades. A non-locking blade knife tends to be very dangerous, especially for kids.

A locking blade will prevent most mishaps. There are different types, but we recommend the button locks as the easiest and safest for kids to use. A fixed blade in a sheath is even better as it's stronger, so it has more use, but often weigh a bit more. However, it's easy to throw them in a backpack if the kid can carry it, but once a survival situation happens, it's best to let the kid wear it on a belt or on a string over their shoulder so it is always on them in case of predators.

*Chopping garden herbs with Uncle Dale. It's good to include a child in as many different parts of a task as you can so they can learn and feel some ownership over the process. Even a very small child can use a razor sharp knife with the correct supervision. (Photo credit Ruth England Hawke)*

*Getting children to carve soap sculptures is fun and it helps them become familiar with using a knife without risk of injury. By carving a bar of soap with a plastic picnic knife, Megan is honing her blade skills in absolute safety with no need for supervision.*
*(Photo credit Lisa Williams)*

*Robin is demonstrating the Blood Circle here. This is a fantastic safety practice that's taught in the Boy Scouts to prevent injury to others when using a knife. The child stands with their arm outstretched and their knife closed in their hand and then turns 360 degrees, creating an imaginary circle. If there is no one within this safety zone the child may open their knife and start using it. If anyone else enters the imaginary circle, the knife must be closed until they leave. I don't know who came up with this idea but it's great. (Photo credit Romy Melville-Evans)*

Just make them rehearse always looking at the knife when sheathing it, stopping for three seconds, then looking again and gently sliding back into place. Enforce this every time they put it away.

Now, back to that inventory, what you have available will determine which one is the priority. If you have a knife already, reach for a stick as soon as possible.

If you don't have a knife, fine for now—a stick is actually easier to produce and handier in most cases. Let's look at what is so important about these two items and ways to go about making them.

## The Stick

Picture a standard, sturdy walking stick as your intended quarry. But this is much more than just a walking cane. This is your all-purpose survival stick.

### Things to Consider in Attaining a Good Stick

- Find one that is about six to twelve inches taller than you.
- Look for the straightest, strongest one you can find.
- Use a man-made material if it's available, like a pipe or metal rod.
- For your best bet, find a strong sapling tree that you can cut to fit.

*A pocket knife is safer for a child than a fixed blade as it can be safely closed when not in use. A folding blade that locks is the safest to use because there is no danger of it getting bumped or caught when you're working and the blade closing on your hand. A liner lock, like in the picture above, is probably the most popular form of locking blade. To close this knife you must push the liner lock down with your finger (Myke is pointing to it in the picture) and while you are doing that, push the blade forward and move your finger out of the way. If you're planning to buy this type of knife for your child it is imperative that the locking and folding mechanisms are smooth and easy to use or your baby could lose a finger. I've come across a lot of stiff, dangerous ones so check carefully.*
*(Photo credit Ruth England Hawke)*

- Select a stick just big enough that when you grasp it, your fingers and thumb touch.
- Choose a stick with a natural fork at the top (or make one).
- Carve a point at the bottom.

This will give you the ideal survival stick, which will provide all sorts of uses. Let's look at some of these criteria, and at some of the various uses of this invaluable tool.

### Height

If the stick is too short, you risk serious injury by having it jam into your eyes or neck if you should fall during night travel or if you're moving under illness or injury. Choosing a stick taller than you will mostly ensure that this will never be a problem.

Also, when it is just a bit higher than you, your stick can serve as a great measuring device. You might determine how deep a river is, and thus whether you can cross it; it may also help you safely find footing while making a river crossing. You can use the stick to determine if you could jump over a chasm—just lay the stick on the ground and see how far you can jump beside it, then use the stick to try and touch the other side of a chasm. If the stick is strong enough, it might even be used as a small bridge. It can help you determine heights—to see if you can jump down from a tree or cliff, etc. It can be used as a pole when rafting.

The stick also gives you extra reach for nuts and fruits in trees. This is one area where the fork at the top is very useful as it can be used to wedge between fruit and the tree. It becomes a digging tool for roots and water. The point makes it a good weapon for deterring any wild animals that might be considering making you their next meal. The fork also becomes a weapon if you need to pin the head of a snake or trap a small rodent until you can finish it off. Finally, the fork might become a bit of an arm rest if you end up using it like a crutch, and this is the only time you should make it shorter than your height.

### The Point

As soon as you find a good survival stick, spend a few minutes carving and shaving down the end into a point. The point will serve as a weapon, as a spear for fish or birds, and as an extra measure of stability as you use it for walking assistance. Now, the point obviously won't stay a point for long if you're leaning heavy on it while walking. I tend to only use my stick as a pacing aid unless I'm tired or pulling uphill or using it to lean on going down steep slopes. I also use the stick to clear brush out of my path or to stir critters from bushes into my trap.

### Sapling

If you don't have a knife, converting a rooted sapling into a survival stick can be a challenge. If this happens, bend it far enough down to still leave you the desired length, say a foot more than you need near the base, then twist it until it gives way. I generally twist it on itself in its roots. Then take a rock and smash the end off where you want it. Then use the rock and rub it against the bottom to make your point. One of the benefits of using a green sapling is that they have more give so they are less inclined to snap on you when under some weight, plus they won't burn as easily when you're using the stick to hold a pot over the fire. But, if you find a nice, good, dry piece of hard wood that works for you, then use that.

## The Fork

I try to find the natural point where the tree bifurcates or splits off for branching, and trim those down by breaking them off to leave me a nice fork for the top. The fork is optional—use what you can find.

## Hand Grip

If you have time, consider making a hand grip area and attaching a "dummy" cord. This is just a piece of string or rope used as a lanyard that keeps the stick tied to you so you don't drop it or forget it. This happens to everyone—even elite soldiers. So it's a good practice if you have the cordage, to tie all your key stuff to you for just such exigencies.

## Other Uses

I've used my survival stick as a lean-to frame to make a quick shelter. You can also use your stick as sort of calendar, by carving a notch for each day you're out there

*A stick is a vital piece of kit, particularly if the end is sharpened into a point. You can use it defensively if you're attacked; you can use it to hunt with; as a tool to beat brush out of your way; to dig with; as a water depth measurer; as a gathering device to knock fruit out of tall trees; and as a walking staff. Notice in this picture that all of the children have spears that are taller than they are, this is a very important safety feature as they are much less likely to impale themselves on the sticks if they were to fall on them.*
*(Photo credit Ruth England Hawke)*

to help you maintain a sense of time. Also, carve your name into the stick in case it gets lost and someone finds it, or to use it as a marker to show that you were there.

# The Knife

If you have one, that's great. If not, look to make one pretty soon into your situation as it is the most valuable tool for survival.

Any metal will be your best resource for making an improvised knife. If you've got a blade with no handle, find a piece of wood to wedge it into, or wrap the handle portion in something safe such as clothing or leaves.

You might find a scalpel, a pair of scissors, or some other similar household item that can be modified, sharpened, and used as an improvised blade. You might find a nice chunk of metal that you can beat with a rock and form into some sort of cutting utensil. Consider using anything metal that can be sharpened—like the zipper toggles on your pack, or the metal pieces of your suitcase, or maybe even your belt buckle or purse strap. Other items that can be fashioned into some sort of cutting or slicing tool include coins, nails, glass, and plastic (if it is thick and strong enough).

One very useful life skill parents can pass on to their kids is knife sharpening. It can be a fine art, and there are a few techniques. Here's my preferred method:

## Sharpening the Blade

Sharpening the blade manually is a bit of a lost art since most modern knives stay sharp a long time due to their excellent machine-made razor edge. Also, many people simply use an electric or automatic sharpener. Those often in the field tend to carry a small sharpening stone for this purpose.

The basic principles of sharpening are fairly easy to grasp, but practice will help to refine your technique. I recommend trying to sharpen some knives at home.

### Steps to Basic Knife Sharpening

1.  Use a rough or course surface to grind down the bulk of the blade's edge, (this is often called a "dry stone") using a bit more strength in the strokes.
2.  Then use a smoother surface to get a finer edge on the blade. This is best accomplished with a "wet stone" (wet it with water) using longer, controlled strokes. Use soft gentle strokes in a sort of arcing motion to refine the edge.
3.  Start by keeping the sharp edge facing toward you while you stroke the blade against the rock away from yourself. Change directions when you turn over the blade to the other side; this gives a sort of saw cross-cut on the blade and the end result is a more razor-like edge that slices more efficiently.

It is key to keep the angle of the blade consistent with each stroke—approximately 20 degrees off the sharpening surface.

While sandstone is not good for making a knife, it's the best for sharpening one; if there's no sandstone, any gray-colored clay-like rock, or rock with glitter in it (such as granite), will work pretty well. The smoother the sharpening rock, the better.

## Natural Materials for Making Knives

Many things found in the wild can be used to make a knife, as well as other weapons and tools, including wood, stone, bamboo, shells, and bones. This can be a fun project for anyone and especially for parents to do with their kids.

### Bones

Animal bones are some of the handier items often overlooked in the outdoors. If you find some antlers, consider yourself lucky, as you'll be able to use them for several purposes. Should you find a carcass—be it recently killed by a predator (make sure they're gone; vultures are a good sign of this) or a rotted corpse—if the bones are good and strong, pick through them for the good ones you can still use. The key when working with bones is to first sterilize them by fire to kill any harmful bacteria.

To make a bone-blade knife, find yourself a strong bone and break it in half with a rock. Take the shard that looks most knife-like in size and shape, and sharpen it up with a stone per the method described above. Then wedge it into an improvised stick handle, or wrap it in cloth or natural materials to protect your hands. Try to keep the outside of the bone as the sharpest piece, as it has a harder surface area than the marrow side and will hold an edge longer. This should last awhile; and when it starts to give, make another.

Bones can be used for many other purposes as well. Some cultures use bones to make alcohol, and some use them as an aphrodisiac. I have successfully used antlers as a good poking weapon. The antlers are tough to break, but you can break them off. Then sharpen up the point a bit and you will be able to use it in a sort of tearing manner to incise game—it's much better than using your fingers. You can also lash a rock into the forks in the antlers to make a club. I have also used dead cattle horns as drinking cups; these come off fairly easily after a certain amount of decay has set in.

Femur bones tend to make great clubs. While shoulder blades can be made into a saw, it takes a lot of work to carve the teeth on the blade, unless you have a knife; best to use it for a club or a modified axe or machete. You can use various bones to make a rucksack frame or other such framing purposes. When you find a nice set of bones, take a moment to study them and then creatively apply them to your problem-solving needs. Jaw bones of big game can be used as a make-shift saw, as well. The skull might become your bowl. Look at how much skin is left on the bones; is it worth salvaging to make shoes or a sack?

Bones can be used to make buttons by taking a small piece, rounding the edges with a rock, and poking or boring a hole in it with a hot piece of steel (like a heated safety pin).

Bones can be used as needles as well. If you can, bore a tiny hole into the top through which to run the line. If that's not possible, make two small cuts in the back end, slightly offset from each other so that you don't cut right through the thing, and then tie your thread material with a small knot so it doesn't slip.

Bones can also be used to make fish hooks. Fish and bird bones are especially good as they are very small and light and have natural points that are easily sharpened. So, dig through any dead bird bones you find. Make them safer to work with by sterilizing them in the fire to burn off any residual flesh; or, at least, let them get good and sun-bleached if time is an option.

*Grandpa supervises while Gabe saws off a dead tree branch. Kids spend much more time indoors than they did just one generation ago, but it's important that they get out and pick up life skills like these. You really don't want an emergency situation to be the first time that your child uses a sharp tool, as that is a dangerous time to learn.*
*(Photo credit Ruth England Hawke)*

Bones can be used to make arrow heads. When you break the bone to make the knife, sift through all the smaller pieces to find any that have a shape you can work with; sharpen them up and make them into spear heads which can be lashed to sticks (for arrows) and spears.

Further, bones can be ground up into a medicinal chalk to help slow diarrhea. Hooves can also be melted and used for glue, but that's only if you have the materials such as an extra pot to boil them down in.

The key is that whatever you find, make it clean and safe with fire or boiling and to use everything, everywhere, all the time. Teach your kids to constantly analyze their environment and seek ways to create new things or improvise with old things.

### Wood

In most environments, wood will be the most readily available resource to use to improvise a knife. It may seem a bit odd at first to think that wood can be used as a sharp-edged tool. In fact, it is more common than you might think.

### Key Factors for Selecting a Piece of Wood

- Find a piece about one-foot long.
- The harder the wood, the better (use the thumbnail test).
- Use live wood, not dead dry wood.
- Select a piece where the grain goes the length of your intended blade, and not horizontal (the grain is the lines of a slightly different color).

Once you find a nice piece of blade wood, the next step is to use a piece of stone to shave it down by scraping the rock against the blade area (the top six inches or so). You can rub the rock against the stick, or vice versa if the rock is too big. The idea is to make one side of the blade the sharp edge, and make the other side flat or blunt.

Rub the intended sharp edge on both sides of the blade so that you have two halves that bevel and taper down to a blade. The trick here is to make sure that the sharp edge does not go to the center of the piece of wood. It should go 90 percent of the way there, but not actually to the core or this will make the blade weaker.

### Burning the Blade

Once you have the foot-long hardwood selected and filed down to a basic knife shape, then it's time to temper it with fire. Place the blade near enough to the fire to get it nice and dried out—this will take some time, maybe an hour or two depending on environment. The drier it is, the harder it becomes. Once it is dry, then work on the actual edge of the blade. You'll want to hold this right at the edge of the fire so it's almost licking the blade, and get it just barely blackened, but not burned. This area will then be ready to make a finer blade by rubbing a smoother stone against it. The same technique for sharpening steel applies to wood. Go gingerly so as to not break the edge, but once finished, this will actually slice pretty well for a while.

It will need some re-firing and sharpening, and eventually will break or give way, but it will be a very utilitarian item for a while, depending on how much heavy use you put it through.

### Shells

On the seashore, wood might not be readily available, but often seashells will be. These make excellent cutting tools. The handle might be trickier to fashion without wood, though you can use cloth or other natural materials. The edges of shells can be sharpened quite nicely against a stone or another shell, and these blades will hold an edge for a while.

### Bamboo

Bamboo makes an excellent blade, and I have used this many a time. The same basic techniques for wood apply to bamboo. Find about a two-foot-long section of bamboo. Break it to get a piece that's about one foot long and about three inches wide—basically make it a width that is comfortable for your hand when you grip the handle area. If the shard is too wide, it's easy to scrape the edges down to a comfortable size. It is better for the bamboo piece to be a bit too wide rather than too narrow, for strength and longevity.

Once you have the raw form of the knife, start to sand down the blade portion. Again, the concept is that one edge should be flat and blunt, and the other edge is to be the sharpened side—do not make the sharpened side bevel above the center point of the blade face. By keeping less on the blade side, this makes the back, blunt side more of a supporting ridge for the knife itself. Remember, at the end of the day, it's only about a centimeter that does the actual cutting work.

As you sand away the bamboo to get the edge, shave down the inside of the bamboo as it is softer. This makes it easier for you to smooth but also keeps the harder, enamel-like surface on the bamboo, meaning it will hold its edge longer and therefore, serve you better.

Once the bamboo is ready, again apply the fire drying and tempering. Then again, slightly char that edge and smooth it into a nice sharp edge.

### Coconut

I've found that a good hard coconut shell makes a good cutting tool. It's probably not often considered because it is curved and, as such, doesn't fit well on a handle.

But a nice triangular shard of coconut shell can be very sharp on one side, and the other two sides will remain plenty dull enough to not injure the hand when working with it.

## Stone

Not all rocks are created equal. Some are inherently better for making into tools than others. So before you start to smash and break rocks, take a good look around. Try and find rocks that are either exactly what you need or very close to it in their natural state. This little bit of looking could save you lots of time and effort.

Once you find a rock that looks like a good candidate for a blade, take into consideration its composition. Stones like sandstone or shale will simply shatter or crumble when you start whacking at them with other rocks. It won't take you long to figure it out, but generally, the dark, harder stones work better for shaping. Most of the rock knives I've made looked horrible, but they did cut and did the work I needed of them. So don't fret if your handiwork doesn't produce a masterpiece—the goal is utility.

Making a knife from stone is one of those tasks best done when you have some time to sit down and work on it. It'll take some refining of your technique to figure the right angles for striking the stone to eventually give you the rough shape you're striving for. As the stone begins to take form, pay attention to the pieces you whack off. You might get a most unlikely looking piece that just happens to be a very sharp and thin-edged fragment. If so, consider stopping and using that as your knife blade, or as an arrow or spear head.

### Rock Tools

- Breaker: This is a large rock, like a sledgehammer, used for breaking a large stone down into manageable knife-sized fragments.
- Chipper: Think an oval rock, like a small hammer, used for further shaping the stone blade down to its useful dimensions.
- Flaker: This is a flat piece of sharper-edged rock that you use to flake off the last bits of stone in order to give your stone knife its edge.

Once you break a starter rock with the breaker, look for the best piece to begin forming. Then use the chipper to give it the basic knife shape. Next use the flaker to create an edge with small taps, at a sharp angle, away from you. Finally, you can try to actually grind this edge against other stone to give it sharpness.

The basic principles of knife-making apply throughout. The ideal length of your finished knife is about one foot—that's six inches for the blade and six inches for the handle. Too long and you run the risk of it breaking while you work on it, which can also cause injury. The blade should actually be a few inches longer, maybe eight inches or so, in order to fasten it to your handle. A knife that is too short is also risky, as you may overextend yourself in an effort to counter its shortness, resulting in a cut or gash.

Once you've chipped and flaked your blade, secure it into a handle. You can wedge the blade into a piece of wood, bone, or antler; or wrap cloth around the end and fasten the cloth with cordage; or tie the blade onto a stick or piece of wood with some lashing. The key is to make the strongest, most comfortable handle you can, as a bad handle can lead to blisters, and then infection. If you're going to wedge the blade into a stick, try to find a stick that is slightly split on one end (or split one yourself ), and slowly thrust the blade into the slit until it's secure. Then fasten it with cordage.

## Improvised Weapons for Survival Defense

Now that we've covered the basics of the two mainstays in the armament of the survivor—sticks and knives—let's take a look at other potential weapons.

### Dirt

Never underestimate the value of good old-fashioned dirt. In a pinch, you can grab a handful of dirt and throw it at a predator, aiming for the eyes to hopefully drive it away. In the absence of anything else, I recommend doing so vigorously and repeatedly! This is a great fallback option to teach your kids, as they will almost always be standing on dirt if they encounter a wild animal.

Also, you can use dirt to try and stun smaller game long enough for you to close the distance and stomp on them. If you don't have any weapons or stones handy—for example, in a desert or beach environment—you can fill a sack or t-shirt with sand or dirt and use it as a rock-like weapon. This can also be fastened to a small stick to make a club or used as a sling-like weapon to be spun around and let loose towards your target.

These methods are best used as a last resort. But it's good to keep in mind that everything can be utilized and exploited, however creatively, for your needs.

### Rocks

If they are around, keep an eye out for the ones that will make better projectiles for your purposes. Your strength should determine the best weight for you to throw. You want to have the ability to give it a good thrust, and potentially to throw it a decent distance, so it should be manageable. But you also want it to do some damage when it hits, so it shouldn't be too light.

Take some time and practice your aim, as no two rocks throw alike. I find the smoother ones give me a bit better aim because there's less resistance as they roll off the fingertips to change their trajectory. I also find the smoother stones are better as your prey is usually some distance away, and there's less resistance on smooth stones flying through the air. Also, a well-placed round smooth rock tends to impact the prey with a core shock that stuns them or knocks the wind out of them long enough for you to finish them off. This is particularly true with birds.

I sometimes find that a rock with a pointy part or sharper angles and edges work better on rodent-like prey as these rocks have a better chance to fracture bones. This means the creatures will either stay in place due to pain or not get as far as fast due to limitations.

You might choose a large rock to drop on prey, or just to have near your hunting site for finishing off what you catch. It's good to have various types of rocks as readily available projectiles in all circumstances. They are good for all the reasons noted, as well as for flushing game out of bushes, or throwing at predators.

## Throw Sticks

Throw sticks are different than your basic walking stick. A throwing, or rabbit, stick is basically a non-returning boomerang. Find a solid stick about two feet long with a bend in it the shape of a boomerang. The advantage of the rabbit stick is that you get more leverage on your throw due to its angle, which means it delivers more impact on the target. Seek out a naturally-curved piece of the hardest wood you can find. To throw it, point your non-throwing arm at the target, then whip the stick either overhand or side-armed, whichever is more comfortable to you and gives you more power and control.

## Clubs

These come in a variety of styles. The simplest is the log-type club, usually a tree branch with the heavier side for whacking and the thinner side for handling (sometimes you need to scrape down one side to get a thinner grip). Keep on the lookout for a good animal leg bone, shoulder bone, or jaw bone that could work as a club. Also look for a tree branch with a natural knot in it—if you can, find a fresh one on the ground, providing it's still strong and solid. If not, try to cut it from a tree. The hard knot makes an excellent weapon as it's very heavy and strong, and is not likely to break on impact or with heavy usage.

The best sticks for clubs are usually harder woods that don't snap on impact. You should try to use a greener stick to keep it from being too brittle and to better hold the rock in place.

The best rocks to use are darker, harder rocks that have an oval shape so you get more force of impact over a smaller surface area.

## Hammer Club

This is great for a number of reasons. Not only does it simply make a great tool—a hammer—but it also makes a great weapon, and is fairly easy to make. Just lash a good stone to the end of your stick and voila, you have a hammer club.

There are three ways to lash the rock to the stick:

### Fork Technique

The best and most practical way is to use a stick with a natural fork in it that will fit your rock nice and snug naturally, then lash it in with your best cordage.

### Split-Stick Technique

Split one end of your stick, wedge your rock into it, then lash it in, putting extra lashing at the base of the split to keep it from splitting the stick further. This method is okay, but I find the stick often ends up splitting eventually anyway, unless you have a lot of cordage and can really wrap it tightly. But the split method is good for temporary uses and when you have limited cordage as the pressure of the split will do most of the work for holding a well-placed, well-wedged rock.

### Bark Wrap Technique

If you find a stick with flexible bark, you can break it and keep a long strip on the end to fold over the rock at the end of your stick. This is not the best technique, as the force of the rock can sometimes snap the bark.

## Hatchet Club

This is similar to the hammer club, but with a rock that has a sharper edge to be used as a hatchet, tomahawk, or axe. Find a rock with a triangular or wedge shape that has more weight at the back and a finer point at the front. Then chip and flake away to give more of a cutting edge. Note that too much edge will tend to disintegrate on impact against any hard surface. It's good for certain types of chopping, such as making a structure with larger logs, like a raft.

## Spears

The basic spear is a long, strong stick with sharp point at the end. In its simplest form it is best used for lunging and piercing mid-sized game such as a small pig or doe. It takes some skill to effectively throw a spear. Because the standard spear is best for lunging and not for throwing, they should be very strong. Further, the point must be sharp and strong enough to forcefully pierce through flesh.

Making a spear is pretty simple. Find a strong, fairly straight, and long stick. Scrape off any knots or other imperfections in the area where you will be holding it, then sharpen the point. That's pretty much it. If possible, you should fire-harden your spear(s) by using the method described above regarding fire-hardening wooden knives.

## Throw Spears

A throw spear is different than a regular spear in that it is a much lighter and, therefore, frailer stick. It would not hold up well against large game. However, with the addition of a good spear head, the throw spear becomes a great hunting weapon for mid-sized game that might be aggressive, like wolverines, boars, coyotes, and bobcats.

The best piece of wood to use for a throw spear is a green (i.e., not dead) hard wood, and about thumb-sized in diameter. You can make these into a very long javelin-like spear (about nine feet) or very short type of throw-dart spear (about three feet). These can be made even more effective when a sort of sling shot device is added, called a "spear thrower." These have many names in many cultures, such as *atlatl* or *woomera*. With a pouch of leather or paracord, it provides more leverage and delivers more power to the throw of the spear, resulting in a more forceful blow to the target.

Spear heads come in a variety of options. Anything sharp is good. Usually, the pieces of rock that are too small to be a knife and too big to be an arrowhead makes a good spear head. Bone can be used—just find a piece about six inches in length and file it down into a long nail-like point. If the bone is wider, you may file it down into two points for a forked spear head or three points for a trident spear head—the more dangerous the working end, the more damage it inflicts, and the greater chance of you dining that day.

Metal, glass, or anything sharp and hard can be made into a spear head. The more weight the better, but too much weight and you'll likely not be able to use it as well.

## Making and Lashing a Spear Head

The lashing is important in order to keep the head attached as it makes its impact upon the game's hide and bones. Any give in the lashing and the whole thing may just be an exercise in futility on your part and lucky for the game.

First choose your material, be it stone/rock, bone, glass, etc. Then, chip it into a basic long arrowhead shape, then file it to a finer edge and sharp point. Next,

*Andrew is practicing throwing a long javelin style spear. A throwing spear is typically much lighter than a lunge spear. They can be long like Andrew's or shorter, around three feet, and more like a dart. They are good for medium-sized game. You can simply sharpen the end and harden it in a fire or you can lash on a spear head made from a sharpened material such as rock, bone, shell, glass, or metal. (Photo credit Jeffrey Coit)*

add a tongue to the base of the spear head that will fit into the stick and help make the lashing that much more secure. Split the end of the spear *slightly*, and wedge the tongue of the spear head into the split. Use cordage to lash the split stick back together, forging the spear head into the stick as tightly as possible, locking it in.

One advantage of the throw spear over the regular spear is range. You can project your reach with a throw spear, but to do so accurately takes a lot of practice. The best way to throw a spear is with the hand catapult method.

Spears aren't the best projectile weapons for a survivor as they take some work to make, and a lot more work to master. It is probably best to use your stabbing spear instead, skip the throwing spear for land game, and make a lighter spear with finer spear points for fishing (a much easier proposition than hitting mammals). A spear with three prongs (nails, long thin bones, pieces of wire, or even three long thorns) for pinning and piercing smaller fish works really well—just keep a string tied to it for retrieval and you're good to go.

## Bolas

Bolas are super easy to make and use, and are fairly effective weapon for hunting. It's just three rocks tied to three strings which are tied together at the other end. The bola is swung overhead and then, after a few whirls, let loose in the general direction of the prey. The concept is that the bolo will either whack the prey with one of the rocks, or, if the rocks miss, the strings have a chance of getting tangled around the animal, giving you time to close in and finish it off.

## Slingshots

Slingshots are a forked piece of wood (or any other material that will do the job) with some rubber, tubing, elastic, or other such material tied tautly to both ends and with a pouch in the middle for holding your projectile. These take a little practice to perfect, and can be quite effective for killing small game. I use it for field mice and birds as it usually delivers enough impact to kill them dead on the spot. Plus a slingshot gives me a good enough range to get close enough without scaring them off. Slingshots are fairly accurate and quiet, so even a near miss will often not cause the animal to scurry away.

## Slings

A sling is any cordage of about two feet in length, with a small pouch fastened to the middle, and with a moderate-sized smooth-edged stone, can become a fairly accurate and deadly weapon with some practice. Tie a knot in one end of the string, tie a loop in the other end of the string, and fasten a pouch to the middle of the string (the pouch can be a piece of animal skin or clothing) into which you'll place the projectile.

Here's how to use it:

- Place the looped end around your index finger.
- Hold the knot end between your thumb and index finger.
- Place the rock in the pouch, give about three good circular swings overhead.
- Let it fly at your target by raising your thumb to let loose the knotted end while the looped end stays firmly around your finger.

Before you start hunting, practice to increase your accuracy and velocity.

## Bow and Arrow

The bow and arrow are the classic weapons of the primitive world. I don't always recommend using these as they are time-intensive to make, but if you find yourself in a long-term survival situation, they can improve your mammal-hunting success. On the other hand, I have made and used many bows for short-term fishing as this is an effective method for rivers or ponds where you can see the fish but can't quite get at them. A good bow will thrust an arrow right through the water and into your prey.

For the basic bow, find a nice strong sapling about four-to-five feet high from top to bottom. Choose a hard wood that is green and fresh. Find a piece that has little or no knots, branches, or sprouts. This will give you a good solid bow. Cut the sapling, then trim and slightly smooth down the outer surface. Leave the middle third of the bow in its whole, solid state for strength and for gripping. Shave the top and bottom thirds so that they gradually begin to taper towards the end of the bow—these two thirds should be about a third of the original thickness of the stick. Shave and taper only on one length side of the bow; the other side should remain completely solid from top to bottom as this will become the backbone of the bow. Then cut perpendicular notches into the top and bottom of the bow, just an inch or two from the ends, for tying your string or cordage.

Start by using the best cordage you have (sinew and paracord woven together is a great combo). Lay the cordage straight out on the ground next to the bow, cut it so that it's just longer than two-thirds the length of the bow, and then tie a strong small loop at both ends. With the shaved length of the bow facing you, bend the bow to about two-thirds of its original length and slide the cordage loops over the ends and into the end notches. The bow is now ready. When not in use, it is best to unstring your bow. This will prolong the life and effectiveness of both the bow and the cordage.

Basic arrows can be made out of any long, thin, strong branches that are as straight and as free of knots or twiglets as possible. Shave or scrape them down to create as smooth a shaft as you can. Cut the back end of the arrow to create a flat tip, then cut a slight horizontal notch across that tip into which the string will go. Then cut or file the other end of the branch to a nice point, harden it with fire, and you have the simplest of arrows. About two feet long is ideal.

You might try making simple arrowheads for your arrows as well to give them a greater efficacy. Take shards of rock, shaved bones, nails, flakes of shells, glass pieces, scraps of metal, or anything you can fashion into an arrowhead shape and wedge in and lash to the point (use the directions for spear-head lashing as a model). Finally, to add finesse and increase control, add two or three feathers to the back end of the arrow to create "flights." These can most simply be fastened with cordage near the back end of the shaft.

Once you've got your bow and arrows made, practice before you start hunting (aim your practice shots at something that won't break the arrows). A bow and arrow works well for all kinds of small mammals. Even if the arrow doesn't kill it

*Myke teaching Gabe to use a bow and arrow. Archery can be an interesting hobby that has great application in a survival situation. A forearm guard is good additional piece of kit. (Photo credit Ruth England Hawke)*

on impact, a good hit will disable the critter long enough to allow you to move in for the kill.

## Blow Pipes

These aren't the easiest weapons to make or use, but I don't want to leave anything out of your mental arsenal of possibilities.

Ideally, you can buy one of these as they aren't super expensive, are very easy to use, and are highly accurate. Blow pipes are also very lightweight and can be folded up and stored.

You can make one if you happen to have some tubing, can find some hollow reeds, or can bore a vertical hole through a length of bamboo. Essentially, you need a long tube (about five feet) that's hollow through the middle and has openings on both sides. If you don't have the materials noted, or the tools to make it, it's best not to try to make a blow pipe—you'll waste too much time and energy.

But if you do manage to get a decent pipe, you'll need some darts. Small nails, paper clips, or other light, thin objects like sewing needles, thorns, fish and bird bones, thin branches, or even wires can be used. Whatever you use, sharpen the point as best you can. Also, the darts will need a base on the opposite side of the point which will create a good seal once placed in the tube, and which will assist the flight. You can make the base from cork, foam, Styrofoam, feathers, etc.—anything light enough to travel quickly out of the tube and through the air. Think three to five inches for the dart length.

To use a blow pipe, place the projectile just inside one end point-side first. Place your mouth around the opening, creating a tight seal with your lips. Aim the blow pipe just slightly above your prey, take a good breath, then release a thrusting puff of air into the pipe to shoot the projectile.

## Nets

If you have the time, the patience, and most importantly the cordage, then a net will be a great multi-purpose tool. Nets can be used for catching fish, snaring birds, trapping small game, as a hammock to sleep in, as a litter for a patient, or as a rucksack to carry your goods on the move. This is why I try to carry the U.S. Army Jungle Hammock at all times, as it does all these things very well. If I don't have it, but have some 550 paracord, I'll use the guts and the casing to make a net. If not, I make string from sinew, plant matter, or whatever I can. Dental floss is a good improvisational material for nets as well.

Start with two ten- to-twelve-foot lengths of strong string for the top and bottom of your net (the main lines), and as many twelve-foot lengths of finer string for the interior of the net (the core lines) as you have. Tie the ends of both main lines to two trees about ten to twelve feet apart so that you've got about eight to ten feet of main line across the top and bottom to work with. Tie one at about eye level and the other just below waist level.

Next, take the core lines and fold them in half so that they're each about six-feet long. Using a prusik knot (refer to further explanation on page 279), tie each of these core lines to the top main line—about one inch apart—until you have as many "pairs" of core lines hanging down across the length of the top main line as are available.

Now you're ready to start making the net. Starting with the far left "pair" of core lines, tie these two together about one inch down from the main line, using an overhand knot. Then take the inside line of this pair and tie it to the closest string from the next pair over, also about an inch down from the main line. Next, take the other string from the second pair, and tie it to the closest string from the third pair. Repeat this process until you get to the end, then reverse direction and continue back the other way. Do this back and forth—creating a diagonal pattern of squares—until you get to the last two inches of core lines. Then tie the bottoms of the hanging pairs of core lines to the bottom main line, and you've got yourself a nice three-foot-wide net.

To catch fish with your net, use sticks to stake it in across a stream, and weight the bottom with rocks if needed. Or, tie small rocks around the edges and use it as a throw net. Or, stake one end down near the riverbank with a vertical stick, tie the other end to another vertical stick, and walk in the water in as wide a circle as you can, coming back and closing in on the original stake.

To catch birds, spread the net across an area where birds fly through often—such as an opening between trees. For small game, you can throw the net over them and tangle them in it long enough to finish them off. Or spread the net out on the ground and tie the ends to a snare-like spring that can spring up and net your prey that way.

## Other Tools

Let's now look at other tools and techniques you can make and employ in the wild using all the materials available to you in nature.

### Latrines

Wherever you are in a survival situation, you'll need to utilize the facilities. This becomes particularly important if you're stuck in a contained area or with a larger group of survivors, or with your family for a longer period of time than just a few days.

*Brian teaching his daughter Olivia to shoot a pellet gun. Primitive hunting is brutal, so using a rifle is far more humane. A pellet gun should only be used on small game such as rabbits, birds, and squirrels. In a non-emergency situation only let a child shoot at an animal if they are completely proficient at hitting a target and intend to eat the game afterwards. (Photo courtesy of Simone Cohen)*

## Urinal

These are not normally needed for most survival situations. However, you might want to pee all around your camp site to mark your territory and keep preda-tors out. If you opt for this, do so outside of your own smell range and a fair distance around your perimeter, such as thirty meters. Try to go downwind from your campsite.

It is easiest to make a hole, keeping insects at bay by having it covered when not in use with another large leaf or piece of wood or sheet of bark. These are good for larger groups staying put a while. Change them around as needed and keep them about fifty meters from the camp if you can, downwind, down range, and downslope of water and camp. Also, it doesn't hurt to throw a bit of dirt on after each use to keep down smells and vectors.

**Cat Hole**

You'll always need to defecate in the field as well, and you *always* have to cover up your feces after you do so. When you're with a family, it is often better to keep the urinal separate from the cat hole. The urinal will see a lot more use and persons suffering from stomach complaints may need to spend more time at the cat hole.

To make a cat hole, dig a hole at least one foot deep and one foot around, and cover it up with sticks, leaves, rocks, or whatever else is available. But always cover it as it not only attracts insects, which then land on you and your food and spread disease, but it may attract larger animals. You don't want to invite such critters to start hanging around your survival camp. So, always go farther away, about a hundred to two hundred meters, from your camp to dig your cat hole in which to defecate. When the hole is filled halfway up, it's time to dig another one.

If you are in dangerous areas, consider having people go out to the cat hole in pairs. People are exposed and vulnerable to animal attacks when in the defecation position. Also, when surviving, people will be fatigued and they might pass out. While it is a bit odd and uncomfortable, try to use buddy teams whenever separating from the group—the more minds, the more hands, the more solutions and help, the faster, better, and easier things are done.

## Hygiene

It is extremely important for survival to maintain good hygiene. Use water, sand, or sun and air if that's all you have. Soap can be improvised by taking animal fat and mixing it with slurry ash from your fire pit (slurry is ash mixed with water), then boiling the lot. Let it cool and harden, then slice it into bars you can use. This will clean you to a degree, but is not antiseptic. Try to add some pine sap or pine needles to the brew when boiling to give it some antiseptic properties. Soap-making is an art, so experiment to find a good mix that doesn't dry your skin too much and cause irritation. Use soap for cleaning all your tools, especially after handling game and cooking food. Some plants make a soapy residue when crushed; experiment, and if you happen upon these, use them.

## Waste Disposal

You will always produce by-products and waste if you are living outdoors. Try not to waste anything. For anything you make that results in leftover bits and pieces, find a use for them or save them. Wood shavings from whittling can be used for bedding, insulation, fire re-starting, etc. Save everything!

For leftovers from animals, try to use or save what you can. Clean bones and cook them over the fire to dry and destroy the small bits of meat left, then store— either in a hole covered with dirt, or in a makeshift sack tied up into a tree. Use parts like offal or guts for traps or fishing, even if it's just to chum the waters and make fish come to you—just be sure to chum the water downstream from your normal water and hygiene areas. Whatever you absolutely cannot use that is organic and will decay and smell and attract insects and other critters, put in a pile for burning. Just make a bigger fire than normal and slowly put the organic matter in the fire. If fire is not an option, then bury it as well as you can, and do so far from your camp.

In short, if it's organic, burn it. If it's inorganic, save it.

## Utensils

Utensils not only help you eat, but also keep your dirty fingers out of your fire-cleaned food and keeps the food from getting under your nails and growing bacteria that could make you sick.

Spoons are primarily for eating soup-type meals that consist of water and a bunch of things you chopped or smashed up that are too small for a fork. Spoons are the hardest utensil to make as they require a good deal of carving, which means you need a blade. To make a spoon, find a solid piece of wood just larger than the size of spoon you want. Scrape off all bark and imperfections, draw or carve an outline of a basic spoon shape, then start whittling. Once you've carved out the shape, start to dig out the bowl. When that's done, sand the entire piece down with your blade or, lacking a blade, a combination of rocks from gritty to fine.

If you need a fork, try to find branch that is already in the shape of a "Y" and use that. Trim and scrape the bark, fire-temper it to dry it, harden it, and take any smell or resin off it. Then use it to jab your chow.

If you're comfortable using chopsticks, they're easy to find or fashion in the wild, even without a blade. If not, try make a "poking" stick by sharpening the end of a strong thin stick in order to stab and jab your food.

Finally, you'll need all types of hanging implements to hold pots, food over the fire, etc. Try to find joints where branches sprout out from a limb and use those as natural hooks. Hard woods with little to no smell are the best choice for these purposes.

## Carrying Tools

Before you make any travel plans in your survival situation, you'll want to make sure you've regrouped and resupplied your family with as many provisions as possible. Sometimes, this means you'll have to devise ways to carry things.

Especially if you're stuck in the wild for some time, you will eventually start making things, and before you know it, you have a collection of stuff. You might just want to store it, or carry it if you're mobile, so some sort of carrying device is always handy.

Whenever possible, keep it simple by using your shirt, poncho, coat, or blanket. If you have nothing, there are almost always plants around that can help out. Look for wide-bladed grass, long thin reeds, willow branches, or large tree leaves such as palms.

If you find natural materials that are good for weaving, you might consider a woven basket of reeds or weaving a sort of bag with leaves. Weaving takes some skill and practice and if you're into it, it's a great skill to have and to teach your kids. When you're stranded for a long time, staying busy by making things is both productive and useful for feeling a sense of control and accomplishment.

*Myke tests the weight of Dominik's pack before a hike through the bush. Children should be involved with the packing of their own camping kit or survival bug-out bags so they know exactly what is in them but it's also very important that they can actually carry them by themselves. (Photo credit Ruth England Hawke)*

*Myke makes sure that the hip belt on Mia's pack is tight. Having a hip belt on your child's backpack, and your own, is hugely beneficial. It causes the weight of the pack to be redistributed from the shoulders to the hips. This means your child can walk with their pack for longer before you end up becoming their beast of burden.*
*(Photo credit Ruth England Hawke)*

## Bowls

Bowls are one of the fundamental implements a human being needs on a regular basis. So they are useful to produce if you are able.

You can make a bowl out of many things. A closed-ended segment of bamboo is easily transformed into a bowl by cutting a hole into its side. You can also make a decent roughly-hewn bowl from a block of wood but that is a time-consuming endeavor and not one I'd recommend for surviving families.

Some tree barks—such as cherry and birch—are just amazing. Neither will burn when placed next to a fire, but water can be boiled through them without the loss of integrity.

Birch bark is frequently used for making canoes as it has such a versatile and utilitarian texture. Birch is a white tree that appears to have peeling bark which look like paper coils when you get up close to it. A piece of birch can be peeled off and rolled up into a cone, or folded into a box shape. Then take a small twig, form it into a one-inch peg, split it halfway down the middle, and slide it over the edges of the bark like a paper clip and it will hold your utensil in its shape. This will hold water very well, and is a great field tool.

# Boats and Rafts

There is a lot of bad advice out there about making boats, canoes, and rafts in a survival situation. These things take a whole lot of time and energy, and without good tools, are extraordinarily difficult to make for a single survivor. So, only attempt to make a raft if you have to make a tremendous water journey, and then, make sure you give a lot of time to make it, at least a week or two. Don't expect to make a raft like the ones you've seen on TV. People tend to forget that when surviving, food, water, and hygiene needs alone take up most of the day. Add to that low energy and lack of physical strength and you'll see that making a seaworthy raft is a very difficult task.

If you're going to make a raft, find the lightest wood you can. Tap all the trees around you and find the lightest, softest ones. Without an axe or machete, you won't be able to cut fresh trees and will be stuck having to find what you can laying around. If you have the time and can make a stone axe, do it, and cut green logs.

The only method I will describe is the basic log raft. Use as many long logs as you need. These should be eight inches or so in diameter—large enough to hold your weight. You'll also need four slightly narrower branches to use as cross beams. In a pinch, the most basic raft of all is just a big log that you hang onto.

*Bowls and cups are an essential part of everyday human life. If you find yourself without them in the wilderness you can make them by burning a block of wood and carving out the burned bits, by folding leaves or bark, or even by molding mud and heating it in a fire. However these methods are time consuming and challenging, particularly for a child, and generally not as effective as using what nature has provided. When you're out on walks have your children look out for items that they could repurpose. This lateral thinking is good survival training. (Photo credit Ruth England Hawke)*

Lay the long logs tightly together lengthwise on top of two cross beams, one on each end. Then lay two more cross beams on top of the long logs, directly above the two bottom cross beams, and fasten those beams together like your life depends on it, because it does. Test it by trying to break it; if it gives way when you push and pull against it, keep working on it until you make it strong enough to pass the test. Once you get moving on the water, you won't have much chance to stop and make corrections.

## Rafting Techniques

There are a few standard rules to follow when taking to water on a homemade vessel. Do not raft at night. Do stay to the inside of river bends. Do not attempt to navigate rapids; stay away from them if at all possible.

## River Crossings

River crossing can be very dangerous. When attempting to traverse a river, especially one with good flow, you'll need some tools. If you have a walking stick (and you should!), you will be using it to propel your raft by pushing it off the river bottom. If your regular walking stick isn't long enough, find one that is.

### Key Thoughts on Rivers

- If you find a river, most of the time it will lead to civilization
- If you encounter cliffs, you must decide whether to climb or swim
- If there are any rapids, avoid swimming and walk around.
- If it's not too dangerous, a raft might be the easiest way to move
- If you have an injured person, a river might be the only way to get them out

An important note on river crossings in the cold: If you only have one pair of shoes, take them off, wrap them and keep them dry, and then put them on when you get to the other side. Or plan to take some time and dry out your feet afterwards if you must get them wet.

Getting your only clothes and boots wet in the cold environments is taking a huge gamble that you won't get caught in a blizzard for a long while afterwards. That's a big risk. If you get caught in a cold snap or just stuck overnight in wet clothes in cold regions, you'll likely not make it to see the dawn if you don't make an emergency fire and get warm and dry. Everything else must wait or the cold will claim you.

# Rope and Cordage

Rope is another important item to have in a survival situation, yet in most cases, you will have to make your own rope and cordage. Luckily, nature provides plenty of raw materials for this purpose. We'll talk about the materials first, then the process of making rope.

## Grass

Grasses can be used for a wide variety of purposes including bedding, roofing, clothing insulation, and to make tools such as brooms, baskets, and blankets. They can also be used to make lashing and cordage. The key to using grasses as cordage is in the bundling. First gather a lot of grass, then make bundles of same-length grass and tie the bundles about an inch from the top and bottom ends, as well as in the middle—make as many ties around the middle of the bundle as necessary. When grass is bundled in this way, it becomes a sort of flexible log and a very useful tool indeed for manufacturing many types of structures and tools, from dome homes to baskets, frames, and seats.

## Other Plants

There are way too many plants for me to list here that can be used for making things. What you do need is to have an idea of what kind of plant can be used, so I make mention of a few of the more common plants here. With that in mind, look for plants like these as your standard to make cordage. Most of these require some beating and splitting. Once they are separated out, I make cordage as with any other fibrous material, as noted below.

## Tree Bark

Many trees have naturally flexible bark that can be peeled off in strands. These strands can then be torn into thinner strips to give the foundation for good cordage. You'll have to practice by peeling some tree bark, but you'll quickly ascertain the good ones in your environment.

*If you don't have access to man-made ropes or fibers you can always make your own cord by braiding strips of animal pelts or strands of vegetation. Thin roots and vines make excellent cordage as they're naturally flexible and can be used straight away without treatment. (Photo credit Ruth England Hawke)*

## Roots

I don't encourage digging for these, but when you happen across them, put them to use. I don't like to use roots for two reasons. First, they dry out fast and that makes them a bit more prone to becoming brittle and breaking. Additionally, it is harder on the environment when you go ripping up root systems. However, it is survival, and it's a brutal business.

## Vines

What I love about the jungle is that vines are everywhere, meaning cordage is readily available. Often vines will have a bark that is inherently superb for making cordage. So, if you find some little vines, use them; they are nature's twine. If you find big vines, peel them first and then use them.

### Facts about Using Natural Fibers to Make Cordage

- Anything green and pliable is possible to use.
- If material is dry, and in the winter, soak the material in water.
- When a fiber is really hard to work with, boil it.
- Test everything with your eyes and hands to see if it's useable before you start working it.
- Test everything after you make it to ensure it's usable.

## How to Make Rope and Cordage

- Once you have the base material fibers selected and prepared, you're ready to begin.
- Take several strands and tie a small knot at one end. Then twist these fibers together to make a strong strand, and knot the other end.
- Repeat the last step until you have a good number of strands to work with.
- Next, take two of the strong strands you just made, and begin to braid them together by crisscrossing them in an overlapping fashion until you get to the ends. If you have a partner, have them hold the starting ends together. If you're solo, pin down the ends with a rock, between your legs, in your teeth, or whatever works for you to keep the ends stable as you twist.
- Make a knot at the other end.

If you need longer cordage, tie two more strands to that end, and start the braiding process again.

## Knots

I am not a knot master. Sailors, scouts, and mountaineers have vastly different needs than basic survivors so they do need to master different ways to work with rope. For the survivor, I find a few can be used to do just about everything you need.

Everything I ever needed to do regarding knots, I could manage with a granny knot—it's as easy as tying your shoes. But, to make life even easier, I found a few more knots that have been helpful so, we'll share here. And these can be fun to sit around the camp fire at night when you can do much else and the kids can learn and practice some different types of knots.

### Overhand Knot

This is the simplest knot. It's the common knot you make in a single rope to keep the end from fraying, for example. Just make a loop in one end of the string, then pass the other end through the loop and pull tight.

### Half Hitch Knot

This one is pretty simple, too. It can be used 90 percent of the time for almost everything. Simply wrap the string around the object, tuck it in on itself, and pull tight. Do this twice when you need real security.

### Square Knot

This is a bit trickier. It's really good for binding two pieces of cordage together.

To make a square knot, just remember: over-under, under-over. Hold one piece in one hand, the other piece in the other hand. Lay one side over the other, it doesn't matter which. Then take that same piece and turn it under the other. Turn it back pointing towards its original start point. Then bring it back under the other string. Then wrap it back around over the other string. Pull them together slowly and dress them up a bit as they come together. They should form a sort of symmetrical square, hence the name.

When it's in shape, pull it to the desired tightness and you have tied a nice square knot. Once you learn this, it helps to do it the same way each time. The good thing is, you always know if you did it right or not as soon as you pull it tight. And if it's not tight, simply undo half, re-do it in the opposite way, and you should have it. You can also remember the square knot sequence as: right over left, left over right—or, left over right, right over left.

Note: The square knot is really just a double version of a half hitch, with a reverse twist!

### Granny Knot

The granny knot is similar to the square knot, except the sequence is: right over left, right over left—or left over right, left over right.

### Prusik Knot

This is basically another form of a half hitch. It is ideal for tying into other ropes without cutting up your cordage. It is good for making a slip knot, as well for emergency ascents. It makes a bight that won't slide under tension, but when loosened it can be slid around and moved easily to a new place on the rope.

To make a prusik knot, make a bight or loop or upside-down "U" with your string. Make it a few inches long so you can work with it. Place it over the rope or object you want to tie into/onto. Then pull the rest of your string through that bight so that it's wrapped around the rope. Then dress it up so it looks neat like a letter "T" across the rope. Pull tight to lock in; loosen to move or slide.

That's all the knots you'll ever need to know. Don't get me wrong, learning and knowing knots is great. And it is true, the more you know about anything, usually the better off you'll be. However, from years of playing and teaching survival in the bush, I have found quite simply that you really don't need to be a rope master to survive and anything that you can teach kids that's fast, easy, and works is likely the better bet for training them.

## Rope Ladders

Rope ladders are great if you have lots of man-made para cord, for example. But for the most part, unless you are going to live in a tree fort for a while, you just don't need a rope ladder. It is far easier to just use a single rope. If it's hard for the kids, make knots in the rope that they can hang onto.

You can also make a lean ladder, meaning a long, strong stick or small tree you chopped, and lean it against your tree with your shelter. It should be strong enough to hold the weight of the family members climbing. Some extra branches to hold on may help or cutting some notches to make as steps or grip can be useful too.

# CHAPTER TEN

# SIGNALS AND COMMUNICATION

For families, communication is one of the most important parts of life on a daily basis and in survival, it is even more crucial. The best plan is always to call for help. That means you have to have the means. We'll look at some of the ways you can have this sort of plan. Depending on your kids ages, tell them to remember the best plan is simple: call home.

Signals are some of the most important tools in survival. Rescue often starts when the survivor sends a signal, be it audio or visual, which catches someone's attention.

The principles of signaling are pretty straightforward: Make yourself seen or heard. So let's look at some ways to make a scene and make some noise, because it's the squeaky wheel that survives.

The first thing you want to do in any potential survival situation is let someone know where you are so they can come help you. The thing is, if you have a working radio or a phone, you're probably not truly surviving so much as just tolerating temporary discomfort until help arrives.

Special Forces makes a habit of always keeping everyone on the team informed. This way, if anything goes wrong, even the lowest-ranking person will still know what the mission is and how to get it done. It's easy to make this a standard for your family, too.

Just start each day with a quick brief on what you expect to do and get done. As things develop, make new plans and estimates. Part of the brief should include meet up spots if there is a break in contact. And part of any family travel plan should always be to leave a written or oral brief of your intended plans and time-lines with loved ones who can initiate a query or a search.

All family members should have multiple layers of communications on them and the family itself as a unit should have multiple layers or backups.

Tip: There are a lot of gadgets to help families protect their kids. So, when you decide to make your family's survival plan, your priority should be to do some research about what is out there, and evaluate it based on your needs and budget.

For example, there are wrist watches that kids can wear that serve as a GPS locator for your child twenty-four hours a day. If the band gets taken off, an alarm signals. If the kid has a fall, the alarm signals. If the kid is in trouble, they can press a button to call for help. It lets you keep in constant contact with your child.

That said, these types of items might not work in a remote area. Check if they operate offline. Check their battery life and compatibility with other systems.

## How to Track Your Family and Call for Help When Needed

Each kid should have these items on them at all times, especially in the woods:

1. Whistle, as audio travels farther in the day than the night
2. Signal mirror
3. Flashlight for night
4. Radio: handheld and local range only
5. Cell phone: consider options that keep GPS function, even out of range. Also consider apps that work off of Wi-Fi, and allow a cell to act like a walkie-talkie
6. A strobe light or laser flare

Note that for all electronics, a dual power source is best. Use batteries that can be recharged by car, home, or sun. The best options will also have a hand crank tool for cloudy days.

The strobe is a great tool as it most definitely catches the attention of the human eye, especially at night. There are great ones out there that actually flash in Morse code.

Newer types of laser flares are also great in that they are bright and go high in the sky or travel a long distance and can be used multiple times. Plus, they are not flammable, explosive, or gaseous.

However, there are some instances where these old-school signals may be your best or only choice. For example, if you're out at sea, you might have a flare gun or pen flare. If you're out in the desert or jungle, you may have smoke flares or smoke grenades. If you're in the mountains, you might have to use flare candles. All of these are a bit dangerous, and as such, are not recommended for kids. But parents should be aware of them and choose what's best for the family PACE-WCS plans.

# Family Emergency Signal Plans

The family as a unit needs a team emergency communication plan. Again, this may seem like overkill, but it is survival and your family's lives that will be saved.

We go into greater detail below, but at this juncture, we just want the family to be assessing and evaluating all this information about communications in the context of a cohesive plan.

So, let's look at the "heavy lifters" for the family communications plan:

## GPS Radio (SPOT, Rhino)

These are some wonderful tools available for families today. There are many brands and prices, but the key thing to look for are the standard functions of the higher-priced models. One of these should be in one of the family backpacks for every outing.

For example, the Rhino 750 has a two-way radio, with a range of about twenty miles, which is pretty good, but it also has a GPS so you will always know where you are. The included maps means you can find your way to safety fairly quickly.

With the Explorer model, you get the GPS function with the extra satellite function that allows you some text service. With the devices that have SPOT built in, that you can press a button and an all-call alert goes out that you are in trouble. This functions as a homing beacon to help bring rescuers to you.

These are fantastic as an emergency device for any family that come in a variety of price ranges.

For those with a little more disposable income, there are watches on the market that have beacon responders, similar to planes. When the plane crashes, the GPS beacon is activated and sends a signal to the satellites, which pick up the signal and then let the emergency services know the exact location where the signal is emanating from.

## CB Radios

These are primarily vehicle radios, as they require a strong battery and an antenna for range. If your family takes many road trips, then these should be a mandatory part of your kit. Cell phone range may drop out in remote regions but the CB will always be able to receive and transmit anywhere you are. The range can be from five miles in thick terrain to fifty miles in open terrain, but if anyone is on that area and has their CB on, they can respond and hopefully, help.

## VHF/UHF

These radios are like CBs for cars. They use slightly different frequency rangers and are mainly used in boats and on aircraft. Usually boat captains or plane pilots will know all about these radios and their ranges and limitations. While it's beyond the scope of this book to teach radio wave theory, a small explanation helps make it more understandable.

Think of the UHF, ultra-high frequency, as free of static, but also with much shorter range. These are often what you'll find on hand-held radios. The VHF, or very high frequencies, will travel a bit farther, but also pick up a bit more static. The HF will travel around the world, if the antenna, frequency, atmosphere and a few other factors are right, but it also picks up the most static along the way.

HF radios, also known as ham radios, are some of the best survival radios around. Of course, these can be made mobile as they are often the only thing that works after large-scale disasters and ham radios operators often become the crucial link for FEMA, the Red Cross, and other agencies when all other communications fail. In family planning, these are best used for the mountain cabin, tree fort, cave hideout, beach house, or whatever your choice for static location may be. They require skill to work but they can truly be the best resource for getting help.

### Satellite Phone (and BGANS)

For the family that wants to plan, some research should be given to having a family satellite phone. There are different sizes, plans, and prices and also different satellites and areas covered. But, getting one of these for your family's travel region is essentially like always having 9-1-1 available. The BGANS is similar to Wi-Fi in that it lets other phones tether to yours for Internet access; the BGANS converts satellite to data and then lets family use their phones, tablets, and laptops to connect to it to communicate through the internet, but it is expensive and connection speed is slow.

Now that we have options, let's look at how things work, and how they don't work without a plan.

When you have no means of direct communication and you're stranded, that's a survival situation, and it's in these situations that signaling becomes important. Now what can you signal with?

First off, take an inventory of any resources you have at hand. Some, like a whistle, are good for signaling over short distances, while others, like strobe lights, are better for longer distances. Some signaling tools are one-time use only, like rocket flares or limited-use, like a beacon with just a few days' worth of battery power.

*Walkie-talkie training for Bella and her cousin. It's very important that not only do your children know what is in your survival kit but that they also know how to use it. Using walkie-talkies can take some adjustment for youngsters who are used to the ease and convenience of cell phones. (Photo credit Ruth England Hawke)*

Simple, low-tech signals like clothes can be laid on the ground to spell "help" or "SOS" without too much effort, or you may be able to arrange rocks and branches in similar fashion (if they'll contrast with the background enough to be seen).

But only go to the effort if you have the time and energy to gather a bunch of rocks and branches, and if you plan on staying put for a while. There's no point vigorously marking a camp if you won't be there long, but it doesn't hurt to leave markers everywhere in hopes of someone finding something to pick up your trail somewhere.

Now let's hope you had some good prior planning and got stranded with some sort of communications, and let's take a look at some of the options out there.

## Radios

If you have a rescue two-way radio, and you can see an aircraft or vessel, be sure to keep the antenna perpendicular or "broadside" to the target instead of pointing it at the vessel you're trying to signal. The strongest signal radiates out from the length of the antenna, not at the tip. This applies to any sort of antenna you might rig up.

It's also good to know that most radios and beacons have only about seventy-two hours' worth of power, so use them wisely. But also know that all aircraft and sea vessels monitor the distress channels, and if you don't think you'll survive for seventy-two hours, it might behoove you to leave it on and hope for a speedy rescue.

Search through your supplies for any type of standard communications items before attempting anything more complicated. Most signaling tools will come with instructions, and even if they don't, they can usually be figured out without much trouble. But even though you can often figure out how to use a signal, you may not know when and where to best use it, and for how long.

Here are some good general rules to follow when implementing any communication plan, especially when the power supply, whether batteries or engine fuel, is a finite resource:

## Where

Always broadcast from the highest, most open, and most likely to be spotted vantage point, where visual signals can be seen from the greatest distance, and broadcast transmissions travel farthest.

## When to Signal

Try to concentrate your power-based communications in the first twenty-four hours, as this is when most search parties will be initiated. Broadcast your signal continuously during this window if you're able.

Consider delaying your twenty-four-hour broadcast period for a day or two if you have reason to believe it will take folks that long to begin looking for you. After the initial broadcast period, you'll need to go into power-conservation mode. This means spacing out the broadcasts and standardizing their length.

### Transmit at Dawn, Dusk, and Midnight

Dawn and dusk are when atmospheric changes can help broadcasts travel enormous distances. At midnight the sky is "stable," as it is at noon. These should be your standard broadcasting times. Should someone stumble across your SOS pattern or beacon, they'll have a better chance of finding it again the next day at a standard time that's easy to remember. For example, if a radio operator thinks he hears an SOS around noon on a particular channel, but he can't tell for sure, he might try the same channel at the same time the next day to confirm.

Transmit from five minutes before until five minutes after the hour and the half hour. Most radio broadcasts begin at the "top" or "bottom" of the hour, so that's when most people start tuning in their frequency. These will be the most likely times for someone to accidentally happen across your Morse code SOS signal.

If you do have a radio, tune to one of the big channels, as these are used to broadcast WWV universal coordinated time, and people all over the world use this to set their watches. SOS tapped out in code has a good chance of being heard by someone on these frequencies.

# Lights

Radio contact isn't your only way to call for help. Any light, even a pocket pen-light, can save you in a survival situation. Although its range may be limited, even a small light in an otherwise blacked-out area can attract attention. Remember to keep your method of signaling handy at all times. That brief and unexpected moment when a plane flies overhead or you glimpse a ship on the horizon or maybe even another flashlight on a mountain across the valley might be your only chance to catch a rescuer's attention.

## Flares

Flares should be fired overhead and at a slight angle away from you, but never directly at a ship or aircraft. Only use flares when you can see the craft you're trying to signal, or, if visibility is poor, when you can hear it. These are single use, so use them wisely.

### Laser Flares

Laser flares are bright and fan out to cover wide areas for long distances, but there's one catch: they often look like disco lights, and thus may not be taken seriously as a distress signal. Still, if you're in a remote area and folks are looking for you, the chances are great you'll attract help.

### Flashlight

The standard handheld flashlight can typically be seen at a range of approximately five miles, depending on weather and terrain.

### Strobe Light

The individual-sized strobes found in many survival kits can be seen for about ten miles on a clear night, and perhaps as many as twenty.

### Vehicle/ Aircraft/ Watercraft Lights

These can be seen for five to fifteen miles over open terrain under various weather conditions. Even if the weather is foul, if SAR crews know you are out there, they will continue to look, provided the weather is not so bad as to put their vessels and

*A flashlight or lantern can save you in a survival situation. A flashlight can be seen as far away as five miles. The Morse code for SOS is an internationally recognized distress signal and it's very easy to teach your children this nine-element sequence: DOT. DOT. DOT. DASH. DASH. DASH. DOT. DOT. DOT. If you're in distress and you want to attract attention it's also good to flash the lantern or flashlight off and on whilst waving it around as people's eyes are drawn to movement. (Photo credit Ruth England Hawke)*

lives at risk. Don't give up hope just because the weather is bad—rescuers might still be looking, and they may still be able to find you. If the weather is extremely dangerous, best to save your lights and settle in to ride out the storm.

**Laser Pointers**

These are often overlooked as a means of signaling, but they have very good range (at one kilometer, these beams fan out to cover about a twenty-inch area that can't be seen from the point of origin without binoculars), and can be used to signal to aircraft and ships at sea. Laser pointers are also visible to pilots who might be flying with night-vision goggles.

However, with laser pointers, there's a danger of damage to the human eye, so don't aim it at anyone's face at close range. Also, civilian laser pointers are many times weaker than the lasers used for military purposes, so the risk of injury is minimal. If you can find a laser pointer in the wreckage, include it in your signaling arsenal.

## Chem Lights

Also known as glow-sticks (or cyalume lights), these have a range of about five miles, and are very effective when tied to the end of a string and swung around in circles. In the early days of night-vision goggles, this was an extremely effective and simple mid-range signaling method. Just remember that once you break your chem lights to illuminate them, you'll only get about twelve hours of light out of them—basically one night's worth. If your supply is limited, try to wait until you're sure you see something worth signaling to before breaking one open.

## Homemade Lanterns

Find some cups, tin cans, or chunks of sandstone, clay, chalk, or other soft stone that can be hollowed out to contain animal fat, engine oil, or any other liquid fuel. Use a piece of twine or cloth cord, or even pith from a fibrous plant, as a wick, soaking it in the oil until it's fully saturated. Position the wick so it hangs partially out of the container while staying in contact with the liquid fuel. Light the wick and you've got a lantern. When protected from the wind and arranged in a triangle, three lanterns can make a very effective SOS signal.

## Fire

This is the most likely resource for the survivor in most situations. If fuel is scarce, fire's use for cooking and warmth must be weighed against its potential use as an emergency signal. Likewise, if your resources for starting a fire are limited, you'll have to make a decision whether to use them now or later. But if your resources for starting and feeding fires are plentiful, you'll definitely want to make signal fires. As a general rule, high points and open areas are the best places to build them.

It's a good idea to build some sort of platform under your fire, especially if the ground is wet, as in snowy terrain, swamps, jungle floors, etc. Platforms also help if you're hemmed in by a lot of dense vegetation. The higher the fire is off the ground, the more likely it is to be seen.

Try to make multiple fires if you can. Make three fires approximately ten to twenty-five feet apart when possible. This arrangement will be clearly distinguishable as a distress signal at great distances. If multiple fires are too difficult to build or maintain in your situation, stick to just one. Also consider preparing a bonfire that you can set ablaze quickly when the moment comes to send a signal.

*Fire is one of the best ways of attracting attention in an emergency. At night the flames can be seen and during the day, the smoke. High points and open areas are the best places to build signal fires. Bear in mind that search-and-rescue planes will search up and down waterways so a river beach is a good place to light your signal fire. If you are able to build three fires about twenty feet apart, this is recognizable as a distress signal. Teach children to throw bundles of greenery on the fire to create lots of white smoke; if you're on a beach, seaweed does the same thing. (Photo credit Mike Mac McAleenan)*

Trees can be used as natural fire beacons. If you happen to find a big, dead tree that's still standing, build up a pile of kindling around its base to make an ignition station for easy and quick lighting. Be sure to protect your ignition station from wind and weather, and keep everything you'll need to light it nearby so you can start your fire—and send your signal—quickly when the moment comes. Opportunity often arrives without warning. Don't miss your chance at rescue due to lack of preparation.

If no dead, dry trees are handy, look for a large, living pine tree. These have a resin that burns very well, making them good candidates for signal trees. Seek out lone trees to prevent the fire from catching and spreading.

In an extreme emergency, you might have to consider starting a forest fire to draw attention to your area. Just know that fire can spread quickly and could very well be deadly. If you find yourself trapped by a forest fire, try to get to water. If you're surrounded, try digging in and waiting for it to pass, but don't expect to survive. This is an extremely high-risk option, and will likely put innocent people, including your potential rescuers, in harm's way. If you do survive, you'll probably be arrested after your recovery.

## Smoke and Mirrors and Other Signals

Many other visual signals are available to you and all should be used at every opportunity and in whatever ways time and resources permit. There is virtually no limit to what you can use to signal for help.

### Smoke

Light is only one aspect of a fire that can be seen at great distances. Don't neglect smoke as part of your signaling plan. Try always to make smoke with your fire, and try to make smoke that contrasts with your environment.

For example, use white smoke to mark your location in the jungle. Green leaves and green plants are excellent for generating white smoke. Just try not to burn any poisonous plants, as the poison can enter your lungs if you inhale the smoke.

Use black smoke in snow-covered terrain. Burning rubber creates a thick, black smoke. Again, be careful to stay upwind, as inhalation can cause sickness.

Petroleum products can be used to not only get a fire started in a pinch, but to create dark smoke. The trick to using any petroleum product is to start with a small amount, wait a few minutes for it to soak into whatever fuel you're pouring it on, and keep the container a good distance away from the flame. Petroleum can be extremely flammable, so use caution and experiment before the actual moment of need.

*In this shot Chase is using a mirror to signal to his friend on the other side of the park by using flashes of reflected sunlight. This is a very effective method of signaling and can be seen many, many miles away. You can buy a special signal mirror which has a hole in the middle for aiming but any mirror or reflective surface can be used. In order to aim the flash at his friend, Chase is using his two fingers as a sight. To do this, position your fingers so your target is between the "V" and then adjust the mirror so the sun beam is reflected across your two fingers and the area in between.*
*(Photo credit Ruth England Hawke)*

## Mirrors

This is a classic. The military estimates the effective signaling range of a mirror at fifty to one hundred miles. That is stronger than any other visual signaling device, and stronger than most emergency radios. Metal shards from wreckage or any other type of metal can be polished to a mirror like surface, if they're not sufficiently reflective already. On a sunny day, metal can reflect sunlight as far as ten miles.

The technique for aiming flashes of reflected sunlight with metal or mirrors is simple. First, if you have an actual "signal mirror" made for this purpose, just follow the directions. This store-bought item has a hole in the middle of the mirror through which you can look and see exactly where the reflected light beam is hitting in the distance. Simply hold up the signal mirror, note where the beam is going, then direct that beam at your target.

If you are using a piece of metal or solid mirror, you will have to aim it manually, but this is not difficult to do. Face the sun, hold the mirror or piece of metal as close to your eye as you can, and aim the reflective surface at something nearby. This will show you the angle at which to hold your device, which can then be turned at an aircraft, ship, or target area in the distance.

Once you've got the beam locked on or near your target, move the reflector just a bit up and down between the sun and the target. This will cause a twinkle that is very bright and will catch the human eye at great distances.

There is a neat trick to use to show your kids these principles of just how far a bright mirror reflection can be seen. The next time your family is on a commercial flight, let the kids sit by the window. Then give them a mission the see how many bright flashes of light they can see in a few minutes. This only works on a sunny day of course, but they should see a handful of bright flashes in just a couple of minutes.

That will help them understand how a simple signal mirror can make such a bright flash that a plane high in the sky can still see them. Remind them that the altitude at which you're flying is a much higher altitude than any search-and-rescue aircraft would be flying. So, if that aircraft is closer to the ground, with crews looking for you, and they see a flash like that in the middle of nowhere, it will certainly get their attention. In this way, you made a potentially boring flight into a training opportunity and a confidence builder for your kids.

## Panel Markers

These are swaths of brightly-colored cloth made primarily for the military with the express purpose of signaling. If you have these, use them. Keep them displayed at all times and deploy them where they're most likely to be seen. You can cut them into strips and tie them to treetops surrounding your position. The breeze will make them move, helping SAR aircraft to locate you.

Panel markers are usually bright orange or yellow or pink and made of tough, weather-resistant material. You can also use them to help construct a shelter.

## Space Blankets

These are thin, lightweight, shiny silver blankets designed for retaining body heat in emergency situations. They make excellent temporary shelters or water catchments, and their reflective side makes an excellent signaling device. The drawback is that they are not very durable and will fall apart after a little use. But even when they do, they can be torn or cut into strips and tied or staked out to blow in the wind.

## Clothes

Even the shirt off your back can be used as a signal. Clothing that's bright, white, or shiny is best, and can be spread out on the ground to spell "help" or SOS. This should only be done when you have enough clothing to spare for warmth and protection from the elements.

## Flags and Poles

These are simple and effective means of sending signals. Any time you can find or improvise a pole in a clearing that can hold up some strip of plastic or scrap metal or cloth to form a flag, you should do so. You might even consider climbing any hilltops near your position and raising a pole on each one with arrows pointing toward your camp. If you've got nothing to make flags with, a grouping of three poles will stand out and draw attention if anyone should come near them. Skin the bark off of saplings so they look white and better contrast with the surroundings.

## Mounds and Shadows

This is another low-tech way to get a signal out, especially when the terrain is bare, as in a desert. You might try stacking three rock mounds. By themselves, they may not really stand out in the terrain, but in the afternoon they will cast shadows, and a pattern of three dark shadows in a geometric shape just might be what saves you. There are specialists who do nothing but study shadows on satellite photos looking for anomalies, and this is the sort of thing they would spot easily.

### Upturned Dirt

If you're in a tundra-like area, and have something to dig with, overturn shovelfuls of dirt so the moister, darker side is facing the sky. The combination of the small ditch you've dug and the dark dirt will stand out against the surrounding grassland. Dig in the pattern of a geometric shape or a word and you'll have a signal.

### Sticks and Stone

If you're really beat up and don't have the strength to try these other methods, simply stack small piles of rocks, or arrange them in lines. You can do the same thing with sticks. Try to make a pattern, or a grouping of three.

### Beach Sand

Try writing your message in the sand in large letters carved with a stick or large shell. Use wet seaweed or sticks to line the letters. These darker materials will help your message stand out.

### Sea Markers

The open ocean can be an especially difficult place to improvise signals unless you have a light or mirror. Sea markers (there are many dyes and powders available

*If you are lost and trying to make your way to safety, always leave an obvious trail for anyone who might be trying to find you. Leaving arrows is an excellent method as they clearly show your direction of travel and their geometric shape stands out in nature. Try and use a color or tone that is clearly visible against the surroundings, like the green arrow on the tan ground above, and always try and leave three arrows in a row to represent the universal distress signal. Also make other disturbances like snapping branches and dropping litter. (Photo credit Ruth England Hawke)*

specifically for this use, which when placed in the sea create a fluorescent cast upon the surface) are only good for about three hours in calm seas, but they can be seen from several miles off. If you have a packet of sea marker available, use it only in clear weather and when you suspect that someone may see it within the timeframe.

## Morse Code

Morse code is an old-school but effective way to communicate that you can use with almost any means of communication. Morse code is also the only signal that will transmit through a nuclear-charged environment when the airwaves are full of static and charged particles, Morse code can still be heard because it is simply a pattern in the otherwise steady static background. (See Chapter 10 for more.)

However, the fact is that you do not need to learn Morse code at all. All you really need to know is SOS. SOS is . . . - - - . . . (dit dit dit, da da da, dit dit dit), and that's all there is to it. Three fast taps, three slow taps, and three fast taps again. Memorize it right now—tap it out on your wrist with your eyes closed.

But even though you don't need to memorize and practice Morse code, you should keep a copy of the full code somewhere. Here's why: Let's say you do manage to make contact via Morse code and someone actually replies. It would be good if you could make out what they are saying, and say something back that might assist in your rescue.

A flashlight's beam can be seen from shore or from the air for a surprisingly long distance, especially when it's flashing, and this is one good way to send Morse code. Also, you can use a blanket over a fire to control bursts of smoke that can send a clear message for a long distance. Even a broken radio or phone can transmit sparks of static that can be controlled to send Morse code.

If you have a radio with no handset, you can use a wire, nail, ballpoint pen, or any piece of metal to short out the pins where the handset would normally be plugged in, and this will create an arc spark that will transmit a break in the static that can be read as code. Experiment with briefly touching one pin at a time, then holding the piece of metal against that pin. Try all the pins until you find the "hot" pin that would normally key the mike or handset. This takes some practice, but you can keep arcing out the handset pin against the sidewall to make the sparks in longer and shorter bursts that will form the basis of your Morse code.

Now you can start learning to communicate basic messages. Just think of a dot or dit as a one-second sound, long enough to say "one" or "dot." Think of the dashes as a two-count, "one and two" or "da-ash." Whatever it is, work out a dots-and-dashes rhythm in your head and practice it.

## Morse Code

Is like a one quick second count in your head

- Is like a one long second count in your head

A *-    N -*    1 *----

B -***   O ---   2 **---

C -*-*   P *--*   3 ***--

D -**   Q --*-   4 ****-

E *    R *-*   5 *****

F **-*   S ***   6 -****

G --*    T -    7 --***

H ****    U **-    8 ---**

I **    V ***-    9 ----*

J *---    W *--    0 -----

K -*-    X -**-

L *-**    Y -*--

M --    Z --**

The numbers are easy, and I suggest practicing those first. For the alphabet, start with the easier and shorter letters, like E (*) and T (-), and work your way through the alphabet. At the very least, learn and practice SOS *** - - - ***

## The Rule of Threes

There are three dots and three dashes in the three-letter Morse code for SOS. That's no accident. The universal distress signal is anything in threes: three fires, three whistle blasts, three rifle shots, three stacks of rocks, three crosses made of sticks, etc. Let this principle guide you in all your communications. Anything presented in a pattern of three will tell observers that it's not mere coincidence or chance, but rather a man-made attempt to send a signal and ask for assistance.

## Arrows

I find that arrows formed on the ground make good markers as they are easy to construct from sticks and stones and they are easily spotted as a pattern that doesn't occur naturally. Always make the arrow's head a triangle, since geometric shapes stand out in nature, and so attract the human eye more effectively.

Three arrows pointing in your direction of travel or toward your base camp is a good survival signal plan. But you should also make a path, or a sign, or a disturbance everywhere you go, at least as much as your energy, time, and resources permit. Every day you should hold on to hope of rescue. Every time you take an action designed to signal or communicate, it's a tangible reinforcement of your commitment to the fight for survival.

## Where to Make Your Mark

When it comes to the placement of your signs, seek the highest point you can get to. In the case of multiple clearings, try to place signs in the areas most likely to be seen first, and if resources permit, mark them all. If there is no high ground nearby, or you can't reach it, use the largest clearing or open space you can find.

## How to Tell If You're Wasting Effort

Any form of communication requires energy. Conservation of energy is a critical component of survival, and your energy reserves should be rationed out only as needed. It won't always be practical to expend the effort necessary to create a signal. Be prepared to prioritize your physical resources over signaling if the situation calls for it.

# What You Need to Know about Changes in the Sky

The truth is, you just don't need to know several dozen different panel configurations or body gestures. For civilian survival, just getting the attention of an aircraft or ship is all you need to do. Rescuers will then send in the right type of craft and personnel to get you as soon as possible, or perhaps drop supplies and messages to keep you alive until they can. A simple waving of the arms, or a nice big "X" to mark the spot, or "H" for helicopter pad is all you really need to know about using panel markers.

## Changes in the Sky

The new system takes advantage of many satellites in the sky, in space, on land, and at sea. These incorporate many systems from beacon transponders, to GPS satellites and many different radio systems. There are used to help find people in trouble, and share the information with rescue agencies and government resources to try and work together to help save lives.

What this means to you is that if you have the means to notify these folks about your emergency, they will likely have the means to help find and rescue you. So, the communications plan for your family is one of the most important parts of your family survival plan.

When all your electronics fail, do not forget to keep all your basic and primitive methods going. The key, as with everything, especially in survival, is to never quit and always keep trying, always do, always communicate, always signal, always transmit, always send a message for help, always keep the fires of hope burning, and never quit.

# CHAPTER ELEVEN

## ACTIVITIES

Some aspects of activities will fall into other categories and some are just mini-survival exercises or practice sessions for various sections of survival. The main idea is to think, prep, and then do something survival based and even occasionally put the skills to a fun test.

*Pushing your children out of their comfort zone is an important step in preparing them to cope with the new and unexpected. Gabe was scared of alligators so I took him on a swamp walk in Florida when we were on vacation, though it was more of a swim for him. Guide Charles O'Connor educated us on the local flora and fauna and Gabe wasn't scared at all even though he was neck deep in water. The unknown is usually much more frightening than the actuality and that is a good lesson to learn.*
*(Photo credit Ruth England Hawke)*

The key in all of this is to first make sure you have all the key areas covered in your plan. That is, make sure you have a plan for what you are going to do if you stay or go, for a short or long period, and if you go, where will you go and how will you get there.

Then, make sure all eight main areas are addressed in your plan, including food, water, shelter, fire, first aid, communications (including signals), navigation (including maps, compasses, and GPSs), and safety (including weapons, tools, alarms, and other security measures). Then make sure you have all the required items within each category, that you know what they are, how to use them, how they work, and have backups for everything.

Then make sure your kids have what they need within each of the eight categories. Make sure they know how to use them. It is not enough to show them or ask them. Ask them questions and try to test them with some degree of stress appropriate for their maturity and skill levels.

## Never Forget to Always Make it Fun

Try to make these activities fun with small rewards, treats, or breaks from chores, extra game time, or something that gives them incentive to push harder and do their best. There is an ulterior motive here: You want to push your kids so you can know how well they can do, and what their limits are by actually seeing it yourself. Also, you want your kids to have an idea of how much they can do. Invariably, if a survival situation ever occurs and they are forced to face these hardships under duress in a crisis, they will know that they can do it. By keeping it fun, you avoid causing fear and panic and instead, make them feel brave and ready for the challenge.

This is a fundamental foundation for teaching kids about survival. The fear is real as is the chance of dying. They will get that well enough should they ever have to face it. They need the confidence that they can face these things, with some degree of competence. The mission is to make them feel like they can rely on their parents, on their family, and if it comes down to it, they can rely on themselves.

As a parent, knowing that kids have these fundamental skills will give you peace of mind should a worst-case scenario happen. Further, because you will have created and rehearsed plans, and briefed kids on the plan for each situation, then you will have the calmness of mind whenever something bad happens

One of the biggest things the parents will have to do to train their kids and make sure the kids are the best prepared they can be, is to constantly update their training to match their age and abilities. Each year kids will gain a new level of knowledge and capabilities. But it doesn't need to be unduly burdensome and painful.

### Survival Gardening

Gardening becomes harder as life has become more urban, technological, and fast paced. Usually, older persons, farmers, and country dwellers are the people doing gardening. But gardening can be done at any home with even a tiny yard. If you have no yard, you can have a mini-garden in your apartment. If that is too small, you can consider guerrilla gardening in the local park, or any green space you can get to. Rarely will you hurt the environment by planting seeds of edible plants.

In this way, you can teach your kids the life cycle of plants, the value of earth, nature, seasons, and help them get better at plant identification.

### Survival Foraging

Whenever you go for walks or hikes or any outdoor activities with your kids, be on the lookout for edible plants so you can do some on-the-spot training with them.

You can also give them the task each time you go out to find at least one to three edible plants. With rewards and prizes, this is a great fun and easy way to train their eyes to be on the hunt for wild edibles.

### Survival Food Sourcing

Another thing you can consider doing with kids is going out and sourcing some food. Primarily, meat if possible and legal. Can they hunt a squirrel with a BB gun or catch a bird with a sling shot? Or they can catch a fish with a pole, spear, bow, or net? This can be a good option for getting kids exposed and trained to find food. Then have kids help clean it, prepare it, cook it, and eat it, so that nothing is wasted.

### Field Training Exercises

Once a year, a little a weekend camp-in at Fort Living Room and The Wilds of the backyard, one day of each, will be enough to dump out the backpacks, remember what's inside, test each thing out, figure out what is the next level-up item the kids can handle in each category, how much more weight they can handle, especially for their own things for their own needs, taking a bit more burden off your shoulders, literally, and making them a bit more self-contained and self-reliant.

For example, one year, you might teach them to use Band-Aids for a laceration. The next year, you might teach them butterfly tape for improvised stitches, the next year medical or super-glue wound closure, and as a teen, you might even teach them how to do medical sutures. There are new inventions and devices that come out every year as our technology grows exponentially. Keeping up with the latest trends in emergency medical and survival technology could give an idea on what to buy, and how to improvise and make things better.

## Survival Toys

There are lots of toys out there that can help kids get into survival and give them real skills as well. A lot will depend on where you live, your kids' ages and interests as well as your beliefs as a parent. I will recommend a few here, and it's up to you to decide what's best for your family:

### Spears

Get kids use to one as a walking stick, reaching tool, throwing spear, or a defense tool.

### Bow and Arrow

Target practice is good fun and family time.

### Sling Shots

A super skill for getting food and predator defense.

### Slings

Truly old school and way hard, but super fun and cool.

### Blowguns

These are remarkably easy and accurate

### Knives

I recommend folding knives for safety which either will have locking mechanisms to reduce risk of cuts, button locks that are easy to fold and don't require the fingers to ever go in front of the blade, or strong hand guards.

Fixed blades may be an easier answer, but the sheath must be easy to put in, hard to fall out, preferably with a safety snap strap or two and a hard sheath that doesn't allow for wear and tear to cut through.

I recommend wearing them on the front of a belt, so the child can always safely remove and replace. Alternative options include a good lanyard or string to keep it on their wrist when in use and tied to their body when stowed. I do not recommend kids have machetes, hatchets, or shovels until they are older, but make that assessment based on your child and your environment.

A simple small knife is good to start getting into whittling, making spears, arrows, walking sticks, and eventually, traps and snares. A knife can provide hours of fun and enjoyment for a kid as it's a simple tool that has great diversity and utility.

### Knife Rules and Safety Brief

Of course, safety and accountability is vital. Knives must never ever be used to harm or threaten harm to anyone. Kids must also be taught the value of all life. They should be taught not to rip up a plant by the roots unless they must. Not to kill any insect unless they need to and certainly, not to harm any creature of feather, fin, or fur unless they are in danger or need to eat to survive.

You as a parent must strongly admonish your kids for any violations of these principles in order to instill in them from the very outset, that even in survival, we must be kind, show mercy, and have honor in all we do. They will only love, admire, and respect you more for these lessons.

### Tarps

These are fun for making shelters and forts. Give a kid a tarp and a backyard, and watch them create!

### Ropes

Ropes, string, and paracord are great for kids to play with. Making swings, bridges, ladders, or just trying different types of knots. Bottom line, cordage makes for a fun toy and good tool too.

### Hammocks

This is an odd one for toys, but there are all different kinds from the Army style jungle hammocks, which also double as a great net, to the swing kinds. Using hammocks is that it teaches kids some principles of how to string them and operate in and out of them as well as getting used to the idea of being off the ground and sleeping in something outside and other than their bed.

### Canteens

Kids often feel special carrying them and it gets them into the mindset of having to have water and having to carry it.

### Flashlights

Glow sticks and lanterns all make for fun outdoors in the dark. Playing hide-and-seek or hunting for prizes in the dark can get the kids accustomed to using them and being outside at night. These games can be played in the house too for city dwellers or in cases of inclement weather.

### Magnifying Glasses

These are fun for many reasons, but also a great way to teach kids how to start fires. They should practice with adult supervision and experiment with how to do it. It's for sure not my go-to for fire starting but it's great for getting them thinking, especially about tinder, and they may need to improvise glasses to make a fire someday.

### Whistles

Granted, these are typically not the most exciting of toys, but varieties that are multi-tools can be fun and it's good for the kids to get used to having one on them and know to blow them three times every fifteen to twenty minutes when lost. Perhaps, play longer distance hide and seek in a big park and find each other by whistle blows only.

### Bags

There are a few ways to go with these as a toy function to get kids into survival. You can have your kids pack their own survival bag and then show you what they chose and why and then discuss the options. You can also have kids find a way to load a bag and then carry it, as a sling or over the shoulder, or have them make a roll with a blanket to carry across their torso, making a frame to carry a heavier pack. You'll be surprised at how much fun and interest they'll have.

### Binoculars

Binoculars are another great tool. Start by having kids learn how to focus both eyes to spot birds or small critters. After they are comfortable with them, kids can be taught to use binoculars to try and find plants or something man-made in the distance like a building or power line.

### Telescopes

Telescopes can be the next thing up from binoculars and kids can then begin to take interest in the skies, the stars, and learning to read weather.

## Games

Lots of board games and electronic games can teach kids good thinking skills as they can see how things fit on a large scale, and in competition with others.

However, real skills can only come from physically doing things, so try to find ways to make games out of training. So many variables will determine what you end up doing as a parent, but anytime you can, make some sport of a task, like who can get the fire going faster, or make a challenging activity like a hike, into a fun pastime then these things help you assess their skills, motivation, capabilities, and limitations. The point is to try and create games of skill with prizes and acknowledgement.

## Skills-a-Plenty

Many normal fun activities teach good survival skills.

### Boating

Boating in all its forms can be useful for kids. Of course, make sure swimming is learned first and always teach safety. Sinking is an ever-present danger and so a life preserver is a must for all water activities.

### Swimming

Swimming is a vital skill. If the kids are good swimmers, and the life vests are not practical for their activities, they must have an IAD, or immediate action drill, trained into their minds. For example, if on a boat, life jackets must be beside them at all times and they must know how to put it on in a few seconds.

This means you have to train kids, practice with them, and occasionally spot test them with a drill. It helps develop healthy habits and makes sure they have the best chances of survival while also allowing for some of life's practical issues.

## Challenges

Challenges are a great way to have fun, get fit, push boundaries, gain experience, and keep everyone thinking, improving, and increasing skills while decreasing response time.

Design a variety of challenges. Make some first aid challenges, practice a fire drill, and remember where the extinguishers are in the house. Does everyone know what to do if your car breaks down, how to fix a flat, how to escape a fire or what to do if you go off a bridge into water?

When you start breaking down all your daily, weekly, monthly, and annual activities into worst-case scenarios and then work out your family's personal response plans, you start seeing right away what things you need and what things you need to do.

## Fitness

A child's fitness can come from many areas, including walking, hiking, running, jogging, biking, skating, skiing, playing sports, hard work outside, or chores around the house. The key here is to make sure that every day there is some sort of physical activity. Generally anything that gets them outside, in nature, getting exercise, and developing numerous other physical and life skills is beneficial.

### Martial Arts

Self-defense skills are important for everyone. It's key that kids are taught some skills of self-defense, the principles of when to use those skills, when to help others with those skills, and when to avoid conflict and run.

I teach my kids that there are many different types of people, including fighters and artists. Learning dancing, writing, drawing, painting, and many other forms make your kids better humans, better at learning, and could be helpful in survival. It may be that it simply helps them pass the time and not let fear set in when stuck inside and they can do nothing else. In short, have your kids learn some martial arts and some of the other arts.

## Diet

In survival, diet is very much impacted by a lot of factors, almost always negative ones. This is usually by virtue of simple lack of food or by the availability of only one type of food. So, it is good to teach kids about the importance of a balanced diet and constantly expose them to new things and have them always try foods. The point of teaching the kids to try new things is to make them less averse to trying new foods when a survival situation might force it on them. Many early settlers died of starvation while surrounded by food simply due to lack of knowledge.

## Sleep

Rest is very important in life, especially for kids as they are growing. In survival, sleep is very, very important for overall health, fighting infections, and engaging in good decision making. Further, rest helps the body and mind better tolerate the inevitable hardships and sufferings that come with most survival situations such as exposure to extreme temperatures or lack of food and water.

To parents I cannot stress enough the importance of making sure your kids sleep and sleep as well as possible. Take and make extra time to make the shelter as suitable as possible, have enough fire to see you through the night, and of course, keep as much food and water available as your situation permits. But even when all these are lacking, make sure the kids get sleep, as it makes a world of difference.

## Core Fitness Activities

### Hikes

Hikes are a great way to get exercise, so take the kids out into their environment and show them the world around them. Use this experience to discuss life cycles of animals, migration patterns of birds, blooming period for plants, the rise and set of the sun, the moon phases, the direction of water flow, or anything else that helps them to better understand their world. Hopefully they will become more curious and start researching the local plants and creatures.

### Climbing

Climbing falls into a few categories, from climbing trees, to scrambling rocks, to rope climbs and even parkour. It's a great skill as it teaches kids to get a new perspective and keeps them fit while providing some action and adventure. Of course, as parents we worry about falls and injuries, and rightly so. However, all we can do is caution them and do our best to supervise and advise, but we can't hold them back too much.

### Camping

Camping and camp craft are the best ways to prepare the kids for the basics of survival. The more they get used to being outdoors, in different environments, under different climates, and different circumstances the better equipped they will be mentally and physically to adapt to the likely unpleasant and potentially volatile circumstances of a survival situation.

When the kids practice the small acts of going to the bathroom outside in nature, doing full body personal hygiene at the camp site, or disposing of waste and storing of food, it shows that you are expertly preparing your kids for surviving.

# CHAPTER TWELVE

# PREPARATIONS

Once you get your family trained in the various parts of survival, it can be an exciting adventure to go out for a survival weekend. Bring everything you need, but only use what you have to. Try to survive the whole weekend without using any supplies you brought or at least minimal supplies should be used. By having everything you need, if something happened, you'd not be in any danger and could just wait it out.

*Myke putting Alex and Dominic through their paces. If your family is physically fit they have a much better chance of surviving a traumatic event. That doesn't mean that you have to put them through Hawke-style boot camp; being involved in a sport really helps as does good old outside play. (Photo credit Ruth England Hawke)*

# Checklist

Be sure to make a check list for everyone and everything.

Do you have a checklist for each disaster that could happen to your family in your area? Start with the most likely ones, then work your way down to the most extreme and worst-case scenarios. After a while, you will have great confidence that you are as well prepared as you can be and the rest is up to fate. Some things for the disasters/emergencies list are:

## List of Disasters

- Hurricane
- Tornado
- Earthquake
- Sinkhole
- Tsunami
- Mud Slides
- Home Flooding
- Large-Scale Fires
- Home Invasions
- Car Stranded
- Car Hijacking
- Plane Crash
- Wild Animal Attacks

- Boat Sink
- Hiking Fall
- Drowning or Near-Drowning
- Public Act of Terrorism
- Bombing
- Explosions
- Train Derailment
- Car Crash
- Life-Threatening Illnesses
- Trauma
- Being Lost

## List Questions to Develop Plans

- What should each child carry with them at all times?
- What should each child have always stored in their pack?
- What should each child always have by their bed?
- What should each child have in their "go" bag?
- What should each parent carry with them at all times?
- What should each parent always have in their pack?
- What should each parent always have by their bed?
- What should each parent always have in their "go" bag?
- What should the family always have in the car?
- What should the family always have in the boat or plane?
- What should the family always have at their vacation destination?
- What should the family always keep at a designated relative's house?
- What is the route for the family bug-out plan?

- What is the route if the family has to walk?
- Are there any cache locations on the route?

### The Snuggle-Bunny List

This is usually the comfort items for kids. A favorite teddy bear, blanket, game, nighttime story, or comfort food or drink all make tough moments in life a little bit easier. Yes, it's a bit more weight and hassle to be sure, but these are the things that could make the difference in kids' morale and spirit. So, definitely take some time to contemplate these special things and make some extra room for them somewhere. Usually, the kids' pack is the best.

Note: In Special Forces, we always tie critical gear to our body or harness when on missions so we don't lose anything vital in a firefight. At home, we also tie Gabe's critical gear to his backpack.

# Storage

We teach some general guidelines to help folks plan for emergencies. No one can ever know your needs, your budget, and your space availabilities like you, so use these to help make your own custom tailored plans.

### On You

We recommend having enough supplies to survive one day.

**Food**

We usually have a small beef jerky and power bar.

**Water**

Keep a large bottle of water to hand at all times. You may also want to keep a condom or zippered bag as a backup canteen, as well as one to two water purification tablets.

**Weapons**

A tiny knife anywhere on you and you're sorted.

**Fire**

A tiny lighter in your pocket and you're covered.

**Medicine**

It's nice to have a few meds like a travel pack of aspirin, Benadryl, and antacids, as well as a vitamin pack. Additionally have a scarf or handkerchief for trauma dressing.

### Signal

A tiny light and whistle on your key chain.

### Navigation

A simple tiny compass on watch, phone, or keychain works.

### Shelter

A torso-sized trash bag covers you.

## In Your Pack

Have enough supplies here to survive three days. Use the same principles as on your person, but obviously, you can carry more, bigger sizes and better quality.

Think of the things you carry on your body as your primary plan. Your pack or purse is your alternative plan. Your vehicle is your contingency plan. Your home is your emergency plan. Your office is your WCS, or worst-case scenario. By following this, you are keeping to the principles of a five-layer plan.

Note: For kids, their school desk or locker could be their equivalent to your office or place of work as the parent.

There are additional locations that you should keep emergency items. In your car, boat, or plane, keep enough to survive seven days. In your office, enough to survive three to seven days. In your home, keep enough to survive thirty days. These are ideals and in actuality, your supplies should reflect your needs, your budgets, your plans, your fitness, skill levels, and the like.

Of course, some supplies do expire, so try to get things that are low maintenance. If they have expiration dates, make a little list of when to rotate supplies. We usually give ourselves a one-month notice for when things are due to expire, but know that most things, if stored well, will last much longer than the expiration date.

## Caches

This is likely one of the very-least-considered survival tools.

A cache is nothing more than a stash of supplies. The word cache comes from special operators working the French Partisans during WWII and means "hidden."

This is a viable option for a lot of people with some planning. Ideally, you just want to stash some extra food and water, maybe a few medical supplies and some electronics like a short-wave radio, and possibly some survival gear or spare ammo.

You want to make sure the cache is well protected from the elements, so waterproofing is important. You want to make sure it's well hidden, be it in a hole, cave, or under a rock or fallen tree, Make sure that you can find it again.

Ideally, you will want to make a couple of these and usually, it's best to put them on a route you plan to walk so you know every few days you will get to a new supply of food and water. This reduces the weight you have to carry on you.

## Bug Outs

When it comes to bug outs, there are bug-out bags, bug-out plans, and bug-out places. First, you'll want to have a bug-out bag that lives by your bed and your kids' beds. These are mainly for if there is a fire or some disaster that forces you to flee in a hurry. Plan and pack well, including entertainment items for the kids.

Having a bug-out plan means everyone in the family knows a keyword or key signal that you have developed which indicates it's time to get out now.

A bug-out place is the first place everyone in the family knows to go if you have to get out of your home in a hurry. Usually it will be someplace simple like the front yard, a creek behind the house, or the corner by the woods.

## Hideouts

Essentially this is the first place the family as a unit plans to go once they escape the house and link up at the bug-out place. Often this will be a relative's house, church, school, or local shelter. By having this place designated, anyone who gets lost or separated has an idea that is where to go next to get re-connected with the family. This is very important for mass-casualty-type disasters.

## Practice

Next phase of the operation is to do some local practice. You might just do a fire response practice, or a mock call 9-1-1 drill. Make sure you kids know where the fire extinguishers are or how to lower the fire ladders from their windows. Do anything that you can as single-skill practice.

### Rehearsals

This is when the family actually goes through an entire scenario. Everyone should ask questions, solve any issues, and then repeat everything in its final form after any tweaks or changes so the kids have memorized the rock-solid plan. Try to have them give you a "brief back" where they tell you the plan and then you ask them the questions. Then you'll know they have it.

### Drill

After the rehearsal, it's good to drill. Drills are announced event activities so the kids know it's a drill and they are ready and excited to do it.

These should not be slow like a rehearsal, but not be full speed like a test. These are slow but sure actions going through the motions as they would need to do in an emergency, making sure not to get hurt, not to take risks, not to rush, and not to break anything.

### Tests

The final phase for any family unit is to be put to the test. These should not be announced. They should be coordinated by both parents so that there is time to execute and evaluate after and then recover so you're re-loaded and ready for the real deal.

First, you sound the alarm or call the code word and everyone springs into action. These should only be done once a year. Otherwise, kids grow weary and they may not be as responsive as they need be, if and when the real deal actually occurs.

With all this done as best as you can, you as parents can know you have done all you can to be prepared and to save your kids. And your kids will be the best prepared they can be for survival. While they may moan and complain a bit, they will also be proud of their parents and themselves.

With that, we are honored to be able to share some of our training and experience from our family with you and your family. We wish you all nothing but the best, peace, prosperity, health, and happiness. But if something else should come calling, we hope this book will have helped, even if only a little. Be well, happy survivalin'!

# APPENDIX

## Hawke Family Survival Kit

- Backpack, medium-sized, easy and light to carry
- Two lighters, one large and one small
- Matches that are waterproof
- Waterproof container for whistle and compass
- Whistle
- Compass, (military or civilian)
- Iodine drops (small bottle to purify water and treat wounds)
- Gauze for bandages, fire starter, toilet paper, etc.
- A small bar of soap, small bar for preventive hygiene and overall cleanliness
- Water (100 ml minimum)
- D-ring for mounting to vehicle or aircraft or holding off ground at campsite
- Magnesium bar for fire starter
- Water-purification tabs
- Electrical tape
- Cravat to serve as a triangular bandage, tourniquet, sling, towel, sweat rag, head protection, and as rag for filtering muddy water or gathering dew
- Toilet paper
- A large zippered bag, for canteen or food storage
- A large trash bag for waterproof bag or rain coat
- Meal bar
- A small Swiss-army knife
- A medium, Leatherman-style knife with pliers, screwdriver, file, saw, etc.
- A large, fixed blade, utilitarian-style, dual-blade knife
- Hammer/hatchet tool for chopping
- A large mag light
- Spare batteries
- Signal mirror

- Multivitamin pack
- Beef jerky
- Machete with saw on other side
- Shovel tool (handheld or fold up)
- Mini mag light
- Strobe light
- Pen flare
- Shortwave radio and transmitter
- Space blankets (one as shelter, one as sleeping bag, two double as litter)
- One hundred feet of 550-paracord
- Fishing kit
- MRE or equivalent
- Canteen-style metal cup
- Alternative hunting items like a slingshot, bb-gun, and bow and arrows
- GPS and SPOT-type beacon transponder/locator
- Satellite phone
- Family hand-held radio
- CB/VHF/UHF Radios depending on needs and mobility
- Possible GPS watches for kids and even adults with beacon transponder
- Net/hammock (back sack, bed, trapping, fishing, etc.)
- Ten safety pins
- Sewing kit
- Water, filter, canteen, and water containers
- Hunting rifle, ammo, and cleaning kit

## Hawke Family Recommended First Aid Kit

- Bandages
- Sterile 4x4
- Ace wraps
- Triangular bandages
- Acetaminophen, aspirin, pain meds, antibiotics, specialty meds, and any others you can use, including charcoals, ipecac, etc.
- Benadryl tabs (anti-allergy, mild sleep medication)
- Chapstick
- Condoms
- Ibuprofen
- Twenty-five sterile 4x4
- Twenty-five nonadherent sterile bandage
- Fifteen Band-Aids of various sizes and shapes
- Other burn, rash, and sting non-prescription medicine

- One anti-fungal cream tube
- Twelve Bismuth tabs (anti-diarrhea)
- Five pairs of gloves for water and waterproofing
- Hydrocortisone cream 1% tube
- Forty-five laxatives
- Twelve motion sickness tabs
- A pair of tweezers for tick, splinter, and thorn removal
- Two types of paper
- Temporary fillings and pain meds
- Eye pads and eye drops
- Sterile eyewash
- Two tubes of insect sting relief ointment
- Eight sterile gel pad, burn dressing
- Tape
- Two rolls of adhesive duct tape
- Two rolls of black electrical tape
- Sunscreen
- One nasal spray squeeze bottle
- One tube of sunscreen
- Thermometer
- One sterile scalpel
- Three butterfly sutures
- A large open pocket
- Tongue depressors (use as small splints and kindling, too)
- Twenty sterile applicators
- Ten safety pins
- 7.5-inch shears that are sharp/strong enough to cut through a penny
- Syringe, 30cc + 18 Gauge irrigation needle (for one wound irrigation)
- A reusable hot/cold pack
- Two sam splint (flexible splinting)
- Sixteen burn bandages
- Four ice packs (chemical cold compress)
- Fifty alcohol swabs/pads
- Twenty pads of blist-o-ban (large) hi-tech, ultra-thin blister
- Duoderm (blister dressing)
- Molefoam 4 x 3.5 (pressure-point padding)
- Polysporin ointment (unit dose) (broad spectrum topical antibiotic)
- Superglue™, state-of-the-art wound closure
- Vaseline tube
- Blood pressure kit

- Cotton balls
- Twelve moleskin, 4 x 3.5
- Steri-strips, minor wound closure (Many new kind make sutures obsolete)
- Five tegaderm, lightweight transparent wound and blister dressing
- Thirty surgical soap packets
- One aluminum cup
- Stethoscope
- Twenty Iodine wipes
- Small pockets
- Sterile saline solution (wound irrigation)
- Flashlight
- Eight molefoam, 4 x 3.5 (pressure-point padding)
- CPR kit
- Retractable knife
- Elastic bandage
- Airway J-Tubes
- Halstead five-inch forceps
- 5.5-inch scissors
- Three six-inch elastic bandags
- Insect repellent, large canister
- Survival blanket
- Blankets
- Iodine tabs in vial
- Candles
- Thirty-day supply of prescriptions

## Recommendations for Local Readiness Training

- Scouts of America
- Red Cross First Aid Classes
- FEMA Volunteer Training
- Local Police Safety Training
- Local Fire Safety Training
- Local EMS Safety and First Aid Training

# REFERENCES

*The Green Beret Survival Manual.* Mykel Hawke, Running Press, 2008.

*Green Beret Survival Handbook.* Mykel Hawke, Running Press, 2011.

*The Green Beret Mini-Book.* Mykel Hawke, Running Press, 2013.

*Foraging for Survival.* Douglas Boudreau and Mykel Hawke, Skyhorse, 2018.

*The Quick and Dirty Guide to Learning Languages.* Mykel Hawke, Skyhorse Publishing, 2018.

*U.S. Army Survival Manual.*

*U.S. Army Special Forces Medical Handbook.*

*SAS Survival Manual.* Lofty Wiseman, Harper Collins, 2009.

*Food for Free*, Richard Mabey, Collins Gem, 2012.

*Auerbach's Wilderness Medicine.* Paul S. Auerbach, Elsevier, 2007.

*Nancy Caroline's Emergency Care in the Streets.* Nancy Caroline. Jones & Bartlett Learning, 2012.

https://www.nfpa.org/Public-Education/By-topic/Top-causes-of-fire/Candles

http://candles.org/wp-content/uploads/2017/08/NCA-NASFM-Hurricanes-Fire-SafetyRelease-Aug-2017.pdf

http://www.redcross.org/images/MEDIA_CustomProductCatalog/m4340090_FireCandleFactSheet.pdf

http://www.fao.org/docrep/018/i3253e/i3253e.pdf

https://www.fema.gov/pdf/library/f&web.pdf

# ACKNOWLEDGMENTS

**From Ruth:**

Thank you to my family. To the loves of my life: my amazing, talented, difficult husband Myke, without whom I'd never know the joys of sleeping up trees full of mosquitoes in strange parts of the world, and our beautiful baby boy frog, Gabriel, who modeled for many photos in this book when I know he'd rather have been playing with his friends.

To my wonderful parents who have always loved, encouraged, and supported me and who gave me my love of travel, and to my brother Dale who is always there for me and his lovely family, Peela, Astrid, Botilda, and Beata.

Many thanks also to my good friends who contributed photographs.

**From Myke:**

For my part, I can never thank my lovely wife, Ruth, enough for all the hardships she has put up with and endured with me, both in life and on our shows. Many times, she risked her life, or almost died, and every time, she suffered a lot of misery, illness, and injury.

I can't ever thank my folks and siblings enough, since I was not easy to live with. But one of my biggest thanks goes out to my grown sons, Tony and Nick, as they taught me more than anything else about what really matters, and that love for them is what help me through in my younger years, through all the wars and combat.

Finally, I can never say thanks enough to my Green Beret brothers, my older brothers who taught me, my brothers with whom I served, those who made the ultimate sacrifice, and those who I taught and are still carrying the torch and going into harm's way.

# AUTHOR BIOS

## Ruth England Hawke

Ruth England is an author, photographer, TV journalist, and TV producer who has spent decades specializing in adventure travel, survival, and wildlife, often under extreme conditions.

After completing a bachelor's degree in photography and film and a postgraduate diploma in interactive design, Ruth trained as journalist with UK news agency ITN and was news anchor for Channel Five News and CNBC.

Ruth also worked as a photographer for the Telagu Film Industry in India and Switzerland. In her early twenties she worked as photographer with the Iban tribe in the heart of the Borneo rainforest. She shoots much of the promotional material for the Hawke Brand.

Ruth's on-camera work has taken her across the globe from the South Pacific to the Arctic Circle. Her work with wildlife includes tracking tigers in Nepal, filming mountain gorillas in Rwanda, swimming with sharks in Australia, and much more.

She has slept rough in the Amazon jungle, the Alaskan bush, the Okavango Delta, the Chihuahua Desert, and survived on such delicacies as maggots, tadpoles, tree bark, and carrion whilst learning primitive wilderness survival practices with her husband Myke.

Ruth was the first female principal on Discovery Channel in their history. CEO Clark Bunting said that she had single-handedly changed the viewing demographic for their network, opening the door for many more women to get lead roles on survival shows and ushering in a new era of almost completely woman leadership in their Los Angeles office.

Ruth's survival show featured many TV firsts such as survival a real forest fire and surviving a minefield. Hers was the first survival show that was completely filmed at sea from start to finish and the first survival show to call in a medic in two life-threatening situations. Discovery UK listed her along with Bear Grylls, Les Stroud, and Ray Mears as one of the great adventurers of their channel.

Ruth was producer on the Discovery Channel show *Man Woman Wild* and Travel Channel's *Lost Survivors*. She has hosted shows on location and in the studio for Fox TV, ITV, Channel Five, Channel Four, Sky, BBC, National Geographic, Discovery Channel, Travel Channel, HGTV, CNBC, and others.

## Mykel Hawke

Mykel Hawke served twenty-five years in the US Army Special Forces (Green Berets). They are the world's only unconventional warfare specialists. Mykel was trained as a jungle doctor (18D), a communication technician (18E), an intelligence specialist (18F), and as a combat commander (18A). He holds multiple black belts, speaks multiple languages, has served and worked in nine conflicts, and has taught survival for twenty years. He has multiple books in survival, language, and other subjects. He's best known for producing and starring in dozens of survival TV shows.

Mykel's background in survival began with growing up poor in the southeast United States. He was born in Kentucky, but also lived in Virginia, North Carolina, Georgia, Texas, and Colorado. His specialty in survival is particularly global due to the nature of his profession. His first unit was a winter warfare team, and he spent a lot of time in the desert, mountains, jungles, and swamps. Myke brings some highly unusual skills to the table for the survival enthusiast because of his medical background and the time of his service. Myke began his service during the Cold War and as a result, studied a great deal about CRBNE (chemical, radiological, biological, nuclear, and explosive) warfare. As a medical service officer (70B), he was taught how to deal with these events from the medical mass casualty perspective. Because of Myke's extreme experiences in combat zones, he also brings to bear the harsh realities of cannibalism, amputations, and death. Myke's survival knowledge comes from having served around the world in combat and having survived in extremes globally.